BROTHERS IN ARMS

Brothers in Arms

Chinese Aid to the Khmer Rouge, 1975–1979

Andrew Mertha

CORNELL UNIVERSITY PRESS   **ITHACA AND LONDON**

First published 2014 by Cornell University Press
First paperback printing 2019
Printed in the United States of America

Library of Congress Cataloging–in–Publication Data

Mertha, Andrew, 1965– author.
    Brothers in arms : Chinese aid to the Khmer Rouge, 1975–1979 / Andrew Mertha.
        pages cm
    Includes bibliographical references and index.
    ISBN 978-0-8014-5265-9 (cloth : alk. paper)
    ISBN 978-1-5017-3123-5 (pbk. : alk. paper)
    1. Technical assistance, Chinese—Cambodia. 2. Military assistance, Chinese—Cambodia. 3. Cambodia—Foreign relations—China. 4. China—Foreign relations—Cambodia. 5. Cambodia—Politics and government—1975–1979. I. Title.
    DS554.58.C65M47   2014
    338.91'51059609047—dc23   2013036443

To Sophie

Contents

Illustrations

Figures

Tables

Acknowledgments

The idea for this book began in March 2010, when an old Cambodia hand, Henri Locard, took me and a few others on a day trip to the Krang Leav airfield, an airport built by Cambodian slave labor under the political authority of the Khmer Rouge but under the management of Chinese technical advisers. We surveyed the airfield and the surrounding infrastructure, taking care to avoid unexploded ordnance, even descending into what initially looked like a cave but was in fact an unfinished underground command center that evoked images of SPECTRE and NORAD. Between avoiding snakes and side-stepping the layers of bat guano in the airless and sticky heat, I could not help ruminating over some fundamental questions: How is it that so few people know about this place? If we know so little about this airfield and China's involvement with it, what else do we not know about what happened during the Khmer Rouge era in Cambodia? Such questions inspired the research that culminated in this book.

When I began, I had the unenviable task of starting at the very bottom of the food chain in what was for me a new area of scholarship: I had no contacts, minimal language skills, and what can only be described as an impressive reservoir of sheer ignorance. In short, I felt like a first-semester graduate student again. And that was just on the Cambodia side. In China, I had to "learn" a new set of institutions, some of which have not existed for decades, involving a subject that officially did not exist. So it goes without saying that I benefited greatly from the generosity of others.

The staff at the National Archives of Cambodia was unflinchingly and unfailingly helpful in providing key documents and data and also worked tirelessly to make sure that I could compile them in a timely fashion. Y Dari, in particular, deserves special thanks. Youk Chhang and the Documentation Center of Cambodia (DC-CAM) were very generous in providing documents for an earlier project, which also proved to be very helpful for this one. Finally, a great number of Cambodia specialists were disarmingly supportive and helped me at each stage. This project would have been inconceivable without them. Special thanks go to David Chandler, Craig Etcheson, Steve Heder, and Henri Locard (whose disagreements with my conclusions never affected his generosity). Others for whom I express my gratitude include John Ciorciari, Lois De Menil, Nic Dunlop, Ben Kiernan, Judy Ledgerwood, Vera Manuello, Philip Short, Laura Summers, Nate Thayer, and Benny Widyono. My research assistant in Cambodia, the promising young scholar Keo Duong, tirelessly enabled me to locate and interview former (and necessarily anonymous) Khmer Rouge officials whom I never would have been able to find, let alone approach, on my own.

In China, I am indebted to another set of anonymous sources who had served as technical advisers in Democratic Kampuchea. They graciously offered their time and shared their recollections, photographs, diaries, and other materials that allowed me to breathe life into the inanimate blueprints, shipping schedules, telegrams, bills of lading, and other documents I had culled from the Cambodian National Archives. These interviewees are extraordinary people who lived through some of the most difficult challenges Maoist China could throw at them, emerging with their intelligence, dignity, and subversive sense of humor intact. They are some of the most impressive people I have ever met throughout my professional career. In thinking about the China side of the equation, I am grateful to the comments and support of Kjeld Erik Brødsgaard, Nis Grünberg, Kevin O'Brien, Michael Szony, and Ezra Vogel. In China and Cambodia and Hong Kong I was able to succeed only through the prodigious talent, stamina, and exquisite good nature of my superb research assistant, Emily Cheung.

At Cornell, I have many people to thank as well. Sid Tarrow inspired me to think "outside of China," urging me to become a "real" comparativist. He suggested fascist Italy; I chose communist Cambodia. I remain ever grateful. Peter Katzenstein compelled me to think about the normative dimensions of what I was doing; he also deserves my thanks. Allen Carlson helped ensure that I did not embarrass myself too much as I ventured into the subfield of international relations. Matt Evangelista, Jonathan Kirshner, and Tom Pepinsky may be surprised to learn that they helped me a great deal in navigating some of the questions that arose along the way, helping to transform what was rapidly turning into a historical monograph into what I hope to be a work of political science. Val Bunce helped me think long and hard about the vast differences between socialist regimes, despite their more apparent yet superficial similarities. Thak Chaloemtiarana and Tamara Loos recruited me into Cornell's Southeast Asia Program, which served as a launching pad into a brand-new scholarly world. Lorraine Paterson showed me how to straddle the moving parts that connect and separate China and Cambodia. Ding Xiang Warner, then the director of the East Asia Program, offered financial and moral support. Ken Roberts and the Institute for Social Sciences also generously provided funds for research assistance, as did Xu Xin at the China and Asia Pacific Studies (CAPS) program. This money was well spent on yet another set of terrific research assistants at Cornell, Wendy Leutert and Lin Fu. My infinitely patient Khmer language teacher at Cornell, Hannah Phan, remains my linguistic lifeline to the soul of Cambodia. She also helped me with the transliteration of a number of Khmer words and phrases to achieve some measure of consistency. Fellow intrepid traveler John Kandel's enthusiasm at the Krang Leav site helped me realize that I might be onto something.

I thank my high school art history teacher, Ruth Chapman, who enthusiastically indulged and supported my fascination with all things Cambodian when I was sixteen. In many ways this book is a tribute to her. Thank you, Ruth.

I am grateful once again to Roger Haydon and the entire team at Cornell University Press for shepherding this project through the publication process without mincing words, as well as to the two reviewers whose comments allowed me to transform a draft manuscript into a much better book.

Despite all the aforementioned help, and even with my best efforts, mistakes inevitably remain. The responsibility for them is mine alone.

My family gave me the time and space necessary to work on this project, supporting me throughout. My inestimably wonderful wife, Isabelle, among a million other things helped me reestablish my priorities; horrified by an impromptu Adirondack cliff dive in the summer of 2011, she told me that such acts of idiocy do not impress her—*writing books* does. Et, bien, *violà!* But the person who has sacrificed the most is my daughter, Sophie Mertha, who can at long last look forward to spending some quality time with the old man. She is an inspiration to me, every day and in every way. I dedicate this book, with all my love, to her.

A Note on Transliteration

I employ the *pinyin* form of Romanization used in the People's Republic of China except in cases of direct quotes or references that use other forms of Romanization, most prominently Wade-Giles, such as in the case of the Chinese shipping vessel *Yong Kang*.

Because Khmer does not yet have a standard Romanized form, I have been forced to make a number of suboptimal editorial decisions. In keeping with the current standard, I have kept widely accepted transliterations of relatively well-known personal and place names. Where transliterated Khmer words are quoted from primary and secondary sources, I have generally kept these as well. When citations use a particular Romanization of Khmer as part of the citation title, I retain the original to avoid confusion. Some proper nouns have more than one common transliteration. For the key term, *Angkar* (Organization), I use the *r* at the end of the word. Vorn Vet is also referred to as Vorn Veth; in this book, I use the former. Van Rith is also referred to as Van Rit; I similarly employ the former transliteration. Ke Pauk is sometimes referred to as Ke Pork; I use Ke Pauk. In the case of Eastern Zone Commander So Phim, there are two common transliterations that conform to the two common Khmer spellings of his name, both of which are in the glossary; I use So Phim. I provide the Khmer script in the glossary for most of the Khmer terms I use in the book.

CHINA'S RELATIONS WITH DEMOCRATIC KAMPUCHEA

The greatest friend of the Kampuchean people is the People's Republic of China, and none other. The People's Republic of China is the large and reliable rear fallback base of the Kampuchean and world revolutions.

—Kaev Meah, veteran Cambodian Revolutionary, September 30, 1976[1]

The Chinese government never took part in or intervened into the politics of Democratic Kampuchea.

—Zhang Jinfeng, Chinese Ambassador to Cambodia, January 22, 2010[2]

When people mention the Khmer Rouge, many might be reminded of the support China once gave it. This is a problem that cannot be avoided. No matter whether China wants it or not, as China's relationships with Cambodia and Southeast Asia grow closer, people will allude to that history.

—Ding Gang, September 27, 2012[3]

A particularly haunting Vietnam War–era photograph, taken by the Japanese photojournalist Taizo Ichinose, who would himself perish behind enemy lines in 1973, shows the road leading to Angkor Thom, the twelfth-century epicenter of Cambodian civilization that today is a bustling tourist site.[4] The road is covered in detritus from the forest and is devoid of any trace of people—but for a human spinal cord mixed in with the debris (fig. 1.1).[5] There is nothing romantic about the image: this jungle evokes Carthage, not Walden. It is as ugly and grotesque an image of a rural setting as can be imagined, one that also perfectly captures the atmospherics of Hobbes's state of nature—the absence of any governing apparatus whatsoever. It is a snapshot of anarchy.

People tend, not unreasonably, to regard Cambodia's rule by the Communist Party of Kampuchea (CPK)—commonly known as the Khmer Rouge—from 1975 to 1979 as one in which the only thing that distinguished the country from such anarchy was its sophisticated killing apparatus.[6] This is not quite right. The

FIGURE 1.1.   The road to Angkor Thom. Photo by Taizo Ichinose.

CPK-led regime of Democratic Kampuchea (DK) is rightly understood, first and foremost, as a regime that killed a vast number of its own citizens and horribly brutalized those it did not murder outright. But it does not necessarily follow that, if we peel away its extensive security apparatus, DK resembled a country-sized extension of Taizo's terrible image. That is, DK was not defined by the negative space of anarchy. It was a state. It was a totalitarian state. It was often a poorly run totalitarian state. It was a state that excelled at fear, death, and hubris far better than anything else. But it was a state defined by a distinctive network of organizations and institutions, not the absence of them.

There is also a historic context to this image that hints at the role of China in the narrative to follow. At the time this photo was taken, not far away at Mount Kulen, the deposed Cambodian monarch Norodom Sihanouk was meeting with the CPK leadership in the latter's jungle headquarters, a rendezvous that had been insisted upon by the government of China. Sihanouk headed a coalition government (Gouvernement Royal d'Union Nationale du Kampuchéa, or GRUNK) brokered by Beijing that, in just three years, saw the transformation of the CPK from a junior partner with a few dozen rifles in 1970 to the coalition's dominant power.

China had been involved in every aspect and at each stage of the CPK rise to power. From 1970 to 1975, Beijing provided GRUNK with an annual budget of US$2 million as well as office space and living quarters at the Friendship Hotel in northwestern Beijing, while Sihanouk himself took up residence at the former French Embassy. Even the Chinese mission to Phnom Penh was physically relocated to Beijing, where the Chinese ambassador to Cambodia, Kang Maozhao, carried out his functions as if he were on Cambodian soil.[7] Beijing continued to provide arms, clothing, and food and even printed banknotes for use upon the CPK's assumption of power. And as relations between the Cambodian and Vietnamese communists began to sour, China's support for the CPK insurgency correspondingly increased.

After April 17, 1975, when victorious CPK soldiers marched into Phnom Penh and other cities throughout the country, the world of many Cambodians was turned upside down: cities were emptied of their residents, who were forcibly relocated to the countryside; markets disappeared; money was abolished (the banknotes printed in China were mothballed); officials of the *ancien régime* were liquidated; and China's influence was radically altered. Up to that point, Beijing had been both willing and able to graft its strategic interests onto the political evolution of the CPK. After 1975, China's apparent willingness to continue doing so never wavered; its ability to do so, however, decreased significantly. To put it somewhat inelegantly, China embraced a sucker's payoff in a Faustian bargain: it justifiably received international condemnation for maintaining the viability of the CPK regime while receiving precious little tangible benefit from its Cambodian allies. And this provides the central question of this book: why was a powerful state like China unable to influence its far weaker and ostensibly dependent client state? Or, to put it in policy terms: exactly what did Chinese development aid buy?

In today's world, as the topic of Chinese foreign assistance grows in importance, the answers matter. The conventional wisdom holds that a rapidly-developing China is currently behind a new wave of economic colonialization, facilitated and nurtured by Chinese foreign aid and assistance. This has raised alarm bells both in these "colonies" themselves[8] and in the policy circles of Washington, D.C., which have seen an emerging consensus that such foreign policy behavior is a manifestation of China's inexorably rising power on the international stage.[9]

This is not inconsistent with the received wisdom on Sino-DK relations. One conventional view is that the relationship was a product of a shared revolutionary outlook and a natural affinity based on the similarities of experiences in the two regimes' paths to power. It argues that DK leader Pol Pot was himself greatly influenced by events in China, some of which—particularly the opening salvos of the Cultural Revolution in 1965—he witnessed firsthand, and by his friendship with Chinese officials like the mysterious and amoral radical Kang Sheng, whose own training in the USSR during Stalin's Great Purge fashioned him into China's Lavrentiy Beria.[10]

Another approach, based on *Realpolitik,* posits that Beijing's relations with Phnom Penh were a function of regional geopolitics, a product of the Sino-Soviet split, Hanoi's increasing dependence on Moscow, and the race between Vietnam and China for U.S. diplomatic recognition.[11] Aside from the sterilizing effect this has on some fundamental normative issues regarding collaboration with the DK regime, this level of analysis tells us little about the actual mechanics of the relationship. Such an approach cannot account for variation in the success or failure of individual assistance projects.

The two lines of argument share the assumption that Beijing, as a regional and a nuclear power, was able to influence a small, poor, overwhelmingly premodern (indeed, medieval) agricultural state of seven million. They do not—cannot—account for China's failure to exploit this asymmetrical relationship. As a result, we are left with an empirical and historical fact bereft of explanation or context.

Still another approach, this one ideational, can be found in Sophie Richardson's *China, Cambodia, and the Five Principles of Peaceful Coexistence*, which centers on Chinese motivations, that is, the "five principles" themselves—mutual respect for territorial integrity and sovereignty, nonaggression, noninterference in the internal affairs of others, equality and mutual benefit, and peaceful coexistence.[12] Although Richardson makes a persuasive case for Beijing's subordination of some of its own interests to the larger contours governing the relationship, her analysis is not engineered to evaluate China's concrete gains from the relationship.

By contrast, the argument in this book will show that in the deeply uneven bilateral relationship, on the policy front at least, it was in fact China that ended up as the subordinate party. Before explaining why this was so, it may be useful to show that the political history of China's relationship with Democratic Kampuchea confirms that the expected outcome—a relationship in which Beijing dictated critical strategic terms to Phnom Penh—never came to pass.

Dynamic Interaction in Sino-DK Relations

For decades China had supported the Vietnamese communists against the French and then against the United States, but as the fraternal socialist ties between the two countries gave way to traditional mistrust spawned from centuries of Vietnamese armed resistance to Chinese regional hegemony, Beijing's suspicions of Hanoi mounted. In 1969, Beijing's relations with Moscow had reached their nadir, when Chinese and Soviet troops stopped just short of limited war along their isolated border in Siberia. By 1975, the prospect of China being boxed in to the north by the USSR and to the south by Moscow's ally Vietnam was becoming increasingly troubling to China's leaders. The establishment of DK in April of that year was an opportunity for China to mitigate the effects of a Soviet-Vietnamese axis. The CPK's growing hostilities against Vietnam, also borne of centuries of ethnic tensions that often erupted into gruesome violence, ensured Phnom Penh's distance from Hanoi and Moscow. The United States, suffering at the time from "Indochina fatigue" after what had been the longest war in its history, largely stayed clear of the fray.

Within days of the fall of Phnom Penh on April 17, Chinese aid in the form of food and technical assistance started arriving.[13] A string of official visits began as well. On April 24, Xie Wenqing, a reporter from the international desk of the New China News Agency (Xinhua), arrived in the Cambodian capital. Four days after that, DK Foreign Minister Ieng Sary returned from China, where he had been living on and off since 1971, accompanied by Shen Jian, deputy director of the CCP International Liaison Department and Beijing's point man on Democratic Kampuchea.[14] On June 21, on a secret visit to China to secure military and nonmilitary development aid, Cambodian leader Pol Pot himself met with Mao Zedong.[15] At the time, Mao's commitment of one billion dollars was the largest aid pledge in the history of the PRC.[16] In August, a delegation from the PRC Ministry of National Defense visited Cambodia to survey DK military needs, followed by a visit by Wang Shangrong, deputy chief of staff of the Chinese People's Liberation Army (PLA), in October.[17]

At the same time, DK began the first wave of political purges, a campaign to liquidate the old exploiting classes—monks, urban bourgeois, intellectuals, and officials of the Khmer Republic. This development was startling enough for ailing, cancer-stricken Zhou Enlai to warn visiting DK officials Khieu Samphan and Ieng Thirith that they should avoid making the same mistakes of immoderation that China had made in the not-so-distant past. Flush with victory, his guests are reported to have smiled at him condescendingly.[18]

A thornier issue was how to handle Sihanouk. The prince, whom many of Cambodia's peasants regarded as a living god, had done more than any other individual to legitimize the CPK. Ousted in the March 1970 action that established the Khmer Republic, the mercurial Sihanouk quickly embraced his former enemies, the Khmer Rouge.[19] After returning to Cambodia in 1975 from a world tour promoting the new regime and finding himself unhappy as a figurehead, Sihanouk sought to retire. Although the top DK leadership was happy to sideline the prince, whom they referred to as "a runt of a tiger bereft of claws or teeth [with] only his own impending death to look forward to," they feared alienating Beijing.[20] From the mid-1960s onward, Sihanouk had enjoyed a particularly good relationship with China's top leaders, including Mao, Zhou, and Liu Shaoqi. He even provided a unique "model" for Chinese leaders to cultivate among the nonaligned developing world: a left-leaning royal sympathetic to China.[21] During a hasty set of meetings from March 11 to 13, 1976, the DK leadership accepted Sihanouk's resignation while severing any contacts between the prince and visiting foreign delegations, particularly from China; this affected such dignitaries as Zhou Enlai's widow, Deng Yingchao, whose request to meet with Sihanouk on a January 1978 visit was denied.

In April 1976, radical leftist Zhang Chunqiao made a secret visit to Cambodia. One top DK Foreign Ministry official said he would not have known about the visit if he had not noticed some children making a welcoming banner for Zhang (as this was a CCP-to-CPK visit, it is not surprising that the Foreign Ministry was kept in the dark). Zhang's purposes in visiting were to demonstrate the Gang of Four's support for Democratic Kampuchea and to assess the situation in the country.[22]

Meanwhile, following a lull in early 1976, aid picked up again, including plans to build a secret weapons factory just outside Phnom Penh.[23] According to a 1976 DK report, China had committed to shipping one thousand tons of military hardware to DK, including tanks and other military vehicles, ammunition, communications equipment, and other materiel.[24] Accompanying this rise in imports was a shift toward domestic economic development through the adoption of a Four Year Plan (1977–1980) along with a new wave of purges, this time focusing on political malfeasance within the regime, particularly but by no means exclusively the cadres of the Northwest Zone. Once again, Beijing chose not to notice.

Did the death of Mao Zedong in September 1976 and the arrest of the powerful leftist faction by Mao's more moderate successor Hua Guofeng one month later provide China with some potential leverage to compel the DK leaders to show a little restraint? Legal scholar John Ciorciari believes so. Pol Pot demonstrated his pragmatic streak when he denounced the "counter-revolutionary Gang of Four anti-Party clique" and demonstrated his support for Hua's actions.[25] But Beijing, refraining from exploiting its leverage, did not discontinue its unconditional aid. On December 10, 1976, a delegation of Chinese journalists led by Mu Qing, deputy chief of Xinhua, visited the country, meeting with the soon-to-be-purged Minister of Propaganda, Hu Nim. Two weeks later, from December 24, 1976, to January 2, 1977, a delegation from the Ministry of Foreign Economic Relations led by Fan Yi met with DK economic czar Vorn Vet.[26]

China did, however, succeed in getting Pol Pot to abandon his tendency toward excessive secrecy and introducing him to the wider world in a lavish high-profile trip to China in September and October 1977. DK Foreign Ministry officials and staff went without sleep for two days and two nights to prepare for the trip, drafting Pol Pot's speech on the declaration of the existence of the CPK. As a former Foreign Ministry official put it, "Before that, it was only *Angkar*"— the term denotes a faceless, omnipotent "Organization"—before adding that it was high time for a publicity tour of this type.[27] It was the first time that people, including members of his immediate family, recognized Pol Pot as the former schoolteacher Saloth Sar. And it was also the first instance that the DK regime volunteered publicly—more than two years after coming to power—that it was led by the CPK. DK's malleability on this issue was a response to China's support of DK against Vietnam. *The Peking Review* described the bilateral relationship for the first time as "unbreakable."[28]

A DK official who accompanied Pol Pot throughout his trip to China recalls that when the Chinese leaders criticized Pol Pot, he smiled to demonstrate that he was taking it all in. Deng Xiaoping in particular castigated the CPK for emptying its cities and for not feeding its people adequately. Pol Pot informed his staff about what the Chinese had said, pointedly without any instructions about how to act on it. To the Cambodians, the message was clear: continue as if the Chinese had said nothing.[29]

But the domestic politics of the two states were not completely independent from one another. Perhaps no single individual in China better symbolized the concept of "self-reliance" than the head of the famous Dazhai model commune, Chen Yonggui. Chen's extended visit to Cambodia in December 1977 underscored the legitimacy of the CPK's own rhetoric of self-sufficient development. His trip was also meant to shore up his position at home and was apparently perceived by the Khmer Rouge leadership as a last, best, and, ultimately, unsuccessful attempt to help strengthen the waning leftist line in China that was threatened by the (re)emergence of Deng Xiaoping and the reform coalition. Pol Pot himself hosted Chen and personally took him all over Cambodia, where the Chinese leader met with a constellation of DK officials, including zone leaders like Ke Pauk, So Phim, and Ta Mok; military commanders like Meas Mut and Thuch Rin; and a number of local DK cadres. On December 13, he went to Takeo, where he was received by General Sombot, Mok's brother-in-law. While there, the embodiment of Dazhai visited the Leay Bo model commune, which boasted nine thousand families spread over four thousand hectares.[30]

At the same time, refugee accounts of the terror inside Cambodia were becoming increasingly difficult to ignore. These were ridiculed by DK leaders—with less and less credibility. Internal political purges continued in DK; in 1977 and 1978 the Eastern Zone bordering Vietnam became the focus, leading to the death of Zone Secretary So Phim, which severely weakened DK's ability to fight Hanoi. Yet even while Phnom Penh undermined its own military capabilities, it ratcheted up its rhetoric and military activity against the Vietnamese. This was happening just as China was seeking to mend its fences with the outside world after two decades of bellicose rhetoric and autarkic policies.

As before, Chinese appeals for moderation were rebuffed. At the same time Chinese aid-based delegations increased, which resulted in mixed signals to the DK leadership.[31] In October 1977, a delegation headed by Qi Duichao, vice director in the Ministry of Communications, visited Phnom Penh to examine ways to rebuild the railway, particularly the Phnom Penh–Kampong Som and Phnom Penh–Poipet lines.[32] And on December 24, 1977, a delegation from the Ministry of Foreign Trade arrived to discuss bilateral commerce.

The steady stream of Chinese visits continued into 1978. On March 4, Communication Committee chairman and railway worker representative Mei Prang[33] received a delegation from the Chinese Ministry of Railways and the newly formed China Machinery Import-Export Corporation. In late July, Pol Pot organized a banquet at the Royal Palace for more than a hundred Chinese technicians working in DK. One Chinese technician recalled that during the banquet, he told Pol Pot of the state of progress at the petroleum refinery at Kampong Som, emphasizing the problems of worker shortages. Not long thereafter, a new group of laborers was sent over to help with the work.[34] From November 4 to 8, Wang Dongxing, Yu Qiuli, Hu Yaobang, and Shen Jian of the CCP International Liaison Department toured the country, visiting the Tha-1 (traditional medicine) and Tha-4 (modern medicine) factories and concluding with a trip to Angkor Wat. Exactly a month later, another Ministry of Foreign Trade delegation, led by Deputy Minister of Foreign Trade Chen Jie, visited Kampong Chhnang and Battambang.[35]

FIGURE 1.2.   Chinese delegation with diplomatic corps and technical experts, PRC Embassy in Phnom Penh, November 1978. Note in the middle of the first row (from left) Hu Yaobang, Yu Qiuli, and Wang Dongxing. Shen Jian is fifth from the right in the first row. Photograph in the author's possession.

During a trip by Nuon Chea, "Brother Number Two," to China from September 2 to 18, 1978, emerging Chinese leader Deng Xiaoping warned him that Phnom Penh must be less provocative toward Vietnam, but China nevertheless continued to send military and nonmilitary aid to DK in increasing numbers throughout this period.[36] China did draw the line at providing troops on Cambodian soil to deter the Vietnamese, despite frequent urgent pleas from Phnom Penh. When the Vietnamese army invaded in the closing days of 1978, Beijing continued its support of DK to the point of waging a short war against Vietnam in early 1979. After both sides claimed victory in an unprecedented war between two socialist countries, Hanoi would continue to be distracted by the CPK insurgency during Vietnam's decade-long occupation of Cambodia.

The Argument

Even before the collapse of its client state—the result of a Vietnamese invasion that Phnom Penh had instigated and that Beijing had repeatedly and unsuccessfully warned its DK allies to avoid—China's provision of vast quantities of cadres, guns, and money had bought precious little. I argue that this outcome was due to bureaucratic fragmentation in China combined with an institutional matrix in Cambodia either strong enough to resist Chinese demands or too weak to act on them. Along the three main dimensions of foreign aid—military, trade, and infrastructure—Chinese assistance was able to shape DK policy in ways favorable to Beijing in trade and commerce only. The other two areas saw at best modest returns for China, albeit for completely opposing reasons. In the case of military assistance, Chinese influence was curtailed because of the strength of DK military institutions, despite the asymmetries of power between the two countries. In the case of infrastructure development, Chinese investment brought even smaller returns because of the fragmentation of the Chinese bureaucracies and their inability to engage their Cambodian counterparts, all of which resulted in complete project failure. In both China and Cambodia, then, the limits of Chinese influence on DK politics and policy were a function of bureaucratic-institutional integrity. Moreover, the Chinese and Cambodian Leninist systems were so different that it was very difficult, if not impossible, for either side to understand the other sufficiently and to exploit that knowledge. Again, the exception is commerce, which remained largely separate from DK domestic politics and which China shaped into an institution that behaved more like a Chinese than a DK organization.

Some might dismiss this argument as not particularly counterintuitive; one should expect, goes this line of reasoning, that the key to understanding outcomes is the interface between the bureaucratic politics of the two countries in question. After all, this is endemic in the policy universe of foreign aid, as anybody involved in such projects will readily attest. It is true that there is an obsession in the social sciences with finding a "puzzle," but although there is something superficial and ultimately unsatisfying about this sort of faddishness, the more important objections to such a criticism lie elsewhere.

The greater challenge involves regarding the DK regime as unique—because of its violent and bloodthirsty nature—while simultaneously focusing on the prosaic aspects of bureaucratic politics. This dissonance renders controversial what would otherwise be a largely intuitive and straightforward—even unsurprising—argument. The notion that different pairings of Chinese and Khmer bureaucratic strength and weakness would produce different outcomes is what a neutral outsider would predict. But what outsider can be neutral about DK policy? In this book, I seek to break through this conceptual dissonance.

Finally, some may object to my leveraging a historical case to make inferences about contemporary Chinese foreign policy behavior. Obviously, the technological aspect of aid projects has advanced in the past several decades. But it has done so without a corresponding change in China's institutional apparatus. Some might argue that China under Mao is not the same as China under Hu Jintao or Xi Jinping. Of course this is true. However, the bureaucratic-institutional analysis that follows is not so much about the policymaking front as the policy execution front, for this is where institutions, precisely because they are so resistant to change, become important as an explanation. Here, the similarities are striking.

Although Chinese behavior is no longer as constrained by the dictates of central planning as it once was, the market has not yet supplanted the most important institutional relationships, modes of action, and investment decisions. Indeed, when we separate out the export-led manufacturing arm of China's economy over the past several decades and concentrate instead on the decisions that have shaped the economy—from the dual-track pricing system in the 1980s, SOE reform in the 1990s, the structure and process of infrastructure investment in the 2000s—it becomes clear that the market remains embedded in the vast Chinese bureaucracy. The dramatic, phoenix-like rise of the National Development and Reform Commission out of the ashes of its previous incarnation, the State Planning Commission, underscores this point.

One of the fundamental tensions of China's reform era has to do with the juxtaposition of an increasingly complex set of demands on the state with a slowly-evolving government apparatus constructed during the high tide of Soviet influence and central planning. Of course, these institutions have changed, morphed, and evolved in some important ways over time. But what is striking is the degree to which they have remained static. One can even argue that institutional fragmentation has, if anything, become even more pronounced: China's fourth generation leaders lacked the gravitas or sheer power that Mao Zedong or Deng Xiaoping were able to wield or perhaps merely lacked the incentivizing leverage of the command economy, in which strategic and scarce inputs could be withheld if downstream institutions showed signs of defecting or vetoing policy in its implementation stages.

A Tale of Two Leninist Systems

The analysis that follows also provides a structured comparison between Chinese and DK domestic institutions. In many ways the two countries' organizational logics were quite similar: both were Leninist single-party systems; both had a significant rural component that made communication with their respective centers difficult; and both systems had considerable concentrations of power housed in their respective party standing committees. And, as I will show, in both cases, institutional integrity demonstrated substantial deviation from the Leninist ideal. However, the ways in which individuals navigated the two institutional environments were markedly different. As a result, the two systems themselves—through the aggregation of individual-level micro-decisions based on managing uncertainty—behaved in fundamentally different ways.

In China, a given administrative unit at any point in the system is often bombarded with requests, demands, and exhortations to undertake all sorts of actions. The logic of the policy stream in China is that any unit enjoys two types of relationships with other units. One is a consultative, nonbinding set of relations, in which the unit in question considers instructions from an administrative superior unit but is not required to implement those instructions ("professional relations"). The other type is binding, requiring the subordinate unit to undertake the orders it receives from its administrative superior ("leadership relations"). Every unit in China has professional relations with any number of other units, but each has *leadership* relations with only one other unit. If leadership relations are decentralized, as in the majority of cases, it is referred to as "leadership across a piece" (*kuaishang lingdao*), while if leadership relations are centralized, it is referred to as "leadership along a line" (*tiaoshang lingdao*). Outside observers, unaware of this distinction, often find Chinese institutional behavior baffling, but for those in the system, it is fairly straightforward and predictable.[37]

In DK—and in Cambodian politics and society more generally—the dominant indigenous organizing principle of interest appears to have been that of a "string" (*khsae*). Local and national leaders oftentimes placed protégés, family members, and others within their "strings" into positions of authority, providing a sort of logic to the formal but increasingly arbitrary organization and constant reorganization of power and authority. Socheat Nhean tells us that this patron-client relationship was endemic throughout the system.[38] Like the informal relations of *guanxi* in China, it could not overcome institutional constraints and imperatives, at least not head-on. Unlike *guanxi,* the concept of *khsae* appears to have been more central to cadres' decision-making, resulting in a less predictable and more corrupt system in Cambodia.

Khmer Rouge Southwest Zone Commander Ta Mok was masterful at creating *khsae* networks. It is worth quoting Ben Kiernan at length to show just how extensive Mok's *khsae* networks really were:

> Mok carefully placed a network of family members in various important positions in his Zone. These included two brothers-in-law, four sons, two daughters, and five sons-in-law. They were all promoted through the ranks, most after serving time in Mok's home district, Tram Kak, known as District 105 of Region 13…Mok's son-in-law, Khe Muth…rose to become secretary of the 3rd Southwest Division. Mok's daughter, Khom, replaced her husband Muth as CPK secretary of Tram Kak District. In 1975 another daughter, Ho, became director of the Region 13 hospital. Two sons, Cham and Chay, also served on the Tram Kak CPK district committee, and a brother-in-law, San, a former schoolteacher, was a leading CPK official. A second brother-in-law, Tith, was CPK secretary of Kirivong (District 109). A third son, Chong, was CPK secretary of District 55 (Prey Krabas). A fourth son, Kol, was a leading official in Kampot province, or Region 35 of the Southwest Zone. A second son-in-law, Boran, begun his career as a courier for the CPK Center and then in 1975 took charge of a new factory in Tram Kak. A third son-in-law, Soeun, commander of Region 13's 120th Regiment, was promoted to division commander in 1975. A fourth, Ren, was a brigade commander in 1975. Tram Kak was the most "ideologically advanced" district in Cambodia…Mok also managed to get family members promoted to positions outside the Zone, through his connections with the Center. In 1975, Ho's husband Yin, Mok's fifth son-in-law, became a commander at Pochentong Airport outside Phnom Penh. Son-in-law Khe Muth retained command of the 3rd Southwest Division and also became CPK secretary of Kompong Som city and commander of the DK navy.[39]

Nor was this something that occurred only in the provinces far from Phnom Penh. Although Pol Pot and Nuon Chea, Brothers One and Two, respectively, refused special protection for their own families, they did have their own factional groupings. Ministries such as Foreign Affairs almost seemed to flaunt their family-based *khsae* networks. Foreign Minister Ieng Sary's wife, Ieng Thirith, was the DK minister of social affairs. Poch Mona, who worked in the Secretariat with her two sisters, Poch Dany and Poch Yamin, was the wife of Ngo Hac Team, who worked in the ministry's Information and Propaganda Bureau. Peh Puriet, who headed the Production Bureau, was the husband of So Se, who worked in the Secretariat. The Civil Aviation Bureau was directly under the control of Ieng Sary and was managed by his nephew, Srey Chanthoeun, among others. DK's Ambassador to China, Pich Chean, was the husband of Yong Moeun, the Embassy's CPK liaison with Pol Pot's all-important Office 870. And the list goes on.

Khsae could also work to identify potential enemies of the regime.[40] Once a single individual was targeted for investigation, torture, and execution, one of the principal goals of the "confession" exacted under torture was to identify the other members of the "conspiracy." Disgraced zone commander and Minister of Commerce Koy Thuon provided the names of thousands of co-conspirators.[41] Although the conspiracies were almost always false and were admitted to as a means to stop the pain of torture or out of fear of execution, the actual "strings" were often quite real.

Sometimes leaders would try to protect those in their *khsae* who had come under suspicion. Former zone commander Ke Pauk—not somebody known for his kindness—provides an example that is representative of other cases I have come across. In his own words: "In February 1977, Phnom Penh sent security trucks to arrest the chiefs of [zone-level] ministries: ministry of agriculture, industry,... and public affairs. I protected the chief of rubber plantations, because I considered him as [a] parent." Ke Pauk's delay allowed the rubber plantation chief to escape to the forest.[42] *Khsae,* then, are vital to understanding the fluid, unpredictable, and ultimately personal nature of the Cambodian political system.

In sum, both countries suffered from subversions of the formal institutional structure, whether fragmented, as in China, or fluid, as in DK. But, as we will see, China, then as now, appears to have had a greater degree of institutional integrity—as measured by regularity, predictability, and functionability—than DK or, for that matter, the Kingdom of Cambodia in the present day. As this book will further demonstrate, however, there was also considerable variation across Chinese and Cambodian institutions, which in turn accounted for variation in policy outcomes.

A Note on Sources

As one might expect, the answers to the questions I raise are not readily available in the public record. Clearly embarrassed by this episode, China has made access to data on the subject difficult, if not impossible.[43] There are clear demarcations of time and space even in the internal (*neibu*) classification system: the period between 1960 and 1990 in Cambodia is off-limits even to those scholars with special access to classified Ministry of Foreign Affairs documents, even while the files on Laos and Vietnam are not so restricted.

I was therefore compelled to turn to sources outside of China. The National Archives of Cambodia house an extraordinary amount of technical material on Chinese aid, including shipping schedules and bills of lading, bilateral memoranda of understanding and trade agreements, and—particularly important—Chinese-language factory and project blueprints. My initial delight in stumbling onto these blueprints was tempered by the fact that that I was unable to evaluate them properly. This was not only because of their technical nature; it was also because I could not assess whether they described large- or small-scale projects, whether they were cutting-edge or not, and whether these were the types of things that China was undertaking in China itself. Native Chinese-speaking engineers not of that generation were similarly unable to make sense of the written record.

A breakthrough occurred when a student of mine mentioned that she had family connections that might uncover some contacts that could breathe life into these documents. While I (figuratively) held my breath, she, over the course of several months, was able to locate a set of individuals who had worked on the projects described in this book as well as other, contemporary ones. These interview subjects, all of them retired technical experts, had worked for government ministries or in attached research institutes. Their recollections were remarkably sharp, but we nevertheless cross-referenced answers across interviews, interviewees, and additional source materials, such as diaries, almanacs, and project plans.[44] All the interviewees were quite forthcoming, with the only constraint being their memory. The questions were, as I have always posed them, more of the "what happened?" or "how did this work?" variety and were not in and of themselves "gotcha"-type questions. Given the advanced age of this demographic and the prolonged exposure of many of them to chemicals and other toxic materials during the course of their work, a great many of them have already died. The pool of potential informants is thus very small indeed.[45]

Back on the Cambodia side, in addition to the National Archives, I benefited from documents held at the Documentation Center of Cambodia (DC-CAM). These included interviews, DK Standing Committee meeting minutes, telegrams, and other key documents. I also was able to draw on a modest network of contacts in Cambodia that afforded me the opportunity to meet with former DK ministry officials from the Foreign Ministry and the Departments of Propaganda and Commerce; soldiers, many of whom were disgraced and forced to build the airport at Krang Leav (the subject of chapter 4); local cadres and foot soldiers at the zone and district levels; an official posted to the DK Embassy in

Beijing; and guards and other staff members of Office 870, which was Pol Pot's administrative unit. These interviewees were far more varied in terms of their initial willingness to talk (almost all relaxed once we began chatting), their ability to recollect details, their suspicion of my motives (some insisted on writing down my name), their knowledge of what happened outside their administrative jurisdiction, and their willingness to share it. A number, however, were extremely forthcoming and provided vivid descriptions and extraordinary details. Some of the Cambodia interviews were in a mixture of English and French; many were in Khmer, in which I was ably assisted by my research associate; and one was in Chinese.

These interviews supplemented the slow but significant trickle of information that the Extraordinary Chambers in the Courts of Cambodia (ECCC) have made available in the form of transcripts from the ongoing trial of Nuon Chea, Ieng Sary, and Khieu Samphan.[46] Although I worked as a consultant at the ECCC, I am legally barred from using the vast reservoir of confidential data that might one day paint a fuller picture of the DK institutional apparatus than what appears in the pages to come. Other ECCC material that is in the public domain has proven to be extremely useful.

The Normative Dimension

Although my approach here is grounded in bureaucratic politics, my focus on the Khmer Rouge provokes expectations about the large normative dimension in which this study is embedded. Democratic Kampuchea was a regime that devastated the country, oversaw the execution and death through violence and neglect of a considerable percentage of its population, and left no enduring legacy in its wake. As a social, economic, and political experiment, it was a failure. Its treatment of the Cambodian people is rightly seen as a vast collection of crimes against humanity that laid bare the ugliest dimensions of the human condition. And throughout its short tenure in power in DK from 1975 to 1979 and its longer existence in the jungle for two decades and then in the courtroom of the ECCC, the surviving CPK leadership has shown no remorse for its brutal behavior.[47]

Without Chinese support, the DK regime would almost certainly have collapsed. The Khmer Rouge inherited a nation that had been devastated by a civil war, U.S. B-52 airstrikes, and various governments that had been unable to rule effectively since the late 1960s. Ironically, it squandered a major source of social and political capital: the goodwill of the people who were willing to sacrifice a great deal for political and economic stability. This wasting of mass support, combined with the liquidation of moderate elements in the regime, sealed DK's fate. As its only powerful ally, China might have moderated CPK actions on either or both of these fronts but did not do so in any effective fashion. Instead, Beijing propped up the DK regime until the very last days of its existence, extending its reign and indirectly contributing to the vast human rights abuses and mass killings that became the defining feature of DK.

If the main question of this book is "what does foreign aid buy for China?" the flip side is "why does China support contemptible regimes?" The answer is elusive for at least two reasons. The first has to do with the fact that Chinese decision-making on policy matters, then as now, is shrouded in layers of secrecy. This can be mitigated somewhat by drawing careful inferences about Chinese interests and motivations and from subsequent Chinese behavior.

The second has to do with how we think about China. Although vast scholarship has debunked the assumption that China is a monolith, it is a difficult one to shake, particularly when attempting to explain Chinese foreign policy. Nevertheless, it is important to emphasize China as a vast network of competing, corrupting, and sometimes confluent interests that strive for dominance in policy-making and policy implementation by taking advantage of the institutional fissures and fragmentation that define the Chinese state. Although the remainder of this book uses this perspective as the principal lens to understand the central question under discussion, this fragmentation of the Chinese state serves another purpose: it helps us navigate—if not quite untangle and certainly not resolve—the normative dimension.

The point of departure is the level of analysis: are we looking at leaders, factions, bureaucracies, or individuals? Each of these broad categories lays claim to a different set of behaviors and motivations. Moreover, various levels of analysis waxed and waned in influence during the 1975–1979 period, arguably one of the least stable in post-1949 China. The DK era, from April 1975 to January 1979, spans a remarkable period in Chinese political development. When the Khmer Rouge marched into Phnom Penh, leftists were ascendant in China as Mao Zedong attempted to enshrine his legacy of permanent revolution; moderates like Zhou Enlai, succumbing to the final stages of cancer, and Deng Xiaoping, only months away from being purged for the second time, were on the defensive. By the time Vietnam invaded Cambodia in the closing days of 1978, Deng and a coalition of reformers had returned from the political wilderness, arrested or neutralized leading leftist demagogues, and moved China to the development trajectory it is on to this day. Thus, during this short time, the whole universe of Chinese political coalitions, configurations, and interests was on display. Each had its own motivations for maintaining strong bilateral relations with DK.

Leftist leaders in China, such as Zhang Chunqiao and Chen Yonggui—who, as noted, visited DK in 1976 and 1977, respectively—embraced the CPK approach to socialist utopianism and appeared to be not much bothered by the "negative externalities" imposed on Cambodian citizens. Indeed, it is unclear if these leftists would have considered such externalities to be "negative." Certainly, if the previous decade in China offers any clue, advocates of the leftist-inspired and -fueled Cultural Revolution had very little concern for the Chinese individuals who were targeted or, later, for the Red Guards who were unceremoniously demobilized and sent down to the countryside. Although it is often forgotten today, the Cultural Revolution was a debasement of the mechanism that separated China from the Soviet (and DK) approach to political conflict. Unlike Stalin and Pol Pot, Mao had developed the doctrine of "rectification" (*zhengfeng*) in the Communist base area of Yan'an in the early 1940s, whereby incorrect political orientations were understood to be a healable sickness rather than an irreparable, inherent personal characteristic of an individual "enemy."[48] By the mid-1960s, this distinction had been all but lost, and the leaders and beneficiaries of the Cultural Revolution increasingly resembled their prior Soviet and subsequent Cambodian counterparts in killing, rather than "curing," their political opponents. The CPK's literalist interpretation of communism, abandonment of the cities, abolition of money, and creation of a truly classless society—all of this inspired Chinese leftists, as it did leftists all over the world, from Noam Chomsky to Malcolm Caldwell, to support the regime on ideological grounds, a stance that required turning a blind eye to individual suffering.[49] For China's leftist leaders seeking a way to inject a second wind into the Cultural Revolution, which was by then in its ninth year and had long since lost its initial momentum, a successful *über*-Maoist regime in Cambodia could strengthen their position at home.

At the same time, with Mao's blessing, Zhou Enlai, Deng Xiaoping, and a number of other leaders had started to embrace a cold, pragmatic calculus with regard to international relations. As Sino-Soviet relations devolved into crisis mode in 1969, China was able to balance the Soviet threat by rapprochement with the United States in 1972. The subordination of ideological purity to pragmatic concerns was apparent when Mao and Zhou unselfconsciously referred to firing "empty cannons" (*kong pao*) of rhetoric in meetings with U.S. President Richard Nixon and U.S. National Security Advisor Henry Kissinger.[50] But it quickly became clear that the United States was unable to prevent the growth of Hanoi as a regional hegemon on China's southeast flank. DK's importance to Beijing increased just as the CPK's own suspicions of Vietnamese intentions, informed by centuries of encroachment and conquest of Cambodian territory, began to escalate. Thus, any moral failings on the part of the DK leadership were outweighed in Beijing's eyes by the benefits of providing a check on Moscow-supported Vietnamese influence in Indochina.

Both the radical leftist and the pragmatist positions pointedly ignored—indeed, prolonged—the suffering of the Cambodian people: the starvation, the killing, and the negation of life as it had existed before 1975. They place China on the wrong side of history, as is the case for many other nations who supported the CPK after 1979, including the United States.

Another—indeed, for this study, the principal—unit of analysis is the Chinese bureaucracy. Government bureaucracies in China and elsewhere are political players, each seeking to promote its own institutional interests and strengthen its standing vis-à-vis competing institutions over budget, influence, and power. The prize is influence over the crafting and implementation of policy. The simple and powerful logic is that the greater the scope of a given bureaucracy, the greater the quantity of resources it commands and thus the greater its political influence. As with the two previous dimensions of analysis, such a motivating factor has little concern for individuals negatively affected by the policy per se. In a way, it is as coldly secular as the leftist and pragmatic positions discussed above. However, for individual projects to work, it is often counterproductive to abuse the people on the front lines, that is, the actual workers. Cambodian workers lived on a starvation diet with no wages, under the constant threat of arbitrary and senseless torture and execution in a disease-ridden environment; their lot ran counter to the organizational goals of the Chinese bureaucracies, which required a healthy and at least somewhat contented workforce. Chinese bureaucracies were thus placed in a politically challenging and internally contradictory position.

It is at the individual level where the motivations of Chinese workers and technicians come into sharp relief. On the one hand, the Chinese shared their work units' preference for well-rested, well-fed workers to see a given project through. But, as we will see in subsequent chapters, they also took some risks by trying to ease the lot of their Cambodian counterparts where they could. They shared food and cigarettes and pointedly never criticized the workers, for no apparent reason other than because it was the "human" thing to do. The Cambodian workers interviewed for this project were strongly unanimous on this point: the scarce glimmerings of humanity they experienced during the ghastly rule of the Khmer Rouge were uniformly extended to them by the Chinese expatriates.

Confronted with this already simplified configuration of interests, it should be apparent that the impulse to simplify further does an injustice to the normative complexities of the relationship. If one focuses solely on the individuals on the ground in DK, the technicians and the skilled workers sent to manage the Chinese-sponsored infrastructure projects and factories, we see rare glimpses of humanity on the part of individual Chinese. Overemphasizing such behavior runs the risk of whitewashing China, which after all propped up and supported an appalling regime. On the other hand, if we focus exclusively on the unqualified support of leftists like Zhang Chunqiao, Chen Yonggui, and others for the horrors inflicted by the Khmer Rouge in the name of socialist purity, we deny the risks undertaken by individual Chinese in DK to help their Cambodian colleagues.

If we step back and use a secular, pragmatic accounting of events, we risk suppressing inconvenient truths. And this, of course, raises all sorts of questions about support from the United States and others for the Khmer Rouge that stretched into the 1980s, long after DK atrocities were a matter of record. The necessarily jarring conclusion is that the topic of Sino-DK relations is complex, complicated, awkward, and challenging to conceptualize, but it is only by embracing and accepting the dissonance that we are able to make sense of it.

Some Implications

Challenges to institutional integrity—and their effects on the structures, processes, and outcomes of Chinese foreign aid and assistance—are a theme we will see throughout this book. The broader implications go beyond the Sino-DK relationship. Institutional fragmentation contributes to an environment in which the leadership in China can easily be overwhelmed with under-evaluated, potentially biased, and even inaccurate information without a way to manage and appraise it. Given Beijing's increasing engagement with the developing world—places prone to political instability—a crisis that threatens Chinese overseas aid, when refracted through China's byzantine institutional network, can easily escalate, leading to policy failure or "gunboat diplomacy with Chinese characteristics" and potentially undermining regime support and legitimacy back home. In sum, contrary to the conventional wisdom of China's inexorable rise, the implications of this study caution that we pay more attention to the way things might go wrong domestically in China and how they could affect Beijing's foreign policy behavior.

THE KHMER ROUGE BUREAUCRACY

The Angkar has the [many] eyes of the pineapple.

—Official DK slogan[1]

The Angkar has the [many] eyes of the pineapple, but none with an iris.

—Counter-slogan whispered during the DK period[2]

In many ways, Democratic Kampuchea (DK) represents a breathtakingly literal approach to totalitarian rule. As with Hannah Arendt's conceptualization of totalitarianism, DK cloaked itself in an ideological foundation that was shared by most of the top leaders and was used to coopt ignorant and uneducated peasants into various positions of authority; like Friedrich and Brzezinski's, DK was formed around a single party that monopolized communication, centralized production, and ruled by terror.[3] Certainly, the overall environment conforms with Benito Mussolini's articulation of "everything within the state, nothing outside the state, nothing against the state" outside of which "no human or spiritual values can exist, much less have value."[4] As far as policymaking was concerned, the pronouncements of Pol Pot and his administrative unit—Office 870—had a force akin to the laws of physics.

At the same time, below the apex of power, much of DK's national and local authority relations can be described somewhat awkwardly as "fluid but never quite jelling" or, more succinctly, as "parochial totalitarianism," in which authority from the top was absolute, and lower levels were governed by a web of authority relations that were constantly in flux. As with Leninist systems more generally, DK ministerial units were largely conduits through which to translate CPK ideological dictates into concrete, tangible policy outputs, but the network of officials that staffed them favored an inward-looking management style in which behavior was intuitive and somewhat flexible rather than overly rigid and formal.

This could be attributed to a number of factors. First, as described in chapter 1, traditional Cambodian reliance on *khsae* networks introduced a strong element of patron-client relations to the DK state apparatus. This tendency was reinforced by the various types of experiences shared by CPK officials during the Party's rise to power, whether they were student networks in France in the 1950s or shared sacrifices in the *maquis*. Second, the brevity of the regime combined with the relentless pace at which it approached its political, economic, and social policies created an uncommon dynamic of intense demands by the state on society, even as the state itself remained unfinished, a work in progress that was constantly congealing but never quite coagulating. Finally, Pol Pot was by nature a micromanager, compartmentalizing the state into an institutional matrix of such bounded cellularity that any challenges to his authority became impossibly remote. Officials and staff knew (or thought they knew) their own responsibilities and understood their immediate surroundings, but they were strikingly ignorant of anything else. Only Pol Pot knew how all the pieces fit together. In practice, this parochialism afforded DK officials a modicum of latitude to bring in their own interpretations of how best to achieve policy goals, as the alternative was complete immobilism. Ultimately, however, there was no tolerance at the Center for failure—whether real or perceived. And the punishment meted out was inelastic with regard to actual behavior or intent.

In this chapter, I describe the DK political and policy apparatus, tracing how power and authority were refracted throughout the system along functional and spatial dimensions, respectively, to underscore the variation in institutional integrity necessary to translate the power emerging from it into concrete policy locally. This chapter sets up subsequent ones by providing the institutional mapping necessary to show where, when, and how DK organizations were able to resist Chinese influence and where, when, and how they were not.

The DK State Apparatus

Cambodia achieved its independence from France in 1953, as King Norodom Sihanouk adeptly manipulated the political confusion left in the wake of French decline in Indochina, abdicating in favor of his father and, as prince, throwing himself into politics. Sihanouk, like his predecessors, sought above all else to prevent Cambodia from being swallowed up by its larger neighbors Thailand and North Vietnam. He was steadfast in claiming Cambodian neutrality in the escalating war between North and South Vietnam, although he also allowed for secret, strategic breaches of Cambodian sovereignty: parts of the Ho Chi Minh Trail ran through eastern Cambodia, and Chinese shipments to North Vietnam were offloaded in Kampong Som and carried overland to Communist guerillas operating in South Vietnam. Sihanouk felt that North Vietnam would ultimately be victorious and did not want to antagonize Hanoi while simultaneously trying to maintain regional balance by forging relations with the West, with sharply varying degrees of success.

Sihanouk's government veered to the right after an uprising in remote Samlaut in 1967, leading to an expulsion of the remaining high-profile leftist members of the government, who escaped to the *maquis* to join others who had fled Sihanouk's secret police years before, and a reestablishment of diplomatic relations with the United States in 1968, which had been strained after the U.S.-linked coup against Ngo Dinh Diem in 1963, and broken off altogether in 1965. As the economy continued to decline, Sihanouk found himself unable to satisfy the growing numbers of disgruntled urban elites. In early 1970, he took an extended trip abroad to France, the Soviet Union, and China. On March 19 he was overthrown by his minister of defense, Lon Nol, and longtime rival, Prince Sisowath Sirik Matak. Although no evidence has come to light that the United States had a role in the coup itself, the U.S. president, Richard Nixon, certainly welcomed it. Nixon, finding Lon Nol to be a much more sympathetic ally than Sihanouk, began sending military aid and materiel, helping plunge the newly established Khmer Republic into a brutal civil war.

Sihanouk responded by announcing an alliance with leftist guerilla elements, whom he had dismissively labeled "les Khmers rouges" just a few years earlier. This coalition government brokered by China that Sihanouk headed, the Gouvernement Royal d'Union Nationale du Kampuchéa (GRUNK), saw the Communist Party of Kampuchea as very much a junior partner that possessed a few rifles and whose activity had mostly been limited to the malaria-infested highlands of Ratanakiri province in Cambodia's remote northeast. Buoyed in part by extensive Vietnamese military assistance, weapons, and training, by 1973, only three years later, the CPK had not simply colonized the GRUNK from the inside, easing its erstwhile allies to the political sidelines, but it also enjoyed an impressive degree of control over large swaths of rural Cambodia. Ith Sarin, who had defected from the Khmer Republic to join the rebels in the *maquis,* was so alarmed at the brutality of the CPK style of governance that he re-defected back to Phnom Penh and wrote a prescient account of what a CPK-led Cambodia might look like.[5] For his candor, he was ignored and even imprisoned by the Khmer Republic. What was clear from Ith Sarin's account—one of the only firsthand accounts of the gestation period of the CPK—was just how quickly and effectively CPK forces were able to control the areas under their jurisdiction, easing out their GRUNK allies by sidelining, purging, and killing them.[6]

The increasingly corrupt Khmer Republic slowly collapsed from within, and when the U.S. Congress forced Nixon to cease the "secret bombing" of Cambodia that had started in 1969, there was little left to do but await the inevitable. After the United States evacuated its mission in early April 1975, there was nothing to prevent the Khmer Rouge from taking over the capital and the country barely a week later. The Khmer Rouge walked into Phnom Penh on April 17, 1975, and within hours began clearing the capital and all of the other cities in the country of their inhabitants and forcing them into exile in the Cambodian countryside, a world that most urbanites found utterly alien. Within days, Phnom Penh's two million residents (due to the influx of refugees, four times what it had been just five years earlier) were gone, and a ghost town of some ten thousand cadres, officials, and support staff remained.

Until the Vietnamese invasion in the last week of 1978, the three years, eight months, and twenty days of Khmer Rouge rule saw a country transformed into a vast rural experiment of arguably the most brutal type of socialism ever attempted, in which misrule, extreme coercion, and neglect led to the deaths of some 1.7 million Cambodians—roughly a quarter of the country's population—through disease, starvation, and political bloodletting.

Consolidating Power

After the fall of Phnom Penh, CPK control over rural areas was complete. Acting on orders from the very top, CPK foot soldiers, many of whom had never seen a city before and whose youth might have been disarming if not for the look of hatred in their eyes, completely demobilized the army of Lon Nol's Khmer Republic. The leaders of the regime who remained in Cambodia, such as Sirik Matak, Lon Non, and Long Boret, were butchered like common livestock. But perhaps the greatest symbolic and substantive manifestation of the CPK's drive to consolidate power was its ability to empty, by force, all of Cambodia's major cities within a matter of days, even hours. Using the fiction of an imminent U.S. attack and demonstrating the will to execute anybody who refused, the Communists were able to accomplish this with almost no resistance.

But in taking over the cities, the troops' behavior suggested deep fissures in the new regime. When the top CPK leaders arrived in Phnom Penh a week later, there seemed to be a noticeable degree of disorganization. Pol Pot himself "may have had no military power base of [his] own; and as Ben Kiernan has emphasized, the various military units were not recognized into a single army until July 1975."[7] Indeed, as Democratic Kampuchea was not formally established until 1976, it took the better part of the following year to fashion the contours of a functioning state apparatus.[8] Initial meetings were held at the abandoned main railway station and at the Silver Pagoda within the Royal Palace, where leaders slept on cots or on the floor.

But the organizing principle of the new regime was enshrined early on in a series of meetings from August 20 to 24, 1975. Discussion centered at the level of the individual citizen, moving outward and upward. The leaders decided that it was essential to condition the consciousness of the people so that their thinking would become indistinguishable from the revolutionary authorities. Specifically, the people evacuated from the cities were to be absorbed into collectives, which were the basic organizational unit of analysis of DK society, with the "base people" at the core, the "new people"—people who did not live in CPK-controlled areas before 1975—on the periphery, and the CPK managing the functions of the collective. The concrete measures designed to achieve this outcome involved consolidating relations between various administrative levels, specifically between the districts, regions, and zones so that the latter would be able to mobilize troops from the districts and regions when necessary.[9] The actual institutional network that emerged to manage these relations as well as make and implement concrete policy was complex and often contradictory.

During a meeting of the CPK Standing Committee (SC) on October 9, 1975, the discussion revolved around the dearth of qualified cadres throughout the country and the degree of autonomy they should be given when implementing policy. Although the outcome of this discussion was ambiguous, there was a clear delineation of the proper communication infrastructure within the country. Information in the form of telegrams was to be forwarded to the cadre or office with the appropriate portfolio (foreign affairs, commerce, and so on), and that person, in turn, would make proposals to the SC, which would then discuss and decide what the policy would be. Also at this meeting, individuals were tasked with specific portfolios and actual physical work spaces were assigned; the date for moving into these spaces was to be October 15, 1975. Individuals assigned to a particular section would usually live with colleagues within the work compound in the newly deserted capital.

The ultimate seat of power in Democratic Kampuchea was concentrated in a surreal environment, in a city built to handle half a million residents that now contained about ten thousand. The various functional units (ministries would not officially exist for another year) were scattered along the east-west axis of the city between the main railway station and Pochentong Airport. Key Party institutions tended to be on or near the waterfront. The diplomatic "compound" of foreign embassies and embassy shops was within walking distance of the Foreign Ministry, although the Chinese Embassy had its own location on the south side of the city. Various factories, warehouses, hospitals, motor pools, and logistics stations were scattered throughout Phnom Penh, but movement was strictly controlled and enforced, although Chinese expatriates appear to have been exempt from the most draconian measures. Particularly sensitive areas, such as the Tuol Sleng/S-21 prison and torture complex, had a buffer zone, constructed with the intention of "keeping outsiders away from the compound [and] clearing the neighborhood."[10] Areas that housed the top leaders were protected by layers of bodyguards and soldiers.

"Angkar Loeu"

At the very top of the system stood Saloth Sar, who had adopted the nom de guerre of Pol Pot, and his top lieutenants, collectively referred to by outsiders as *Angkar Padevat* ("the Revolutionary Organization") or simply *Angkar* ("the Organization").[11] Sometimes, this group was referred to as *Angkar Loeu* ("the Upper Organization") in order to distinguish it from other nodes of functional or regional authority. The phrase "being sent to *Angkar Loeu*" quickly became a euphemism for torture and death. More prosaically, such as in telegrams from local areas or from the front, this top stratum was called "Office 870," or simply "870," which according to Justin Corfield and Laura Summers, was a "security code number used by the...CPK in the 1970s as a way to designate the Standing Committee of the Central Committee and especially in the field of radio communication." Oftentimes, "870" simply referred to Pol Pot or, when he was incapacitated, to Nuon Chea. Political Office 870 was headed by Soeu Vasy (a.k.a. Doeun) and was responsible for matters of policy.[12]

The "K" Offices[13]

Pol Pot regularly lived and worked in a location referred to as K-1, just across from the Russian Embassy near the riverfront. Pol Pot's bodyguards would wake up at 5:00 a.m., cleaning the facilities, watering the vegetables in the garden, and preparing the morning meal. Pol Pot was known to be very punctual. He would work from 7:00 to 11:00 a.m. and then from two to five in the afternoon. He spent much of his time writing.[14]

It was at K-1 where Pol Pot met with leaders from the district, sector, and zone committees and where SC meetings were convened. Close to the Royal Palace compound, where Pol Pot spent much of his childhood and adolescence, it consisted of two rows of buildings; meetings were convened in the north building. Zone and region meetings were held in the downstairs area and would involve between ten and twenty cadres. These meetings would take place every few months and would last about five days. SC meetings took place on a similar schedule, though each lasted only a single day. These were, like the meetings of zone and regional leaders, held at the K-1 meeting room on the ground floor. Participants would arrive by their personal cars, bringing nothing other than their notebooks and pens. Pol Pot's secretary, Comrade Pun, recorded the minutes.[15]

Guards were not allowed to come close enough to hear the meeting discussions; they were required to stay twenty to thirty yards away in order to prevent information leaks. The guards knew that they would be removed from their posting if they violated this rule. Indeed, security at K-1 was formidable: there was a ten-man inner perimeter guard team, as well as a thirty-man outer perimeter or second squad. This inner layer was physically separated by wooden planks and barbed wire into which non–inner layer guards did not intrude. The second layer was secured by four towers that were placed around the two squads and were manned by about sixty guards. A third layer, known as Y-10, of about one hundred guards was based just over a mile from K-1. Y-10 was in charge of protecting the top leadership when they were walking around Phnom Penh, moving between buildings. Y-10 also had a courier function.

K-3 was where President Khieu Samphan lived, and where he prepared and filed documents and stored the meeting minutes. In Craig Etcheson's account,

> K-1 was near the entertainment hall, while K-3 was behind the Palace. Pol Pot went back and forth between K-1 and K-3. Haem [Khieu Samphan] was at K-3, along with Nuon [Chea] and Van [Ieng Sary]. Meetings took place at different locations, depending on the situation … K-1 was Pol Pot's residence … whereas K-3 was where Nuon and Haem lived and worked. Pang's headquarters was at K-1, with Pol Pot, while Haem was with Nuon Chea at K-3. Pang was in charge of all the K Offices. It was Pang who arranged meetings, but Haem who chaired things politically, but under Pol, who was in charge of political meetings together with Nuon. Haem chaired the meetings of Party branches of the K Offices. Haem was superior to Pang. I believe that the reports from the provinces came to Office 870.[16]

Office S-71, headed by Comrade Pang, and tasked with more administrative and support responsibilities—"protection of the central office and cadre, welcoming guests, communications, logistics, food, transport"—was in charge of the "K" offices.[17] Pang, as office chief (*kanak montie*), would issue verbal commands in five-minute assembly meetings in which the day's tasks would be assigned.

> Pang would tell two or three of us to collect vegetables from the vegetable supply in K-1 and another few of us to take fish and pork from Prek [Phneou], which was a little bit far from the office—about 10 kilometers. When I got the order to take fish and pork from Prek [Phneou], Pang would issue me a travel letter. It was not [a] very formal letter: he just wrote "this letter allows comrade … to take pork." It contained his signature, and the guards who resided along the road clearly knew who he was and what his signature looked like. I sometimes had meet-

ings with Pang and transmitted his orders to my team. I received all my orders from Pang except direct orders from Uncle Pol Pot, but only when he needed me to prepare the meeting room.[18]

K-4 was a logistics office, and K-5 and K-6 were political or Party schools. K-7 was a courier and communications unit located near the Royal Palace. K-11 was the unit responsible for medical affairs, and K-12 was a motor pool located between Pet Lok Sang Hospital and the New Market, which warehoused trucks for transporting food, clothing, and other essentials to the zones. K-12 was also in charge of providing vehicles for official visits for foreign dignitaries and guests and of storing gasoline for vehicles and auto repairs.

The old U.S. Embassy was the site of K-18, the office responsible for internal and external communication (thirty people in each), which included radio and telegraph repair units. A Comrade Phong was the chief of the telegram unit, and Comrade Yous was his deputy. Altogether there were about ten people on the telegram team. Others would type code as well as decode the various messages that passed from K-1 to the zones and regions countrywide. Pol Pot would provide a bodyguard with introductory information for zone and regional leaders. The bodyguard would take this information to Phong without knowing the content. Pol Pot normally received telegram messages once every two days. Sometimes his bodyguards would be instructed to take telegrams to Nuon Chea. Communications between senior cadres in Phnom Penh were transmitted through messengers.[19]

According to Etcheson, "the SC maintained at least six re-education camps (K-9, K-10, K-13, K-15, K-16, and K-17) where persons under the SC's immediate authority would be sent for 'tempering.'"[20] K-9, K-10 (an agricultural work tempering site near Prek Phneou, Chraing Chamreh), and K-13 were reeducation and production units; K-15 and K-16 were units for the reeducation of returnees, and K-17 was a reeducation center for intellectuals and diplomats. K-8, K-14, and K-19 were all agricultural production offices. Office K-17 in Boeng Trabek was where youth were housed and trained in foreign languages, with an emphasis on Chinese.

In sum, the K offices formed the inner sanctum of power in Democratic Kampuchea. They provided security, logistics, food, and materiel to the top CPK leaders, and they formed the physical space where they worked and, in some cases, resided.

The CPK Standing Committee

The Standing Committee of the CPK Central Committee was the highest decision-making body immediately below Pol Pot and his ruthlessly efficient deputy, Nuon Chea, who were also secretary and deputy secretary, respectively, of the SC. The SC also included, at various times, Son Sen, Ta Mok, Ieng Sary, So Phim, Vorn Vet, Ros Nhim, Chan Chakrey, and Cheng An.[21] Pol Pot, Nuon Chea, and the first three were "full-rights" members (*samachek machchhem penh sith*), while Vorn Vet and Son Sen were "reserve" or "candidate" (*samachek triem nai kanak kammathekar machchhem*) members. Full-rights members could "consider and discuss and join in decision making" in all matters of state; candidate members could participate but without decision-making authority.[22] As in other socialist systems, in theory the Standing Committee disposed what the larger, more representative Central Committee of the CPK proposed; in practice, the SC made the decisions that were implemented functionally through the ministries and spatially through the local governments: zone, region, district, subdistrict, cooperative, and village.[23] This was true of policy as well as of politics: the top echelon directly or indirectly micromanaged almost all of the policy intricacies of the regime.[24]

> The CPK SC controlled the appointment of senior officials to the Party, government and military. As seen in the decisions that the SC issued on 21 April 1976, the Standing Committee appointed leading officials to government posts, including secretaries and deputies for commerce, industry, transportation, energy and public works, and appointed and removed senior military officers of the General Staff. The CPK Statutes required that Zones and Sectors obtain the approval of the Central Committee before appointing cadre to leadership positions. In unusual circumstances, such as following the 1977 purge of the Central Zone, the Standing Committee also had the authority to appoint chiefs of zones, sectors and districts, as well as zone ministerial personnel.... The Standing Committee required regular reporting from subordinate organizational units, as provided for in the decisions of the Central Committee reached on 30 March 1976, which instituted a "regime of weekly reporting to Office 870...on the situation and the work of the Zone"...while lower echelons regularly reported to the Zone leadership....The SC also had direct contact with personnel from the Sector, District and [commune] levels. District secretaries came to Phnom Penh at least once a year to attend Party conferences.[25]

The Central Committee included Pol Pot, Nuon Chea, Ieng Sary, Khieu Samphan, Koy Thuon, Ta Mok, Ney Saran (a.k.a. Ya), Soeun, Ke Pauk, Soeu Vasy (a.k.a. Doeun) as well as certain other zone secretaries and district leaders—more than thirty people in all. There was also a military committee under the CC, which included Pol Pot, Nuon Chea, Son Sen, So Phim, Ta Mok, and, later, Vorn Vet and Ke Pauk.[26]

At SC meetings various ministers and upper-level CPK cadres would present reports outlining suggestions based on their functional or administrative portfolios, after which Pol Pot would respond by announcing his decisions in a rambling and expansive tour of the DK policy universe, often emphasizing mundane details and putting them on an equal footing with key broad policy statements. Unless he asked for comments or suggestions or after he considered them, Pol Pot's pronouncements were synonymous with policy, whether domestic or foreign.

Spatial Power Relations

Within the very first hours in the existence of the unnamed new regime, the cleavages undermining institutional unity manifested themselves. The various CPK forces approached Phnom Penh from all directions and met in the city proper:

> Phnom Penh [was] divided into five sectors held by different forces under autonomous commanders. The northern sector of the city was occupied by troops from Kampong Cham, Kampong Som, Pursat, Kampong Chhnang and northern Kampong Speu, thus from the West, Northwest, and North (here part of Kampong Cham) zones...the center sector of Phnom Penh south of Kramuon Sar as far as the Independence Monument...[was] occupied by troops from the Southwest...[while] the western side of the city was occupied by troops from the south...[and] the southern sector of the city...[was occupied] by Southwest zone forces.[27]

According to Huy Vannak, "The CPK designated Phsar Thmei," the iconic New Market, as the starting point for "the evacuation to various provinces. The Khmer Rouge split the populace into seven groups, and divided up the spoils of war for each zone."[28]

In the absence of the top leadership—Pol Pot and his lieutenants did not enter the city until several days later—military commanders sought to consolidate their power by taking over as many neighborhoods as possible and by anticipating (and improvising) the immediate policy imperatives of the new regime—that is, evacuating Phnom Penh—ranging from the particularly brutal to the more benign.[29] There were even somewhat conflicting reports of armed skirmishes between various Khmer Rouge regiments.[30]

Variation in the evacuation orders from city to city was equally pronounced. While the port city of Kampong Som was quickly and ruthlessly emptied of its residents on April 18, Battambang, Cambodia's second-largest city, was not evacuated until a week later, despite a concentrated effort to coordinate the "liberation" of Cambodia's cities to coincide with the fall of Phnom Penh on April 17.[31] Kiernan argues that evacuation of the cities in the northwest was delayed because "poor communications between the Center and the distant Northwest Zone, perhaps a loss of radio contact, may have kept the Zone ignorant of Center policy," but there was "also a suggestion of Northern recalcitrance."[32] Siem Reap, the town adjacent to Angkor, gave residents a full day of decidedly feudal celebrations before forcing them into the countryside:

> When the KR entered the city on 17th April 1975... [a] revolutionary committee was formed at Wat Damnak. The next day [the Venerable Put Ponn] and the two other monks were taken by *moto-remorque* to within the first walls of Angkor Wat to attend a big celebration in honour of the victory. There were many people present and a platform had been built in front of Angkor Wat temple for officials.... Put Ponn was placed where some fifty to sixty monks had been assembled. The victory was announced with great fanfare, to the sound of traditional music heard in pagodas. Speeches celebrated the greatest victory in thousands and thousands of years. Slogans were shouted, revolutionary songs were sung and playlets that described the revolutionary saga were performed. The monks were required to say the *chéakyoantao (jayanto)*, the traditional prayer celebrating victory.[33]

One of the differences between China and Democratic Kampuchea was the former's ability to move from a regionally based system of authority to one in which such power was consolidated at the Center. From 1949 through 1952, China was divided into six military regions led by trusted leaders while the Center attempted to establish a governing apparatus without having to worry about centrifugal forces nipping away at Beijing's ability to govern. Once central institutions had been put into place and the regions consolidated, Mao recalled the regional leaders—Gao Gang, Rao Shushi, Lin Biao, Peng Dehuai, and Deng Xiaoping—to the capital and provided them with important leadership positions in the central government and Party apparatus, in part to ensure that they would not establish "independent kingdoms" (*duli wangguo*).

This did not occur in Democratic Kampuchea. Throughout the civil war from 1970 to 1975, CPK forces were regionally based and largely autonomous from one another. As a result, even during the fall of Phnom Penh as described above, the various regional military leaders scrambled to establish footholds in the city in order to ensure and even leverage their power in the new regime. Conflicting orders from various military units guarding their "own secured" districts in the capital (as well as their different subsequent policy preferences), as documented by Michael Vickery and others, underscores the significant degree of autonomy among these military leaders who subsequently moved on to become zone commanders, although military divisions were carved out of these regional armies to form the centralized Revolutionary Army of Kampuchea (RAK) forces.[34]

That said, it is best to avoid overstating the independence of zone leaders and the autonomy of locales from the Center. Zone leaders were extraordinarily powerful right up until the moment they were not. That is, the Center did not hesitate to exercise its authority and purge those zone leaders who aroused suspicion: Northern Zone Commander and, later, Minister of Commerce Koy Thuon was executed in 1977; Eastern Zone Commander So Phim committed suicide rather than face execution in 1978; Northwest Zone Secretary Muol Sambath (a.k.a. Ros Nhim) was targeted in 1978, as was Northeast Zone Secretary Ney Saran (a.k.a. Ya).[35] In other words, Phnom Penh was able to use its authority and its control over the consolidated central military forces to impose its will. Thus, there were two types of military-based authority relations in DK: those that were centralized, directly under the General Staff, and those that also were led by their regionally based zone commanders. When they came into conflict, the former trumped the latter.

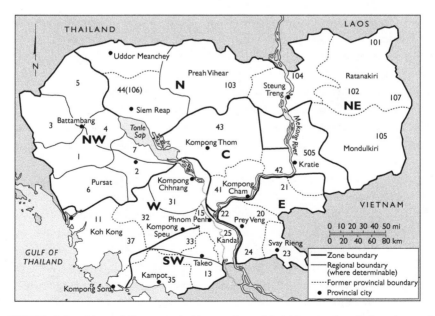

FIGURE 2.1. Map of Democratic Kampuchea. http://www.yale.edu/cgp/maps/bigmap02.gif.

DK had seven *phumipheak* or "zones" (North, Northeast, Northwest, Central, East, Southwest, and West) in addition to the Center (Phnom Penh), the Kratie autonomous sector 505, the Siem Reap/Uddor Meanchey autonomous sector 106, and the Preah Vihear autonomous sector 103.[36] In addition, the Kampong Som port was under a separate administration (*phumipheak piseh*) directly controlled by the Center and not through any zone.[37] According to Corfield and Summers, zones were "governed and administered by a revolutionary committee and territory based divisions of the army."[38] They were further divided into regions (*damban*), which were then divided into districts (*srok*) and then into subdistrict communes (*khum*) or cooperatives (*sahakar*).[39] Finally, there were individual villages (*phum*).[40]

Zone-based divisions included Division 1 in the Northwest Zone; Divisions 2, 11, 12, and 117 in the North Zone; Divisions 3, 4, and 5 in the East Zone; Division 174 in the Central Zone; a division in Kampong Cham, and Division 335.[41] In 1976 and 1977 autonomous sectors 106 (Siem Reap and Uddar Meanchey) and 103 (Preah Vihear)—and, after 1977, 105 (Mondulkiri) and 505 (Kratie)—were directly controlled by the Center.[42] Zone secretaries were automatically on the Central Committee, while some, including Southwest Zone Commander Ta Mok and Eastern Zone Commander So Phim, were on the Standing Committee. In addition to this top-down institutional arrangement, near the 870 logistics office K-7 in front of Wat Unalom in Phnom Penh were representative offices of remote provinces like Mondulkiri, Ratanakiri, Kratie, and Preah Vihear.

Communication was through messengers, who used bicycles and motorcycles (and even a speedboat to communicate with Autonomous Sector 505), but the most common means was a network of telegrams. There is a widely held impression that the CPK did not possess a paper trail distinct from that monitoring the torture and confession of political opponents. In reality, there was a considerable amount of written communication. It is worth quoting the Extraordinary Chambers in the Courts of Cambodia, Closing Order of Case File No. 002 to understand the byzantine nature of communications within the secretive DK regime:

> After the fall of Phnom Penh in 1975, the central telegram unit that had operated in the "liberated areas" was moved to Phnom Penh. About 40 children were recruited from the provinces and were taught the basic working techniques of telegram communication (coding, typing, etc.) as well as sometimes French and English. On 9 October 1975 the Standing Committee decided on the functioning of the telegram unit. The telegram unit, which was divided into two sections (one responsible for transmitting and receiving the telegram, and the other for the encoding and decoding) was code named K-18 and was located in Phnom Penh at the old United States Embassy (now the Fishery Administration).

Office K-18 was composed of an internal communications section with [Comrade] Oeun in charge and an external communications section with [Comrade] Rim in charge. Approximately 20 to 30 persons worked in each of the two sections. Subsequent chairmen of the telegram unit were [Comrade] Yos (also mentioned as deputy chief)....Within the zones, a telegram unit consisted of a telegram coder, a transmitter or operator and a typist or secretary. Outgoing messages from the Centre were first sent to the telegram coding unit which was located at the Party Centre office K-1 to be encoded into number codes. The encoded message was then forwarded to the operation group at K-18 that transmitted the messages to the recipients in coded form, where they decoded it into plain text. Incoming telegrams from the zones arrived at K-18 and were written down by the typist group. The encoded message was then sent to K-1 for decoding and transmitted to the receiving Party cadre. Incoming telegrams were forwarded to other cadre upon the decision of Pol Pot and his staff, who received copies of all messages. Where the word "document" was attributed to a message, this implied that it was to be kept in the archive of the respective telegram translator. Copies of the coded and the text versions of the telegram had to be kept for six months before they were burnt.[43]

Zone commanders gave orders to the sector; the sector secretary would transmit them to the district; the district secretary would do the same to the commune; and the commune secretary would pass the orders on to the village or cooperative. The zone leaders appear to have had more direct control over their jurisdictions than did the Standing Committee members in their functional contours of power. According to a March 30, 1976 CPK decision, "at the base-level structures (subdistricts and districts, regions, and zones) decisions rested with the zone standing committee."[44] This suggests that administrative levels below the zone were more akin to implementing bodies than decision-making ones.

That said, each administrative unit all the way down to the village had a set of three-person committees charged with specific responsibilities that mirrored the configuration of ministries at the top, with some modifications. These committees each had their own "offices," which were oftentimes just traditional wooden houses. Committees for education, agriculture, public works, energy, and transportation existed at every level from the zone down to the village. Social affairs for all intents and purposes stopped at the communes, as that was the lowest administrative level that had hospitals or clinics. Industry had committees all the way down to the village level, but that was true of local industries only, not of factories with considerable investment from the Center; the former (for instance, clothing) were under local authority, the latter (rubber) were not. Transport at the local level would take the form of, for example, managing and coordinating oxcarts to deliver fish and rice, while public works would take the form of repairing a stretch of road that was firmly within the jurisdiction of the administrative level in question, that is, the village.

There were no formal commerce committees below the Center, as *commerce* referred to international imports and exports and was managed vertically, never horizontally.[45] Indeed, unofficial communication between horizontal units was forbidden: "Witnesses indicate that there was a strict policy of no communication between the zones: the communication between the zones would be sent via the Centre. No contact schedule table or decoding table existed for telegram communication from zone to zone, thus making such contact impossible."[46]

Although quite dangerous, unauthorized transactions did, in fact, occur, albeit only among particularly risk-acceptant CPK cadres. One such case is the barter exchanges that occurred between commerce officials from Kratie with their counterparts in the Central Zone and that had emerged out of official economic interactions between Kratie and the Center:

> In the Central Zone, I met a person named Chey who firstly was a chief of commerce. Chey and I decided to trade 10 elephants for 30 horses. In addition to this trade…Chey asked me: "Do you have fish paste to eat, brother Chuon?" I answered I had a little. Chey added: "If you have not, I will give you a tonne of it." After bartering, I returned to my place with a tonne of fish paste. Half a month later, in June 1977 I met Chey again to decide when we should take elephants and horses to Chuon in Kratie. The barter was to be done on 15 June 1977. [In addition to officially-mandated commerce], I asked…"Do you have motor's [sic] pistons? Please give me one."…Comrade Chey answered: "I have not any piston. If you have nothing to ride, take one motorbike, Honda 90." I said: "If you give it to me, it is easy for me."…[So] there were a Honda 90 and a tonne of salted fish. Chey told me that: "From now on, we should constantly stay connected with one another." I replied: "Yes." In late June, 1977, I collected materials in Phnom Penh by travelling along the Mekong River. When I was back from Phnom Penh, I met comrade Chey again.[47]

Subzone policy that spanned horizontally across two or more administrative levels almost always originated from the zone level; exceptions included emergencies or work that remained within a localized jurisdiction. In the case of a dam, for example, the zone leader would discuss the matter with the zone's public works committee, which, in turn, would bring it to the district chief of the affected areas. The district chiefs would then discuss it with their public works committees, and so on all the way down to the village.

There were at least two exceptions to this. First, political work, that is, propaganda, was the responsibility of the committee running the entire administrative level; there was no separate functional "propaganda" committee. So this was a simple top-down process; in the event that a committee at a particular administrative level was unable to perform this function, the administrative level immediately above would temporarily undertake the necessary propaganda work.

The other exception was agriculture. This is the key to understanding why agriculture was such an important part of the DK economy, yet did not have its own ministry. It also explains the hideous mixture of top-down pressure and extreme decentralized authority that more than anything contributed to the widespread starvation of vast segments of the population in DK. State extraction of agricultural commodities, particularly rice, proceeded as follows. The commune's agriculture committee would ask the village, How much do you have? Then they would ask, How much are you willing to give to *Angkar*? The decision was placed upon the head of the village leader. Above the village level, each administrative level would simply combine the output provided by their subordinate administrative levels and send it upwards. The zones would then arrange delivery of the goods to the State Warehouse, which was often the principal locus of direct interaction between the local governments and the functional units of the Center.[48]

Functional Power Relations

Across DK ministerial units, there was a considerable degree of variation in institutional integrity along a number of dimensions.[49] These included the Party status and rank of the person holding office. Some were led by full members of the Standing Committee, such as foreign affairs under Ieng Sary, while others were managed by individuals who were not even on the Standing Committee as "candidate" members, like social affairs under Ieng Thirith, information and propaganda under Hu Nim, and education under Yun Yat.[50] Other dimensions included the perceived value of the institution's mandate, whether the institution existed physically as a bricks-and-mortar structure, the complexity of the institution's responsibilities and the human capital necessary to carry it out, and the degree to which such an institution was directly under centralized control or was firmly under the grip of the zone commanders and other military and regional cadres.[51] Thus, in order to analyze policy outcomes, it is necessary to understand more than merely the policymaking process, which was almost always the domain of the SC. The nexus for policy implementation and enforcement is equally important.

Throughout the DK regime, the intersection of politics and policy in the implementation of central mandates is striking. At the Standing Committee meeting held from August 20 to 24, 1975, it was decided that all machinery, particularly tractors, must be placed under the control of the zone-level authorities and that zones establish a set of work sites and repair facilities for existing equipment, with an eye to transforming these repair facilities into production factories in their own right at some point. Zone commanders enjoyed a particularly expansive degree of power, as mandated in that same meeting: the "new people," that is, those expelled from the cities, were to be organized as a "membrane," as a "buffer" between the more trustworthy members of society and "counterrevolutionary phenomena." If this outer layer of society were to become "infected," then they would be "vanished."[52] In order to ensure such an outcome, it was necessary to consolidate authority relations (and troops) between the various administrative levels of the state, essentially to centralize relations from the districts, up through the regions, and concentrate them at the zone level.

At the March 8, 1976 Standing Committee meeting, Pol Pot asserted that with the promulgation of the DK constitution, "the curtain will fall completely on the old regime." Establishing government institutions would, he argued, show the outside world that "we have prevailed, that we are not unruly, that we behave appropriately in domestic and in international matters." By announcing the governance structure, he continued, DK would compare favorably with Vietnam and even China, as neither had made its constitution public. At one point, he appeared to be protesting too much when he warned cadres "do not speak in a casual manner [*niyay leng*] when discussing the [People's Representative] Assembly" because people should not have the view that "the Assembly has no value [*kmean domlai*]" and "that we are being deceitful [*bonlem banla*]." In fact, all "governance" would remain the task of the Party: the People's Representative Assembly, the mechanisms of elections, and the role of the State Presidium were fictions for external consumption, even if the functional government organs were not.[53] But although government institutions were considered "totally belonging to the party," the relationship—often in the form of the individual leading a given ministry—like everything else in DK, was hidden by several layers of subterfuge.[54]

As noted, government ministerial units in Democratic Kampuchea ran the gamut of an astonishingly diverse set of dimensions; no two were the same—or even similar—in terms of how they were organized.[55] One trait they seemed to have in common is the somewhat fluid nature of responsibilities and authority relations, as exemplified by the Ministry of Foreign Affairs.

The Foreign Ministry (B-1)[56] was run by Ieng Sary, who also led the International Relations Committee of the CPK. B-1 was divided into two parts. The first was an "office," which was headed by So Hong, the secretary-general. The other two leaders were Phi Phuon (a.k.a. Chiem) and So Se. The second section was made up of bureaus and handled various responsibilities related to general diplomatic matters, although there were no organizational divisions along regional or country lines—Ieng Sary kept the power to manage personnel in his own hands. In fact, he managed the brain trust of the entire ministry, including Thiounn Prasith, Keat Chhon, Chan Youran, Suong Sikoeun, Peh Bunret, Ok Sakun, So Se, So Phan, and, until his arrest in March 1977, Toch Kham Doeun. Each of these individuals had one or more portfolios but not necessarily a formal office to go with them—responsibilities were not fixed. Rather, they were appointed to a given task by Ieng Sary, who, for example, selected Thiounn Prasith to represent DK at the meeting of nonaligned nations in Colombo, Sri Lanka, or appointed Keat Chhon to head the delegation to the United Nations.[57]

The departments were divided into the following: the General Political Department, the Secretariat, Protocol, Information and Propaganda, and Production.

- *The Secretariat* included So Se; In Sopheap; Poch Dany; Poch Yamin; Poch Mona, wife of Ngo Hac Team of the Information and Propaganda Bureau; and Laurence Picq, Suong Sikoeun's then-wife and only Western member of the DK state. The Secretariat assisted the other offices in managing the inward and outward flow of documents, letters of congratulation, preparations for international conferences, national ceremonies, and the Military Days of friendly nations as well as the many letters exchanged across all the embassies and to and from foreign governments. This section was also responsible for coordinating communications between embassies inside and outside of the country, especially in the area of making recommendations on economic and commercial decision-making.
- *The General Political Department* was the most authoritative body, containing most of the ranking officials, including Thiounn Prasith, Keat Chhon, Chan Youran, Suong Sikoeun, Peh Bunret, Ok Sakun, So Se, So Phan, and Toch Kham Doeun. It was in charge of the core Party organization in the field of politics within B-1.
- *The Protocol Department* was headed by Ni Kan, with Suong Sikoeun as his deputy, and was in charge of establishing the reception procedures for foreign diplomatic delegations, receiving guests, and arranging cars and managing houses appropriate with regard to proper protocol, all the way down to the gifts that were given in diplomatic exchanges, which were

goods ("statuettes and clothing") that had been pilfered from private homes in Phnom Penh after the evacuation.

- *The Information and Propaganda Department* was headed by Suong Sikoeun and also included So Phan, Ngo Hac Team, Long Norin, Mak Ben, about twenty people in all, including Suong Sikoeun's secretary Chhuon Sikhorn, who headed the Kampuchea Press Agency, which had direct authority relations with Pol Pot. This office was charged with disseminating the "collective ideas of the new Kampuchean society" and the "guidelines and tasks to defend the nation and protect the interests of the revolution" to help unify the carrying out of policy by the ministry.
- *The Production Bureau* was led by Peh Puriet, who was the husband of So Se. Farming was under the committee of comrades Sarng, Sim, Inn, Leng, and Choiy in the spirit of self-reliance and ran agricultural and animal husbandry facilities to provide food for ministry personnel and for foreign guests in DK. There was also a diplomatic store, which was run by comrades Reoun [chief], Thy [deputy], Cheat, Lim, and Hau.

These units were not in separate buildings but rather in designated rooms or desks.

In addition, there was a Civil Aviation Bureau that coordinated the weekly Phnom Penh to Beijing flight and was directly under the control of Ieng Sary and was managed, as noted, by his nephew Srey Chanthoeun. It managed security, the sale and distribution of tickets, and the logistics of greeting and arranging transport for foreign visitors and guests. There were also at least two visitor reception houses directly managed by the Foreign Ministry: House Number 1, near Wat Phnom, and House Number 2, formerly the Hotel Le Royal, where the waitstaff alone numbered more than fifty. There were also foreign ministry guest houses in Svay Rieng, Kampong Thom, Kampong Chhnang, Siem Reap, Battambang, Pursat, and Kampong Som.[58]

All in all, including support staff (cooks and the like), there were around a thousand people working at B-1. The Foreign Ministry had clearly delineated responsibilities and a somewhat well-defined internal division of labor. What is clear, however, is that it was in a constant state of "jelling," but it never quite congealed into a clearly articulated, concrete institution. Other ministries shared this trait of fluidity and institutional conditionality, punctuated by the imposition of various degrees and manifestations of centralization and decentralization.

Degrees of (De)Centralization

Some ministries can be understood as having been relatively centralized, that is, with comparatively clear, relatively unambiguous lines of authority from the top of the system all the way down. Others are best understood as being more "decentralized," that is, with functional responsibilities housed with the local authorities, usually at the zone level. The somewhat loose governing principle appears, at least in part, to have been that the more "productive" the functional system in question, the greater the tendency toward centralization, while the more the functional system was seen as "consuming state resources"—a characteristically distasteful euphemism for providing for the citizenry—the greater the degree of decentralization. Of course, there were exceptions, but this overall logic appears to hold, especially as we go down the administrative hierarchy to the local level.

The contrast between factories as centralized units and hospitals as decentralized units demonstrates how this logic was implemented. In the centralized context of the productive factory, factory managers coordinated directly with the ministry over the supply of raw materials, factory inputs, and food for the workers. By contrast, hospitals were seen as consumers of state assets, not as a productive part of society. Thus, hospitals and other decentralized operations were squarely under the jurisdiction of local officials: resources necessary for hospitals to function were doled out by the local government at the same administrative level in which the hospital was located, that is, a district hospital would receive any and all operating wherewithal through the less resource-rich district government.

It is important not to shoehorn these institutions into too stark a division of centralized vs. decentralized units. The common thread—insofar as one can generalize at all about these offices—is that authority relations remained unfixed and that specific responsibilities, whether of an individual or an office, were solely based on the appointment power of the individuals at the top of the system—specifically, Pol Pot and Office 870 and, to some degree, the ministers or section chiefs of a given unit.

There are three ways to approach the dynamics of these authority relations. First, the power of appointment meant that people could take on one or more "portfolios" as a specific task dictated, at least within the unit in which they were embedded. Second, and related, much like the Chinese military from 1965 to 1988, formal ranks did not exist below the top leadership level in a given unit; a person's authority rested on the nature of his or her given appointment, that is, a formal title had little meaning relative to the scope of a given appointment. Third, unlike in China and other socialist systems with strong Leninist parties, there was not necessarily a clear distinction between government and Party jurisdictions. In the broadcasting office of the Ministry of Propaganda (K-33), there were two section chiefs—Comrade Han, who was trained as an engineer in Germany, and Comrade Vay, who was educated in Hanoi. Han was the "government" or "technical" leader, and Vay was the political leader, the de facto if not de jure Party secretary. Vay outranked Han, even though they were coequal chiefs of K-33.

But such distinctions, which form the basic organizational DNA of the Chinese (and Soviet) political systems, were quite rare in DK. The only systematic relationship that approached the Chinese parallel structure was in the military, but even there it was different: the leader of any given CPK military unit was the "political commissar," and the deputy leader was the one versed in military strategy and tactics.[59] In fact, each of the former Khmer Rouge cadres interviewed for this project found the distinction between government and Party bewildering.

The Ministry of Defense: The Apogee of Centralization

At one extreme, the most unambiguously centralized of all institutions in DK, the Ministry of Defense, was run by Son Sen. As the body in charge of internal and external security, it was the most powerful of the government ministries. Unlike its Chinese government counterpart, the DK Defense Ministry was extremely influential and thus in tension with the regionally based armies under the command of the zone secretaries. As articulated in the closing order of the Extraordinary Chambers in the Courts of Cambodia (ECCC):

> The appointment of zone secretaries would typically be made by the Centre. Implementation of decisions of the Central and Standing Committees was performed by the secretaries of the zones and the autonomous sectors. Policies and instructions of the Central and Standing Committees were disseminated to the zone and autonomous sector secretaries who, in turn, would disseminate them amongst sector and district level secretaries for implementation. Conversely, the subdistricts reported back up to the district committees, which reported to the sector committees, which in turn reported to the zone committees. The Statute of the CPK states that the tasks and functions of the zone committees were to "lead the implementation of tasks," according to CPK policies, in the sectors, districts and subdistricts. As such, they were empowered to "designate new work according to the Party line," meaning that the party line should be implemented "according to the political lines of national defense and the construction of Democratic Kampuchea," in other words that the zones were responsible for the internal security situation within their territories. Further to this, the zone committees were authorized to "administer discipline in the zone framework."[60]

Son Sen belonged to the Military Committee of the Central Committee, along with Pol Pot, Nuon Chea, So Phim, and Ta Mok. More to the point, perhaps, Son Sen also served as Chairman of the General Staff (GS), the central commanding unit of the Revolutionary Army of Kampuchea responsible for "planning, operations, intelligence, and logistics." The General Staff and associated subordinate units, Offices 62 and 63, employed some 4,500 people.[61] The GS had an extensive communications network, with RAK divisions and independent units anchored by meetings with division commanders and Chairman of the General Staff Son Sen as well as one-on-one meetings between individual commanders and the chairman.

The Logistics Committee of the General Staff managed everything from repairing weapons and vehicles to construction to transport. As Etcheson describes it, "The General Staff monitored a variety of statistics related to the military, including food consumption, weapons allocations, and military equipment. It also advised on issues relating to food production. Finally, the General Staff was responsible for political education for division and regimental military cadre and carried out periodic General Staff study sessions which were attended by hundreds of individuals from RAK units all over the country."[62] In short, the GS centralized a set of functions under a well-oiled military chain of command.

The Ministry of Social Affairs: The Epitome of Decentralization

Decentralized ministries had limited authority over their functional counterparts in the localities.[63] This is because the main responsibility for those functions rested within the authority of the regional leaders, particularly the zone commanders. The Standing Committee would give the orders to the Central Committee, which included all zone commanders, including the two on the SC, after which point they would be passed down within the zones. In these functionally decentralized policy areas, zone commanders trumped the ministries when it came to the local implementation of policies that were functionally, but not politically, within the purview of the latter. There were, in addition, special administrative regions that were directly governed from the Center. However, this often meant that these areas were largely left to their own devices through benign neglect from Phnom Penh. As we will see in chapter 5, this was the case at Kampong Som, and it helps explain in part the failure of the petroleum refinery project there.

At the other extreme from the Ministry of Defense was the Ministry of Social Affairs (K-2). Led by Ieng Sary's wife, Thirith, the ministry was in charge of "supporting schools, clinics, and vulnerable groups having few of the usual resources."[64] In practice, much of the ministry's work focused on medical services and the production and warehousing of domestically produced and imported Western and Chinese medicines. Communication between units of K-2 was managed by a group of child telephone operators who were located about two buildings away from Ieng Thirith's office. All requests had to be approved by the chairman of the K-2 Office Committee and, if it was an important request, by the minister herself.

Throughout the entire 1975–1978 period, most medicine was imported, mainly from China, and stored in Phnom Penh and the port city of Kampong Som.[65] In addition, an unspecified number of Chinese surgeons and other medical professionals were working in DK hospitals as well as at P-5, a medical study site. K-2 ran the several hospitals located in the capital but had no direct authority over medical services elsewhere in the country. Production schedules were determined from above and were to be followed by the letter without question. In Phnom Penh, hospitals (renamed "P" units[66])—including the former Calmette Hospital (P-1) for children of ranking cadres between the ages of three and seventeen; Lok Sangk (P-2); Preah Ketomealea (P-6); and the former Khmer-Soviet Hospital (P-17)—were generally well run and well stocked. If sick or wounded people from the countryside were lucky enough to get to one of these Phnom Penh facilities, as was the case with soldiers as hostilities with Vietnam escalated after 1977, they could receive fairly good treatment.

In addition, the ministry supervised pharmaceutical production facilities.[67] These included an oxygen factory (Kh-1), the pre-1975 Enapha pharmaceutical plant opposite the train station (Ph-1); the pre-1975 Pasteur facility on Chroy Changvar, which specialized in viruses and bacteria (Ph-2); the CPC pharmaceutical plant (Ph-3); the pre-1975 Dumex pharmaceutical plant, a block of fifteen two-story apartments on Kampuchea Krom Street where medicines collected after the fall of the Khmer Republic were warehoused (Ph-4); the anti-malaria office and medical training facility (Ph-5, located at P-17); the Edina pharmaceutical production facility in Tuol Kork, which was a production laboratory for cholera vaccine, BCG, serums, and animal vaccines (Ph-6); a small factory opposite P-1 used for packaging pharmaceuticals (Ph-7); the pre-1975 pharmaceutical factory at Teuk Thla, also tasked with animal husbandry (Ph-8); and pharmaceutical factories for traditional medicines (Ph-11 and Ph-12). Th-2, Th-3, and Th-4 were also traditional medicine factories.[68]

On the eastern bank of the Prek Kdam were produce-growing sites (cabbages, squash, pumpkins, and the like) associated with K-2. Sites at Akreiy Ksatr and Ta Khmau also produced vegetables, not to be confused with the "tempering" facilities there, as there were a number of production units in Ta Khmau.[69] Each ministry had such food "support units."[70]

In major cities and even in some districts, medical care was far better than what was available to most Cambodians, although still inadequate. In Battambang, Chinese physicians practiced and trained Cambodian medical personnel.[71] Indeed, in Ta Mok's Southwest Zone, there seems to have been some effort to create a basic medical infrastructure, at least down to the district level, such as in District 105:

> The hospital had a staff of 96 people, of whom 16 were male. Twenty-five were engaged in producing medicine. The Staff was organized in groups, 30 for treatment, 10 for laundry, 10 for cooking, the rest for home visits. Every week the tasks were rotated. The staff were taught by [a medical professional trained at the zone hospital]....Those who were literate, mostly young women who had completed secondary school, got whatever technical training he could provide and were appointed group heads. He had established four medical groups: malaria, maternity, general diseases, and cleaning equipment....He also sent serious cases to the Zone hospital. The Zone hospital, however, was no better than his, its chief was the younger sister of Ta Mok who had no education or medical experience; but they had more medicine than he had.[72]

As another doctor at the time put it, "The main thing was that patients had enough to eat" in the hospitals.[73] But this was not true across the board, as a Comrade Yan, a medical staff member (*montie pet*) at a district-level infirmary recalls:

> The staff consisted of 25 persons, and they ate very well indeed: six chickens a day and a pig per week, lots of rice and vegetables. Yan herself also lived well, being allowed the chicken entrails that the "doctors" did not want. The 150 or so patients, on the other hand, were served thin rice gruel and a few vegetables. Yan was allowed to use 60 cans of rice per day for the patients (which equals about 200 grams per person), but she often managed to add some extra rice, at considerable risk to herself.[74]

Below this administrative level the quality of medical care deteriorated rapidly, or the variation between the few good hospitals stood in contrast to the overwhelming number of practically medieval facilities. The *montie pet* under the direct jurisdiction of local leaders often lacked even the most basic resources, medicines, and medical expertise. They often had to make do with arbitrary injections and with the infamous "rabbit pellets medicine," herbal remedies made ineffective by manufacturing them in pill form rather than as a tea or as a broth. Minister Ieng Thirith did bring her concerns to the attention of the top leadership following an inspection tour of the Northwest in 1976. However, according to Elizabeth Becker, rather than improving the medical situation of the Northwest Zone, Thirith's trip had the effect of providing a pretext for the subsequent purge and execution of Zone Secretary Ros Nhim in 1978.[75]

Between the Two Extremes

Some DK Ministries defied a simple bifurcation between centralized and decentralized functions, combining or blurring the two. The ministry of propaganda and those ministries charged with economic matters are two very different manifestations of this institutional complexity.

The Ministry of Information and Propaganda (and Education)

The Ministry of Information and Propaganda (K-33) was initially run by veteran Cambodian revolutionary Hu Nim.[76] Functionally and in terms of authority relations, it appears to have combined Party and government functions; in China, by contrast, the Ministry of Culture is a government institution, while the Department of Propaganda is a Party institution, although the two have very close ties. The DK Ministry of Propaganda was divided into more than a dozen sub-units (K-25 to K-37) that were spread out all over Phnom Penh.

- K-25 was the office in which the political journals *Revolutionary Flag* (*tung padevat*) and *Revolutionary Youth* (*youveak chon youveak neary padevat*) were published. It was located at the printing house of the former *National Liberation* newspaper in front of the Olympic Stadium. The chief of the writers' group was named Chhay. K-25 itself was governed by a Comrade Nut and his deputy, Comrade Pis. K-25 was also where leaflets were printed, including the infamous ones used to alert people to the "treachery" of Eastern Zone Secretary So Phim, thousands of which were printed and then dropped from airplanes. (Usually, leaflets were packed in boxes and sent to local leaders, but the Center no longer trusted local CPK cadres, especially those in the Eastern Zone, to transmit this message in 1978).
- K-26 and K-27 were actual printing houses. K-26 printed newspapers and was managed by Comrade Chamm. It was located north of Wat Sampao Meas and northeast of the Olympic Stadium. K-27 was the printing house for magazines, as it contained an offset printer. It was also where glossy foreign-language publications, often in French and English, were printed. The cover pages for domestic magazines were printed at K-27, while the inside pages were printed at K-26. The K-27 office was managed by Comrade Phoung and was located at a former military court near Wat Koh.
- K-28 was the place where official documents were printed. It was housed in the former Henry Printing building near the National Museum and the University of Fine Arts. This office was managed by Comrade Phall, who was later succeeded by Comrade Thun.

- K-29, on the site of today's Royal University of Phnom Penh, was located at the former Phnom Penh University and French Language Institute. This office, managed by Comrade Chamreun, had multiple purposes, including ink manufacturing, and it was the meeting site for political education and training meetings within the ministry.
- K-30 and K-31 had educational functions. K-30 was where textbooks for education were printed. It was also where all infants of personnel from K-25 to K-37 were raised communally, that is, by the ministry and not by their parents. K-30 was located along Monivong Boulevard in a former pedagogy school, and the office was managed by comrades Say and Ly. K-31, located at Chamkar Mon, was managed by a female cadre, Comrade Phong, and was a primary school for the children of ministry personnel. During the DK period, each ministry was required to set up an educational institute to teach the children of ministry staff.
- K-32, located near Monivong Bridge south of what is today the Kbal Knal Causeway, was referred to as "the office of art" (*montie silapak*). It was divided into two sections. The first was tasked with writing stories and composing poems. The second comprised actors who performed the writings of the first group, traveling ceaselessly throughout the various localities of DK. The format mostly followed Chinese propaganda themes: fighting enemies, building the country, encouraging people to work harder, and so on. The leaders of K-32 changed so often that my source did not remember their names.
- K-33 was Radio Kampuchea, DK's radio station, located near Wat Phnom on the site of today's headquarters of Cambodian National Radio. It was managed by Comrade Kol, who was succeeded by Chhoy and then by Comrade Kut. Broadcasts were initially aired only in Khmer. Later on, languages also included English, Vietnamese, and Khmer Krom (the local dialect of Khmer spoken in southern Vietnam) in order to garner support from Khmer and Vietnamese living in border areas. Toward the end of the regime, there were also preparations to broadcast in Thai.
- Office K-34, located east of the former Phnom Penh University, probably in front of what today is the National Pediatric Hospital, was managed by a female cadre, Comrade Khheoun, and was in charge of producing documentary and propaganda films, mostly dealing with dam and canal construction. Films about the ongoing military campaigns against Vietnam were also a mainstay. Toward the end of the regime, there were plans to start television broadcasting. It was likely the case that offices K-35, K-36, and K-37 were involved in preparations for television broadcasting and extending the reach of radio broadcasts.[77]

As noted, the journals whose circulation was restricted to Party members, *Revolutionary Flag* and *Revolutionary Youth,* were printed in Office K-25 and disseminated by the ministry of propaganda.[78] Pol Pot reportedly wrote much of the copy for *Revolutionary Flag* himself. Indeed, according to one cadre, "articles were sent to K-25 for printing without any editing." It generally took about a month to produce an issue of *Revolutionary Flag.* Yun Yat, who was Hu Nim's successor after his arrest in April 1977 and whose Ministry of Education was then merged with the Ministry of Information and Propaganda, wrote most of the copy for *Revolutionary Youth;* staff would contribute poems to fill out the journal.[79] The content of the magazine was included in newspapers, which were open-circulation, and official radio broadcasts that were piped into the fields and work sites. In such cases, editors had to change some of the language, for example, changing the Khmer word for "Party" (*kanakpak*) to *Angkar* (the sinister, omniscient, and mysterious "Organization") for public consumption. The July 1976 issue (Number 7) of *Revolutionary Flag* provides a particularly illustrative case of the power of DK publications. It was the information source for production goals ("three tons per hectare"), confessions of disgraced cadres, and general political education. That said, only CPK cadres of a certain rank and higher had physical access to the actual publications.

Sometimes official journals were used in strategic, political ways aside from merely disseminating the CPK policy line. The June 1978 special issue of *Revolutionary Flag,* which was followed up with a circular and a political study session at the end of the year, sought to "defuse tensions within the minds of the people," suggesting a political loosening up, if not an actual amnesty, following a particularly bloody series of political purges. S-21 torture center commandant Duch (Kaing Guek Eev) realized that this was a sham when Nuon Chea sarcastically responded to Duch's relief about the new policy: "Comrade Duch is now knowledgeable—too knowledgeable about the party line!"[80]

Policy documents, as well as carefully vetted domestic and international news, were disseminated through a public radio system:

> Radio was seen as the principal method to disseminate the revolutionary idea among the people by the leadership.... Chinese experts were consulted for the technical establishment of radio broadcasting.... [At the] Ministry of Propaganda there was a group of writers, the interview section, the writing section and the editing section. Radio broadcasts featured international news extracted from the international radio and domestic news published by the Ministry which circulated mainly around the praise of rural cooperatives and the achievements of the regime the [*sic*] Party line, the leadership of the Party and speeches, the

defence of the country and followed an educational purpose. Broadcasts also featured English and Vietnamese speaking programs and there were preparations to broadcast in Thai. Special programming intended for Khmer in Vietnam...was broadcast about the Khmer-Vietnamese border conflict, the relocation of Khmer Krom to Phnom Den in Cambodia and the alleged persecution of Khmer Krom by Vietnam. Confessions of Vietnamese prisoners of war, who had been interrogated at S-21, were broadcasted over the radio, in an attempt to show that the Vietnamese had entered Cambodian territory.[81]

The propaganda minister normally called the chief of each office to have meetings. Afterward, the office chiefs would hold another meeting with their subordinates to pass on the information. Each office provided written reports to the minister. At the beginning of the regime, interaction between various personnel and offices was more open, but after the 1977 purges began, communication among staff members became much more restricted, rarely more than what was absolutely necessary for work to be done.

Below the Center, there were no counterpart offices at the zone level and below, but each zone did have its own newspaper, independent from Phnom Penh, that did not report to the Propaganda Ministry. The Eastern Zone had a newspaper called *Light of the East* (*ponleu bophea*). The newspaper was written in longhand; in fact, my source said that he could recognize the newspaper from the Eastern Zone because of the style of handwriting. These zone newspapers reported on agriculture and defense issues within their respective zones only.

Although K-33 did not appear to have had the same reach as its Chinese and Soviet counterparts in the scope of these regimes' respective institutional infrastructures, its functional importance in collecting and disseminating political and policy lines was substantial. Functionally, if not structurally, then, it was a centralized institution.[82]

The Economic Ministerial Units

The economic portfolio for Democratic Kampuchea belonged to Deputy Prime Minister and full-rights Standing Committee member Sok Thuok, better known by his nom de guerre Vorn Vet. He sat atop a bewildering array of shifting units that held a number of different official designations ("ministries" [*krasuong*], "committees" [*kanak kamatika*], and "sections" [*kanak montie*], which I refer to as "ministerial units") that changed over time, merging and decoupling seemingly at random. The units more clearly designated as "ministries" were Industry (under Cheng An), Commerce (under Koy Thuon), and Public Works (under

Tauch Pheaun). Agriculture (under Nuon Son, succeeded by Comrade Lvei) had its own committee but did not have a formal ministry associated with it. Similarly, the Railway Committee was not a formal ministry, even though it was very large, and increasingly important. Units that did not have a "minister" and were thus not considered ministries were under the dual leadership of the assigned committee and directly through 870. These included railways, agriculture, energy, and rubber plantations.

Moreover, these units were not of a piece; some were more centralized and under the day-to-day control of their superior ministries and the Standing Committee, while others were decentralized under the authority of the zone commanders and other local leaders. In general, commerce functions were centralized, agriculture and public works were decentralized, and industry was both. In other words, agricultural production and water management were handled in a structurally decentralized milieu, while commerce and much of industry were coordinated directly with the Center. For example, the group in charge of the January 1 Dam project was the Central Zone committee of Ke Pauk and the leaders of Sectors 41, 42, and 43. The three sector committees were responsible for mobilizing people to construct the dam, coordinated by the local office of public works, which was led by one of the two technicians assigned to the project.[83]

THE MINISTRY OF COMMERCE

The first minister of commerce was Koy Thuon. The Ministry of Commerce, referred to as K-51, and the Commerce Committee were originally two separate units institutionally and politically, although they merged during the latter part of CPK rule. After Koy Thuon's arrest and execution in 1977, he was succeeded by Commerce Committee chairman Soeu Vasy as commerce minister. After Soeu Vasy was himself arrested, the position remained unfilled and was instead administered by the chairman of the Commerce Committee, Van Rith. Of the four people mentioned above, only Van Rith was not on the Central Committee, indicating the newly subordinate nature of the CPK Commerce Committee. Another indication is that on commercial documents, the authorship of the document was by the Commerce Committee, while the document itself was on Ministry of Commerce letterhead, suggesting the former was subordinate to the latter.

K-51, according to Etcheson, was divided into two sections, foreign and domestic. Domestically, K-51 had jurisdiction over coordinating a number of markets and production facilities. On the foreign side, the Banking Committee handled foreign banking matters and was led by Sar Kimlomouth; two units, BOTRA and FORTRA, were devoted to foreign trade; IMEX coordinated foreign exchange questions; the Ren Fung Corporation in Hong Kong, the Poipet

Gate governing trade with Thailand, and the unit responsible for shipping which "coordinated arriving and departing ships from China, Hong Kong and North Korea."

As suggested above and as will be seen in detail in chapter 6, once the regime consolidated its governing apparatus, the commerce units became the primary node of communication with China on all issues of trade and the single place where China was able to exert significant influence on the DK regime.

THE MINISTRY OF INDUSTRY

The Ministry of Industry was housed in the former French and Japanese embassies and Lambert Stadium, also called the "Old Stadium," in the north of Phnom Penh. Led by Cheng An, the ministry was charged with managing light and heavy industries as well as food processing facilities. Factories under the Ministry of Industry were denoted by code names beginning with the letter "D"[84]: These included D-1, formerly a factory for aluminum pans refitted with rotary hand harvesters and *kapok* shellers; D-3, a metallurgy factory with around seven hundred workers; D-6, a factory manufacturing water pumps that employed about three hundred people; and D-7, a factory that produced rotary pumps and small mechanical harvesters, to name a few. "Logistical" units "carried 'Y' code names,[85] and included units like the Y-2 garage, which was a motor pool and auto repair shop."[86] Technical units were denoted with a *T* and included units like T-4, a unit that manufactured parts for and repaired weaving machines[87]; a laboratory that was used to analyze minerals; railway workshops used to manufacture railway parts; and rice mills, one located near the Khmer Distillery Company north of Phnom Penh and the other in Ta Khmau.[88]

Of course, there were factories all over the country. A former tobacco plant in Kampong Cham was converted into a soap-making factory; Battambang boasted textile works; Battambang, Koh Kong, Kampong Som, and Siem Reap were among a number of areas with small-scale machine tool manufacturing facilities; there was a glass factory in Steung Meanchey, a tire factory in Ta Khmau, a cement works at Chakrey Ting, and a rubber factory and medicine factory in Kampong Cham.[89] Southwest Zone leader Ta Mok reportedly "ran" a factory near National Route 4 that manufactured ammunition cartridges, a product of assistance from China and Czechoslovakia.[90] The Industry Committee also had jurisdiction of up to one hundred hectares in Kampong Speu province, which tens of thousands of laborers cleared of the termite mounds that dotted the landscape and converted to rice paddies.[91]

Factories (*kamachip*) were organized as *sahachip* (the corresponding agricultural unit was *sahakâ/sahakar*) under a manager (corresponding to the *kamaphibal*, "cadre," in agriculture). The factory committees (*kanak kamatika*) consisted of a chairman (*prâthien*), a vice chairman (*anuprâthien*), and a "steward" (*kanak sethekec*). Workers were divided into production groups (*krom bangka bânkaeun phal*) of ten to twelve people or teams (*puok*) of three or four. Like agriculture, industry used military terminology in terms of organization as well as reporting and other communication.[92]

THE STATE WAREHOUSE

The State Warehouse "ministry" (*krasuong khleang roth*) was located a block away from Wat Unalom and supplied goods to organizations located in Phnom Penh and to the various zones. During the first year of the regime, it distributed food to all the ministries.[93] By the second and third years, however, some of the ministries attempted to grow more of their own produce, catch their own fish, and even manufacture goods in order to become more self-sufficient, as described above with the Foreign Ministry.[94] Run by Ta Reoung, the State Warehouse contained several offices—accounting, clothing, construction, *krama* (the Khmer all-purpose scarf, so ubiquitous it necessitated its own separate office) and so on—each of which was run by a one- or two-person committee.

The Ministry of Commerce deposited goods imported from abroad at the State Warehouse, as did the Ministry of Industry, which deposited goods produced in the country (salt, batteries, clothing, tires).[95] These goods were stored in nine warehouses situated on the waterfront, each one specializing in a particular commodity (agricultural products, industrial tools and materials, and so on).[96] The release of goods from the State Warehouse followed a protocol of 870 requesting the Ministry of Commerce to report what it had in its stocks. The Ministry of Commerce would turn around and do the same with the State Warehouse. Then, the State Warehouse would give replies to both the Ministry of Commerce and to 870 directly. 870 would issue its directives, and then, as shown in table 2.1, these imports were distributed by ministry and zone via the Ministry of Commerce.

Goods were always to be (re)distributed through the zones by a straightforward procedure. For everyday goods and commodities, amounts were calculated based on the number of people in a zone. Zone commanders would send their requests for non-regular items directly to 870, which would consider the request and then issue a letter to the State Warehouse, which would coordinate with the zone "commerce" office in Phnom Penh and the central transport unit. The Eastern Zone had its office near Wat Unalom; the Southwestern Zone had its office near the Central Market, and so on.[97]

One former cadre who managed such an office was dismissive: "It's called 'commerce,' but it's really only 'transport.'...My position resembled an elephant but I was really only a mouse" (*domnaeng robos knyom thom doch domrei tae*

Table 2.1 Chinese imports distributed by DK sector and zone, 1978 (in US$)

Ministry of Railways	36,842,068.28
Ministry of Commerce	30,234,034.36
Ministry of Industry	18,305,958.93
Ministry of Social Affairs	5,526,039.74
Ministry of Energy	1,300,881.70
Ministry of Public Works	851,978.13
Ministry of Land Transport	174,825.72
Ministry of Education	168,258.76
East Rubber Plantation	143,343.87
Ministry of Agriculture	107,915.92
Guards	101,176.06
Kandal Rubber Plantation	99,247.90
North Zone	45,920.29
Northwest Rubber Plantation	29,462.40
State Stocks	18,182.34
Kampong Som Port	16,566.66
Ministry of Transport	8,357.58
North Rubber Plantation	7,991.65
Northwest Zone	5,789.12
Sea Transport	4,692.60
Post and Telecommunication	4,447.87
Sea Fishing	4,053.35
Total	94,001,193.23

Note: On January 1, 1978, 100 CNY = US$59.40.
Source: Cambodian National Archives, File N-71, B-16.

theatpit touch doch kandol). He coordinated with the various warehouses and arranged the transport of goods to his zone. The zone itself had very little warehouse space, so it depended on regular infusions of resources from the Center, which were managed and coordinated by the zone commercial offices in the capital. The offices had anywhere between ten and thirty people but no formal organizational subdivisions or even any real division of labor; the office chief would simply assign people to tasks.

Although one might expect organizational turf battles in such an environment, the political imperatives from Office 870 largely preempted them (the transportation bottlenecks were a different story). The lines of immediate authority were similarly unambiguous: the office chief of the zone commerce offices was an employee of the zone, not of the Center. He simply filled an order that had already been decided upon by the zone and 870, communicated to the State Warehouse, and arranged for delivery. Sometimes goods were delivered by rail, which was slower than by truck, a function of how the goods were prepared for transport by rail. Each jurisdiction that received goods was allocated a railway car in which the collection of goods would be loaded for transport. If the railway car was not filled, it would wait until it was full. If there was more than one railway car's worth, the balance was kept at the warehouse until the next full carload was ready for transport. In arranging for transportation, the zone commercial office and the State Warehouse would simply request the railway to transport the goods. The zone office staff would then inventory the goods. One of them would also be sent along on the train to make sure that all the goods were delivered to the specified locales. In addition to railways and trucks, transport by water was also an option, but one my source used quite rarely.[98]

TRANSPORTATION

Before the internal bloodletting crippled the functioning of the ministry, industry expanded to the point where transportation warranted its own units. In 1977, a Transport Committee was established within the Ministry of Commerce, which was further divided into the river, land, and rail sections.[99] Given Cambodia's river system and its poorly developed road network, water has traditionally been a key mode of transporting people and goods around the country. The water transport branch of the Transport Committee underscores the high prestige the water transport infrastructure enjoyed in DK.

By April 1975, the Mekong and Bassac rivers were full of sunken ships, casualties of the civil war, a sign of the challenges the regime faced in reestablishing a viable water transport system.[100] The Water Transport Committee oversaw ship assembly factories, a fuel transportation section, a printing house, a marine transportation unit, and a ship piloting company, B-17, which was the epicenter of DK's river transport facilities (*rong deuk cânchun choeung tuk chak*). Established along National Route 5 between Phnom Penh and Battambang along the Tonle Sap River at Prek Phneou eight miles north of the capital, the facilities included the following units (*montie*): boat repair (60 workers), automobile repair (70 workers), boat building (180 workers and another 60 to cut wood in the forests), and a sawmill (60 workers). The spouses of the mostly male workers were attached to activities related to construction sites, such as making *krama*, clothing repair, gardening, and cooking, assisted by a group of fishermen attached to the Water Transport Committee.

Land transport, always marginal in Cambodia, was decimated in the civil war and by the U.S. bombing campaign, which, at its peak in 1972–1973, reached a monthly average of 137,000 tons. Roads and bridges were destroyed.[101] Phnom Penh had been in a stranglehold for much of the civil war, and the land transport infrastructure was particularly heavily damaged. Not surprisingly, the two roads that were given priority were National Route 4, linking Phnom Penh and Kampong Som, and National Route 5, connecting the capital with Battambang. Dozens of Chinese technical experts assisted in this project. Ultimately, roads were repaired or newly constructed only insofar as they allowed trucks to move about the country. When the Vietnamese invaded in 1979, the best roadway they encountered was the road linking the Krang Leav airfield to the capital. The road was folded into the military-led airfield project, however, and was not under the direction of the Land Transport Committee.[102]

Finally, the ministry worked with the railways.[103] According to one CPK cadre who had worked in Phnom Penh during the DK era, railways were "practically a ministry because the scope of work was large and the status of the railroad chief [Comrade Prang] was the same as that of a minister."[104] Built in Cambodia during the colonial era, the narrow gauge rail had largely been destroyed during the civil war and by the U.S. bombing raids. Rebuilding and expanding Cambodia's railway network and replacing it with standard gauge tracks was a priority for the new regime; Chinese technicians oversaw the project of blasting tunnels through mountains in order to lay track for the standard gauge rail and double tracking. Other countries, including Romania, provided assistance to supply railway carriages.[105] The railway branch oversaw several sections including a train repair section, a new railway construction unit, a tractor-driving section, and a motor pool and oversaw railway units, including ones in Phnom Penh, Phnom Pitch Nil, Sdok Ach Romeas, Doha Kancho, Samrong, Kereru, Trent Trying, Caring Lea, Bamako, Kampong Som, and other locales.[106] These were also associated with the infrastructure projects under the Public Works Committee.

THE PUBLIC WORKS AND ENERGY UNITS

The other ministerial unit of interest in this study is the Committee of Public Works. The Public Works Committee (S-8)[107] was run by Tauch Pheaun, who had risen to the level of minister faster than had his counterparts, in part because he was highly educated in the field of public works.[108] The unit was in charge of overseeing bridge construction, dam building, roads, transport, and water. The first three of these were largely the responsibility of the local leaders in whose jurisdictions these projects were being undertaken.

As we will see in chapter 5, energy was also a key part of the economy. In addition to a small kerosene unit, the Public Works Committee supervised the construction of three power plants in the country, Plant Number 1 (at Phsar Touch), Plant Number 2 (Chang Angre), and the never-completed Plant Number 3 (Kirirom). Although energy also included the oil refinery at Kampong Som, the actual port was, according to Etcheson, "a separately organized unit unto itself, controlled from Phnom Penh and overseen locally by Meas Mut, the Division 164 Secretary who ran the DK navy. Accordingly, the port work force was organized along strictly military lines."[109]

Conclusion

It took some time to establish them, and even after they were up and running, they were unable to function effectively because of the deadly political atmosphere, but the state bodies in Democratic Kampuchea did provide a modicum of governance. Indeed, it is tantalizing to ask, Could the state institutions have evolved into a viable governing apparatus? As soon as its forces arrived in Phnom Penh, the CPK squandered the initial political capital afforded it by Cambodian citizens, who felt that anything would be better than the ineffectual Khmer Republic. But even without it, the CPK might have been able to use its sheer power over its people to craft functioning institutions.

By the latter half of the regime, however, the intuitive and flexible approach to governance and administration had ossified into a rigidly cellular and risk-averse collection of individual officials throughout the system, all of whom had little reason to trust any of their colleagues. Ultimately, the CPK imploded on itself as the search for enemies seeking to undermine the state led to a series of purges that decimated its ranks. From 1976 onwards, the principal political targets—and the vast majority of people tortured at the S-21 prison and subsequently executed at Choeung Ek or on the actual grounds of S-21—were DK cadres and their families. These included the committee heads of agriculture (Nuon Son, executed 1976), rubber plantations (Phuong, executed 1978), and railways (Prang, executed 1978) as well as ministers of commerce Koy Thuon and Soeu Vasy (both executed 1977), Minister of Public Works Tauch Phoeun (executed 1977), and Minister of Industry Cheng An (executed 1978). The latter, as he was being driven past the D-3 metallurgy factory to be killed, reportedly shouted out, "I am Cheng An. Rebel, everyone! Don't follow Pol Pot....He is a murderer!"[110]

The purge went all the way up to the top, eventually consuming Vorn Vet as well.[111] According to Ke Pauk, who was in the capital to attend the fifth meeting of the general assembly:

> Pol Pot told me to stay waiting to see a movie. I was wondering of [sic] what was going on. I decided to stay in the building of the Central Committee. To my amazement, at one in the morning, they captured Ta Keu and Vorn Vet. After that, Pol Pot questioned me whether I saw the movie. I had thought it was a motion picture. In fact, it was the scene

of arresting Ta Keu and Vorn Vet. They accused Vorn Vet of working with both China and Vietnam and that he wanted to become the prime minister.[112]

In addition to engendering crimes against humanity, the policy also made it impossible for DK institutions to function. As leaders and their *khsae* of followers were constantly being liquidated, it became increasingly difficult to identify the person in charge of a given unit. In such a climate, few if any undertook the kind of risky, proactive initiative necessary to make a bureaucracy a tool of human will and ingenuity, rather than the other way around.

But even this was not constant across institutions. As I have argued, DK government offices varied along a number of dimensions. Some were viable governing institutions, while others were virtually ideas scribbled on paper; some were managed by the top leaders of DK like Son Sen and Ieng Sary, while others were headed by individuals who did not even sit on the Standing Committee; some were enormously complex in their duties and responsibilities, while others were relatively straightforward; some enjoyed centralized control that bypassed the authority of the zones, while others were under the thumb of the zone secretaries. And some were so badly damaged by political purges that they effectively ceased to operate, while others continued to function until the very end of the regime. Variation in institutional structure had a profound effect on policy not only in terms of actual policy success but also in terms of helping (or undermining) DK's ability to push back against China's attempts to influence it. However, as the next chapter makes clear, Sino-DK policy outcomes were also influenced by variation in the institutional integrity of the Chinese bureaucracies charged with providing DK with foreign aid and assistance.

THE BUREAUCRATIC STRUCTURE OF CHINESE OVERSEAS ASSISTANCE

No life in Cambodia was more comfortable than that of a Chinese diplomat in Phnom Penh. The embassy was cool in the hot season. There was a swimming pool large enough for exercise and ample space for the staff. The mission had its own Chinese chef, and food was flown in weekly from Peking.

—Elizabeth Becker[1]

When the weather is good, we are drenched in sweat; when it rains, we are drenched in water [*qingtian yishen han, yutian yishen shui*]. We haven't sweated so much in a month back in the Mainland as we have in Cambodia. However, in order to give glory to the motherland, we must work together. The material supply chain is giving us trouble, though: material from the Cambodian side is incompatible with what we have....In terms of sanitation, there is a problem with flies around the food....We need to improve the sanitation here. We should be giving the workers here what they need. I have three children, and my wife is ill with heart disease back home. Originally, the time that I thought I was going to stay in Cambodia was not very long....Reports of problems seeking resolution are bounced from one office to another.

—Chinese technician, on conditions in DK[2]

For many of the thousands of Chinese technicians, skilled workers, and other expatriates, working in Democratic Kampuchea invoked an uncomfortable sense of déjà vu.[3] Although most of them were still in their thirties or forties, they had already gone through enough political convulsions to last a lifetime. As members of the intellectual class (*zhishi fenzi*), they had become a lightning rod for criticism and a perennial target for political purges, especially after the Anti-Rightist Campaign (1957–1958) in which intellectuals, who had been encouraged to criticize the Party just months before during the Hundred Flowers Movement, were purged en masse from their workplaces and sent to undertake hard labor for decades to follow. Those who were not targeted remained under suspicion, and many were attacked in force during the Cultural Revolution (1966–1977). Those who survived with their careers intact lamented the ways in which their training was being used for projects that enjoyed political cachet but were ill advised from a technical perspective, such as building petroleum refineries inside caves and hollowed-out mountains, following Defense Minister Lin Biao's orders.[4]

Cambodia was an environment about which they could not help but be ambivalent. While able to exercise their skills in the service of development goals and relatively unencumbered by the political changes unfolding in China, they nonetheless found themselves working in a violent and uncertain political mael-strom in which their skills could not overcome the technical and administrative shortcomings of their Cambodian colleagues and institutions.

Since many DK workers were themselves unaware of the specific nature of the political violence taking place, it might be tempting to infer that the Chinese experts were even more ignorant of what was happening. From what these tech-nicians have told me, this is not quite accurate. The Chinese could not speak with any degree of certainty about what was happening around them as far as actual killings were concerned, but their acute political antennae—forged over decades of political turmoil in China—indicated something sinister was afoot. From time to time, the Chinese would be told that a person had "disappeared" (*zheige ren bujian le*) or had been "cozying up to Vietnam" (*qin Yue*), which often resulted in the same outcome, death. Years later, they bandied about other euphemisms— close cousins to what Hinton calls "the semiotics of terror"—that suggested as much: "being transferred to Phnom Penh" (*shuoyao qu Jinbian/yaodiao ni dao Jinbian*), "the forest is big" (*senlin da*), "particularly large coverage" (*fugai-mian tebie da*), "digging a pit" (*wo ge keng*), "the entire family gives you a burial" (*quanjia dou gei ni mai le*), and so on, denoting the practice of victims digging their own graves as well as the scope of the violence. They recalled hearing such expressions when Cambodian colleagues—such as the original director of the oil refinery—stopped showing up for work.[5] Others, like those housed in barracks near the execution and mass burial site of Choeung Ek outside Phnom Penh, likely had a better sense of the scale of the killings, given the regular nocturnal deposits of truckloads of S-21 prisoners scheduled for execution.[6]

A common question that people raise is, What did the Chinese know about the killings? The question implies that they could have done something about it. Although they were not in physical danger, they risked being recalled and pursu-ing a career under a political cloud back home if they protested the conditions in DK. Moreover, such activity would almost certainly mean a death sentence for the Cambodians who had worked with any of the Chinese who might lodge such a complaint. As a result, the Chinese tended to do what very little they could, oftentimes surreptitiously sharing their food and cigarettes with the Cambodians under their jurisdiction and making sure never to point out any shortcomings to the workers' CPK overlords.[7]

Conditions on the Ground

The Chinese experiences in DK were complex and often contradictory. Some expatriates fondly recall a Cambodia very different from other, non-Chinese observers, even to the point of waxing nostalgic about it. One recalled walking into any store in 1978 in Phnom Penh and simply taking as many bottles of beer and Coca-Cola as he wanted, apparently not realizing that because the CPK had emptied the cities immediately after the fall of Phnom Penh on April 17, 1975, urban areas throughout Cambodia were in a state of suspended animation— those beverages had been sitting there undisturbed for up to three years.

Since they were considered foreign experts, they were treated quite well. In their work units (*danwei*) at home, working abroad was considered a prestige assignment. By the mid-1970s, despite their suspicious class background, there was a growing recognition in China that this class of technical experts had an important role to play in China's reemergence from a decade of self-imposed autarky. Accordingly, Chinese expatriates were paid double by combining the 300 yuan (around $160 US) they made each month abroad with their original salaries, which they were allowed to keep. The Cambodians provided all food outside of the embassy free of charge, and meals, often consisting of shrimp and fish, were served several times a day. In addition, cooks were brought over from China to prepare food at the project sites. Even so, the Chinese were still displeased over the lack of certain staples, particularly *mantou* (steamed buns) and vegetables; eventually, on their annual trips back to China to visit their families, they would bring back canned vegetables and other necessities. This was not entirely lost on the Cambodians, who were understandably resentful about seeing the Chinese experts eating what was to them an obscene amount of food.[8]

Expatriates' living conditions were often better than what many of these workers could expect in China at the time (air-conditioned rooms, paved roads, fresh seafood); even today, some of them mused about just how highly developed Cambodia was, particularly the colonial- and Sihanouk-era building and infrastructure projects that had survived the 1970–1975 civil war.[9] In areas where viable infrastructure remained, such as at Kampong Som, the Chinese resided in the accommodations that the French employees of Elf Aquitaine had enjoyed ten years before. They were separated into building complexes consisting of conference and activity rooms. The two floors of each complex were air-conditioned at night with eight bedrooms on each floor. Four people would occupy one bedroom, an arrangement the Chinese, so accustomed to close quarters that they felt ill at ease by themselves, adopted quite willingly; there would often be dozens of people in a single building complex. Electronic appliances like televisions, radios, washing machines, telephones, cassette players, and movie projectors—luxury goods in China at the time—were all readily available. There were also baskets of music cassettes that they could listen to.

Some Chinese made do with less plush accommodations. Those working on the Krang Leav airfield lived in a building reserved for foreign experts about three kilometers east of the site, outside of the city of Kampong Chhnang and not far from the field kitchen and barracks housing the Cambodian labor pool.[10] Although one could see the residence from the airfield, they had no contact with the Cambodian workers except on site. Every morning at 7:00 a.m., four or five small buses would arrive and take the hundred or so Chinese to various sections, including the control tower, airstrip, garage, a concrete road to and from Kampong Chhnang, and a testing ground for assessing the correct pressure for the concrete.[11] Chinese advisers working with a DK military battalion in Kandal would have breakfast where they were staying in Phnom Penh (K-7, a unit under military control), be taken to the site by bus, train the Cambodians for two hours, and then be back in Phnom Penh by lunchtime.

When civilian Chinese experts visited Phnom Penh, they stayed at places like the "Blue Hotel" near the Central Market or the Number 5 Guesthouse, with two people in each room, air-conditioning, and mosquito nets, and they would eat at the embassy.[12] Although the Chinese were more or less free to walk around the empty city of Phnom Penh unsupervised by the CPK, they were informed that they did so at their own risk. They were strongly inclined to adhere to the *liangren tongxing zhi* policy, a double supervision-cum-buddy system for workers posted overseas in which accounts by the two or more individuals could be checked against each other for consistency in case any "problems" arose. In an environment where an individual's loyalty could be questioned at any time, this became a means of voluntary self-protection as well: a single person would have nobody to vouch for them, were anything to happen, whereas traveling in packs of two or more gave individuals the security of having a witness.[13] This was the practice of Chinese expatriates in other foreign countries, not simply DK.

There was also a weekly plane, a Boeing 707 that could carry Chinese experts and diplomats to and from Beijing and Phnom Penh. Part of the cargo were Chinese movies, which were shown every week at the embassy.

Compared to the suffering of the Cambodians, the Chinese lived a life of literally unimaginable luxury. Yet for many of them, especially those outside Phnom

Penh, working in DK was also considered a hardship assignment. Many of the Chinese, from work units like the design or construction institutes in Luoyang and Lanzhou, respectively, based in the northern China, were not used to the extreme heat and humidity of Cambodia. And although the food they were provided was infinitely more nutritious and tasted better than the watery gruel their Cambodian counterparts consumed, it was very different from what they were accustomed to eating at home. Not surprisingly, a number of the Chinese experts also became ill, quite a few with dengue fever. The Chinese also recall what they referred to as the *hanmahuang,* a bee-like insect, was also a particular nuisance, providing painful stings that could not be avoided by the knee-high boots the Chinese wore.

They were also frustrated by their inability to communicate with the Cambodians. Although DK had sent a large number of young people to China to learn Mandarin, the Chinese on the ground had to make do with ethnic Chinese Cambodians, whose Mandarin was often spotty and lacked the technical background to assist with more complicated instructions. As one Chinese technician put it, "Normally we just try and use hand gestures, but that is not possible when it comes to complicated directions."

Since many of the experts were on a long-term assignment of a year or more, they were anxious about a number of issues back home as well. Many of them lost spouses or other family members while abroad, and this raised the issue of who would look after their children. At a meeting at Kampong Som on December 1, 1978, one of the technicians reported:

> In the past year, five of the workers have had close family members who have died back home. One [worker] knew that his wife was sick when he left China to come here. Now his wife has died, he has four children (the eldest is nineteen), and his 80-year-old mother takes care of the house. [Another] comrade…also has a wife who has died, leaving three children; but his work has not been affected. There is also a comrade…whose father has died, but he doesn't know it yet. The father of [another worker] in the Lanzhou group has also died. Others who have had parents-in-law pass away include [three more workers] in the Lanzhou group.[14]

Another issue that occupied their thoughts was their "place in line" with regard to benefits meted out by their work units back home. The work unit was the economic, political, and social center for these workers, and by being physically absent, they became anxious that benefits for which the work unit had a monopoly in China at the time—housing, promotion, pay raises, and so on—might be denied them and given instead to those who were physically in

China and could offer suitable inducements to decision-makers in the upper management of the work unit. Given the complex bureaucratic politics of the Chinese foreign assistance institutional apparatus, such uncertainty should not be surprising.

The Bureaucratic Structure and Process of Chinese Foreign Assistance

At the apex of the bilateral relationship were the party-to-party linkages between the International Liaison Department of the Chinese Communist Party and DK's Office 870, which in practical terms was synonymous with Pol Pot. Shen Jian was the CCP ILD point man for Democratic Kampuchea. Office 870 decided on the specific aid programs, often in consultation with the Standing Committee. Members of the various functional arms of the state—Son Sen (defense), Vorn Vet (economics), and Ieng Sary (foreign affairs)—were the conduits between the CPK and Office 870, their government, or functional portfolios, and the Chinese bureaucracies that administered and managed actual foreign aid packages and projects.

In practice this meant, for example, that the DK Ministry of Foreign Affairs (B-1) had almost no direct contact with the Chinese Embassy in Phnom Penh or with the Chinese experts living in Cambodia. Foreign Minister Ieng Sary was a conduit along two separate tracks of authority relations. The first was between the Standing Committee/Office 870 and B-1; the second was the authority relations between the SC/870 and the Chinese Embassy in Phnom Penh.[15] In other words, apart from issues mostly of protocol, B-1 had nothing to do with the Chinese assistance projects. The node in which they intersected was Ieng Sary himself. In the three cases under review in the chapters to follow, the Krang Leav airfield was fast-tracked through the military institutions of the two countries; the oil refinery at Kampong Som was beholden to the ministerial units of industry, commerce, public works, and energy; and commerce between China and DK was primarily handled through the DK Ministry of Commerce.

The basis for nonmilitary assistance was established in early 1976, when Foreign Trade Minister Li Qiang led a Chinese trade delegation to DK to forge a set of bilateral aid and commercial agreements. The two sides agreed on a loan of 140 million yuan and US$20 million.[16] How it was to be utilized was left to the DK leaders, as stipulated in the resulting agreement: "It will be up to the Cambodian government to decide how the [Chinese] military equipment and supplies are allocated and used. China will not interfere, nor impose any condition, nor demand any privilege."[17] Of course, then as now, the assumption was that China would maintain its influence by servicing these projects long into the future, thus locking in DK dependence on China. And the DK leadership was almost certainly aware of this, as Pol Pot himself argued; despite the statements from China and other countries of unconditional aid, aid was always conditional, but as long as DK remained vigilant, "anything that serves our revolution, benefits our revolution, we can take [from them] and thank them."[18]

How this aid was disbursed and managed, once the negotiators went home, became the domain of the various bureaucracies whose policy portfolios intersected with the substance of the specific agreements.

The Ministry of Foreign Economic Relations

It is not far from a novel idea that Chinese bureaucracies were involved in statecraft and foreign policy. But it is quite another thing to identify which institutions were involved and in what specific policy areas. Doing so allows us to examine variation in bureaucratic fragmentation and link them to policy outcomes. Although there is some confusion—even among the Chinese who served in diplomatic assignments abroad and who generously spoke to me for this project—about the various configurations of ministries and other bureaucratic units that were involved in various aspects of overseas aid and assistance—there are several that were key players in the analysis to follow.[19]

The first is the Ministry of Foreign Economic Relations (*duiwai jingji lianluo bu,* or *waijing bu* for short) under the leadership of Fang Yi, Chen Mohua, Wei Yuming, and Han Zhongzheng. Created in June 1970, the Ministry of Foreign Economic Relations was an outgrowth of several similar bureaucratic units (1954–1960: Ministry of Foreign Trade/*duiwai maoyi bu;* 1960–1964: General Bureau of Economic Cooperation/*duiwai jingji lianluo zong ju;* 1964–1970: Revolutionary Committee of Foreign Economic Cooperation/*duiwai jingji lianluo geming weiyuanhui*). Like its counterpart ministry today, the Ministry of Commerce (*shangwu bu*), the Ministry of Foreign Economic Relations was charged with the transfer of international economic assistance outward from China, which by 1978 had become integral to the DK policymaking and policy implementation apparatus.

In addition to providing the interface with its Cambodian counterpart (the DK Ministry of Commerce), the Ministry of Foreign Economic Relations was also responsible for coordinating (*xietiao*) a dizzying array of Chinese functional line ministries as well as the even greater number of design, planning, and production units that were attached to these ministries. It would contact the appropriate ministries, working primarily with the Foreign Affairs bureaus (*waishi ju*) of each ministry. The leading cadre of the project group (*xiangmu zu*) in the foreign affairs bureaus of the various ministries would then outsource the project through ministry unit enterprises and institutes (*shiye jigou*) to undertake the design (*sheji*), construction (*shigong*), and operation (*shengchan*) of the project. Many of these units, scattered throughout the country, were among the 156 projects that had been built with Soviet assistance during the First Five Year Plan (1953–1957) and had been extended inward into the country as a result of the Third Front construction (*sanxian jianshe*) in the 1960s and 1970s.[20]

For example, in restarting Cambodia's rubber industry and making it a viable source of exports of natural rubber needed by China, Beijing was engaged in several projects, including the Phnom Penh Natural Rubber Factory, the Kelie Natural Rubber Factory, the Mianmo Natural Rubber Factory, and the Dabao Natural Rubber Factory.[21] These projects were ultimately managed by the Ministry of Foreign Economic Relations, but the ministry directly in charge was the Ministry of Chemical Industry (*huaxue gongye bu*). Through its Foreign Affairs Bureau, the Ministry of Chemical Industry would coordinate with a set of institutes and enterprises embedded within the chemical bureaucracy to set up operations in DK, such as the Guilin Natural Rubber Design Institute (*Guilin xiangjiao sheji yuan*). It also included the Number Five Machine Industry Survey Team (*diwu jixie gongye bu kancedui*), which was attached to the defense bureaucracy. This facet of the relationship predated 1975, as an interview with a Comrade Saom, a worker at a Kampong Cham rubber factory, indicates. Saom pointed out that in 1973, Chinese advisers taught CPK cadres how to dig trenches around the factory to provide defenses against assaults from the Khmer Republic forces. During the DK period, Saom added, "small teams of Chinese visitors, dressed in white uniforms, stopped by on a regular basis to inspect the factory, a few times a month for visits of between four and five days."[22]

Sau Pauch worked as a mechanical engineer and repairman at a large tire factory in Ta Khmau in Kandal province. He recalls that about ten Chinese advisers began to visit the factory in the late summer of 1975; he never saw any other foreigners. The number of advisers increased threefold the following year, each one staying for about three months at a time. The truck drivers who delivered rubber from Kampong Cham to the factory told Sau Pauch that "a shipload of Chinese" was working in the rubber plantations in that province.[23] The factory where Sau Pauch worked employed three hundred workers, and anywhere from 75 to 90 percent of the tires it produced were exported to China. Another worker at the factory, Sao Yon, recalls that there was a political element to Chinese advice: the Chinese advisers insisted that the factory apply "Maoist" Chinese industrial methods instead of the Czech and East German practices used before 1975. DK officials always obeyed the suggestions the Chinese offered, even though Sao Yon regarded them as "interns who had recently graduated from university and knew much more about theory than practice." Indeed, one interviewee dismissed the Chinese as interlopers who came only to take photographs of the production lines and who repeatedly demonstrated their ignorance of rubber manufacturing.[24] These workers appeared to have had little patience for leftist politics: Sao Yon admitted he had actually killed fifteen Khmer Rouge soldiers when GRUNK forces attacked the factory in June 1972. He received a monetary reward and a certificate from Lon Nol, as well as from the U.S. ambassador. During the DK era, he claims, a photograph of him receiving the award even adorned the factory wall.[25]

The Chinese Ministry of Communications was an important player as well. Among other projects, it played a part in the special port facilities for the petroleum refinery at Kampong Som through its Foreign Affairs Bureau in Beijing and its subordinate units, such as the Shanghai Number Three Network Bureau (*Shanghai disan hangdao ju*) and a design institute in Guangdong province. The Ministry of Communications was also instrumental in rebuilding DK's railway system, although the actual construction designs for overseas railway projects were handled by the Ministry of Railways (*tiedao bu*) and its Foreign Affairs Bureau and channeled through the Beijing Engineering Team Four (*Beijing gongcheng disi dui*) and the Luoyang Railway Design Institute (*Luoyang tielu shejiyuan*).[26] Cambodia's railway network, never terribly well developed, had been severely damaged during the civil war and by the U.S. B-52 strikes. China supervised the construction of a standard gauge line along National Route 4 as well as one between Phnom Penh and Kampong Som via Veal Renh and Kampot.[27] A DK Commerce Ministry employee, Kan, recalls that trains would periodically depart from Phnom Penh to Kampong Som, sometimes with as many as thirty railway carriages full of goods to be exported to China.[28] As we will see in chapter 6, the Ministry of Communications was also an important player—along with the Chinese Ministry of Foreign Trade—in building DK's international commercial infrastructure.[29]

From 1958 to 1979, hydropower and other electricity projects were within the purview of the Ministry of Hydropower and Electricity (*shuili dianli bu*). DK's electricity grid had a capacity of one hundred thousand watts, enough for a million people, far more than enough for the ten thousand or so people still living in Phnom Penh; the Chinese experts noticed that although there were few people on the streets, Phnom Penh was lit up at night, and the air conditioning at the embassy and in the associated guesthouses were running at full blast—it is tantalizing to speculate that there were plans to repopulate the cities, at least in part. One Chinese expert noted that there were new single-family houses being built in Phnom Penh, which seems odd unless there was some sort of plan to repopulate the capital.[30] Nevertheless, there was an electricity plant group

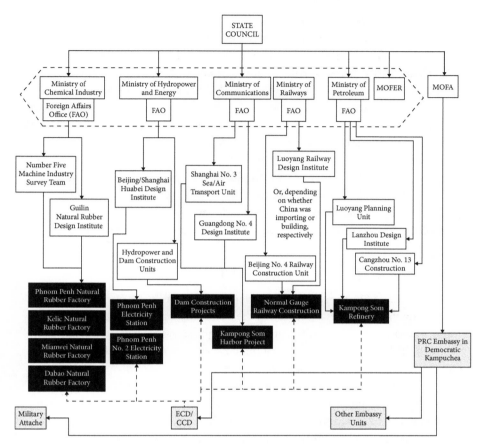

FIGURE 3.1. Partial institutional structure of China's foreign aid projects to DK (bureaucracies in white; projects in black; diplomatic units in grey)
Source: China interviews, November 2011; and Cambodian National Archives, "China" Files 1–32.

(*dianchang zu*) that was responsible for recovering Phnom Penh's electricity capacity. North Korea did assist in some of the externally aided projects involving dam-building and irrigation, but the scope of Beijing's assistance dwarfed that of Pyongyang's.

The flagship foreign aid project, however, was the oil refinery at Kampong Som, the subject of chapter 5. The person in charge of this project was based in the Chinese Ministry of Petroleum (*shiyou bu*). He is said to have coordinated with the foreign assistance (*yuanwai*) departments at the construction unit in Cangzhou (*Cangzhou shisan huajian*), the production unit in Lanzhou (*Lanzhou lianyou chang*), and the planning unit in Luoyang (*Luoyang lianyou chang sheji–yuan*). Although none of these units was physically located in Beijing, they were nonetheless under the direct control (*chuizhi guanli*) of the Ministry of Petroleum and referred to colloquially as *tui'er,* or "errand boys."[31] It was the ministry, and not the local governments within whose physical space these units were located, that handled the *bianzhi* for the three units (*bianzhi* referring to personnel and budgetary allocations within the Chinese bureaucracy that are the basis for authority relations).[32] At each of these units, there was a leader (*zuzhang*) who would be in charge of the specific oil refinery project. The person in Lanzhou, for example, was simultaneously the assistant to the minister of petroleum (*buzhang zhuli*) and the factory manager (*changzhang*) of the oil refinery in Lanzhou. Even though this individual was part of the Ministry of Petroleum, he was physically located wherever the subordinate units were.

The Chinese Ministry of Foreign Affairs

Although these directly subordinate enterprises and institutes were directly controlled by the ministries and received their *bianzhi* from them and not from the local governments within whose jurisdictions they physically occupied, and even though the Ministry of Foreign Economic Relations was the coordinating mechanism for all the ministries involved in these foreign assistance projects, it was the Chinese Ministry of Foreign Affairs that managed them on a day-to-day basis once they were on the ground in Democratic Kampuchea. This was because the vast majority of communication between Chinese technicians on the ground on the one hand and the ministries in Beijing on the other were stovepiped through the Chinese Embassy in Phnom Penh.

The leader of a given project would communicate with the project team on the ground through a relatively formal process. While he remained in China, he would receive a semi-regular report from the team leader of the project based in Cambodia. These reports, like all official and personal communication such as letters to family members had to go through the embassy, which was the singular node of communication. There was a special courier team (*xinshi*) that was in charge of bringing letters from Cambodia back to China. The content of these reports mainly concerned the progress of the project and sometimes discussed and raised problems and difficulties that they faced and equipment that they lacked. According to my Chinese sources—who were demonstrably not skittish about politics—these reports were entirely technical and were devoid of political content. Upon receiving the reports, the project leader would report to his superior, a *chuzhang* in the ministry's Foreign Affairs Bureau, who presumably would run it up the chain of command. The project leader was simultaneously

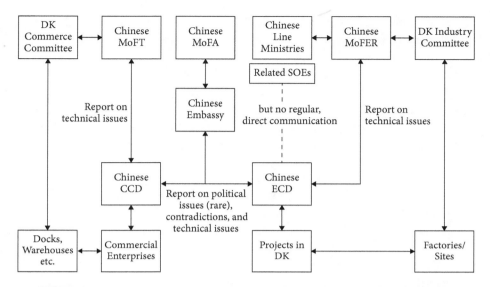

FIGURE 3.2.   Authority and communications framework, Chinese experts in DK
Source: China interviews, November 2011.

in charge of several other Chinese aid projects in other countries and thus tried to ensure that most problems that emerged were handled and resolved locally, which they usually were. As a result, however, the project leader—unless he physically paid a visit to the project site—was often unfamiliar with the day-to-day local conditions surrounding a particular project at any given time.

Indeed, much of the information about the status of a given project was to a great extent localized, albeit within a complex network of units housed in the Chinese Embassy. The ambassador was commonly referred to as having "overall leadership" (*quanquan lingdao*) of the embassy, but in reality his job was very difficult because of the great number of cross-cutting lines of authority with which his subordinate units confronted him. Of the several units that worked in, through, or with the embassy, he had direct control over only three units—diplomatic sections—that functioned to collect data on the situation in Cambodia (*shouji qingkuang*). In the bureaucratic vernacular of my interviewees, which I adopt here, the aid projects were organized at the embassy level into one of three "consultation departments" (*canchu*): one for economics (*jing canchu*), one for trade (*shangwu canchu*), and one handling military matters (*jun canchu*).[33] The ambassador was their administrative leader (*xingzheng lingdao*) but had more contact and had more of a supervisory role than a nominally (non-*bianzhi*-granting) superior unit might otherwise have because he was in charge of the sovereign entity of the embassy on foreign soil.[34]

The Economics Consultation Department reported everything to the ambassador, including technical information about the progress of the project as well as any political issues that might arise. The ECD also reported technical issues to the Ministry of Foreign Economic Relations, which, having bankrolled the projects, had a strong interest in how they were going. But the Ministry of Foreign Affairs, the superior unit to the PRC Embassy, did not report directly to the other Chinese ministries—such as the Ministry of Petroleum—that was done through the Ministry of Foreign Economic Relations. Trade appears to have been handled through the Commerce Consultation Department, with a similar bifurcation of primary contact through the ambassador and secondary contact, in this case, through the Ministry of Foreign Trade. The Ministry of Foreign Trade presumably did not handle military purchases and trade, as there were separate accounts for military and nonmilitary assistance from China to Democratic Kampuchea via the Military Consultation Department, or Attaché.[35]

The ECD, therefore, was the point unit on the ground for all projects being undertaken in the country in question. In the case of Vietnam, where there were a lot of aid projects before 1975, the ECD was so large that it took up a separate building in the embassy to house all of its personnel. In extreme cases, if there was an unexpected technical problem that occurred on the ground, the team leader would send a report to the ECD as well as to the Foreign Affairs bureau of the ministry to which the project was attached. The latter would then try to resolve the issue by directing the specific enterprise or institute planning and executing the project, for example, to send an extra person or an extra piece of equipment. When there was an emergency, or if an unforeseen need arose regarding technical issues, there was no direct method of communication between those on the ground and their actual host units under the ministries' foreign affairs bureaus.[36]

As for the main method of communication—that is, through the embassy—a committee of five or so people (*zongze weiyuanhui*) at a project site with each individual representing an enterprise or institute in China, would meet regularly. The oil refinery team, for example, included representatives from Luoyang and Lanzhou and met every Sunday to talk about progress. These discussions included both technical and "social" or "political" topics, such as highlighting model workers or, less often, cases of malfeasance. Unlike at home, where vast resources, opportunities, and costs were squandered on the politicking that rocked the Ministry of Foreign Affairs and, indeed, the entire government apparatus, Chinese domestic politics do not seem to have gotten much in the way of project goals in DK. After Mao's death in September 1976, political discussions tended to revolve around Vietnam, the rise of the reform faction in China, and the leadership changes of their Cambodian counterparts (particularly as they kept disappearing) and even then, only relating to the success of the projects in question.[37] The notes of an attendee of a Party committee meeting in early December 1978 give an idea of the dull, apolitical atmospherics of the time:

> The political work done here is quite weak. There are people from many *danwei* [work units] here, and people have spoken quite freely about their own situations without paying attention to the consequences [that is, the resentment that arose because of the differences in pay and in housing that came up during these conversations]. Some of the workers are asking us to resolve issues relating to salary and housing, as well as to transfer their work. Some of the complaints are related to daily life, such as movies. Others related to work, such as disputes between individuals. In terms of management, we have only started to pick up on these.[38]

The discussion at this meeting then moved on to the conditions at the work sites. The years of 1977 and 1978 had been very hot and conditions were bad. Several individuals were acknowledged for their ability to cope under these conditions; for instance, a Comrade Zhao was singled out as a particularly good team leader, the comrades from Luoyang were commended for their loyalty to their principles, and a Comrade Wang from Yumen was praised for his work ethic. Finally, there was a brief summary on some of the changes happening domestically in China, specifically the speech Deng Xiaoping delivered at the Third Plenum of the Eleventh Central Committee that signaled the shift from the previous Maoist policy line to the trajectory of economic reform, as the participant noted with glee in his diary.

But the main content of these discussions was technical in nature. When bilateral cooperation was needed, if it was a small problem such as tensions between Chinese and Cambodian workers, the team leader could simply contact his Cambodian counterpart to resolve the issue locally. Of course, this raised a set of challenges, as in the case of the Cambodian manager of the oil refinery project at Kampong Som, who was only nineteen years old! If the problem was more demanding, they would go through the ECD or through their aforementioned DK counterpart, which, in turn, could raise the issue with the DK Ministry of Commerce directly.[39] As we will see, this, too, led to some problems, as the political climate and increasing purges in DK claimed one DK contact person after another, leaving the Chinese quite at sea.

Each of the on-the-ground representatives of the enterprises and institutes directly attached to a specific ministry was required to submit a weekly report to the ECD on the progress of their respective project, a description of any problems they were facing, and what they needed from China. Although only one of these representatives would meet with the liaison at the ECD, the others would be available to answer any specific questions, as all of them would make the weekly visit from the project site to the Chinese Embassy in Phnom Penh. The ECD liaison for any given project was an individual assigned to several such projects. Occasionally, the on-the-ground representatives would meet with Ambassador Sun Hao himself. Sun would inform them of the situation in China. He would also take the opportunity to commend exceptionally good behavior or mention undesirable behavior, such as inappropriate behavior with local Cambodian girls.[40]

Communication and Lines of Authority: The Case of Kampong Som

This section traces a prolonged inspection trip of a senior technician from Beijing to Democratic Kampuchea to observe and evaluate the situation at Kampong Som and the process by which information was collected and made its way up the system. The purpose is to provide a helpful illustration of the structure and process of communication flows as well as of authority relations in the context of foreign aid and assistance from Beijing to Phnom Penh—and beyond—during that time.

Although most issues did not extend beyond the ground in DK, sometimes problems, questions, and clarifications needed to be communicated as high as the ministry level in Beijing. When this occurred, information would then be relayed downward. Sometimes, however, they required the dispatch of an official to observe the facts on the ground and compile them into a report, "to be sent down to the countryside," as it were.

On November 11, 1978, an official in the Foreign Affairs Bureau of the Ministry of Petroleum was called to a meeting about a report on some challenges faced by Chinese technicians working in Cambodia. The deputy director of the Foreign Affairs Bureau stressed that during the investigation of these issues, the problems should be brought up with the Cambodians, but the Chinese had to be absolutely clear about what Pol Pot's views were. He added that the team to be dispatched to DK for this purpose should take a written document with them to present to the ECD at the embassy because "it is hard to deal with the issue verbally. It would be much easier with a written document."[41]

That same afternoon, there were further discussions on the electricity problem. The Chinese Ministry of Hydropower and Electricity wished to move two six-thousand-watt units to Phnom Penh and to use four train generators to produce electricity in Kampong Som. They reasoned that building an actual electricity plant in Kampong Som was unnecessary, and not doing so would save up to seven million yuan. In addition, the DK leadership wanted to build a reservoir (1,400 meters wide by 12 meters deep) in Kampong Som and could divert the money saved to that project. The deputy director said that he would like to push the Cambodians on building an electricity plant at Kampong Som as per the original agreement as well as to insist on a prior agreement with the Ministry of Hydropower and Electricity to provide a two-way power supply line, presumably to the oil refinery. An inspection trip was clearly warranted.

A week later, the team took the 8:10 a.m. flight from Beijing to Phnom Penh, arriving at 1:10 in the afternoon, where they were met at Pochentong Airport by members of the ECD and the Cambodian counterpart to the Chinese delegation leader. After their ECD colleagues helped them settle in the guesthouse, they relaxed by watching a film. The next afternoon, they reported to the ECD group at the embassy and members of the technical team. The ECD head, a Comrade Zhang (not his real name), expressed the hope that the delegation would be able to help coordinate and resolve some of problems that they had been facing.[42] He concurred with the instructions under which the delegation operated, which he reported to Ambassador Sun. Sun told the delegation that they should feel free to contact him or Comrade Zhang with any problems, underscoring the need to "keep up a united front" on the Chinese side in their communications with the Cambodians. He offered the ECD to be the main conduit with the Cambodian side.

The meeting with the Cambodians took place later that day, just before a 7:30 banquet dinner in honor of the delegation's visit. A member of the ECD provided a brief introduction of the responsibilities of the delegation's work to the Cambodian side. When the Cambodians asked if it would be possible to finish the refinery within the year, the Chinese said that given all the work that remained, it would not be possible. When the Cambodians asked if it could be finished by 1980, the Chinese were noncommittal, stating only that they, too, were very concerned about the progress as well and would endeavor to increase the pace of work while subtly injecting their concerns about the managerial and technical training aspects of the refinery. The banquet was attended by Foreign Minister Ieng Sary and cadres from the relevant ministerial units coordinated by the DK Ministry of Commerce.

Two days later, after a bumpy ride on National Route 4 in which the car broke down, the delegation arrived in Kampong Som. Over the next several days, the delegation surveyed the oil refinery, the port, the warehouses, and the surrounding areas. As early as the first day, it was clear that the content of the report would be dictated by three factors: the instructions by ECD head Zhang and Ambassador Sun, the pre-banquet discussions with the Cambodians, and the overall situation as surveyed by the delegation. An accompanying letter, more technical in nature, was directed to the Ministry of Petroleum. By the end of the meeting, they had hammered out a basic draft of the report.

Over the next few days and weeks, there were many discussions about the best way to achieve results. One option was to get the Chinese Embassy Party Committee to communicate directly with the Industry Committee within the DK Ministry of Commerce, as communication through Party channels would permit a more frank and less euphemistic manner of communication. Government-to-government communications were not working very well, as they involved "going over the same problems repeatedly, baby steps by baby steps" (*nimen zai xiamian duo tan yici bu buxing duo tan yiguan yiguan lai*). But there were also questions about where the government and CPK distinction actually lay. Regardless, whatever problems needed to be resolved, they would have to go through channels specified by the embassy.

After a month of inspections, consultations, and meetings, the delegation presented its report to Ambassador Sun, the ECD, and the technical team on December 22, 1978. The report was divided into two sections. The first emphasized those things that needed to be handled back in China among the various ministries and institutes. These included issues with material supplies, transportation, the quality of workers from the Chinese labor pool, and medical care, including doctors and ambulances (they had been making do with a small jeep). Indeed, this last item had already fallen afoul of bureaucratic paperwork: the ECD had already stamped the request, but the Ministry of Foreign Economic Relations wrote back indicating that it required a request at the embassy level, not at the level of the units within the embassy, which were beholden back home to ministries other than the Ministry of Foreign Economic Relations.

The second section concerned issues to be brought up with the Cambodian side. The first problem was the quality of the Cambodian labor force: at present, the report noted, there were about 560 people, half of whom were female and about a sixth of whom were under eighteen. The workers lacked tools of their own and had almost no technical proficiency—they were literally peasants from the fields. The next problem had to do with the lack of a command system for the construction team to manage and facilitate technical transfers, while another had to do with the dire need of translators and interpreters. Finally, local materials were not being provided in a timely manner, causing all sorts of delays. There were a number of issues involving food and sanitary conditions as well as a number of specific technical matters. The delegation requested that the embassy decide which issues should be broached immediately and which ones could wait.

In response to the report, Ambassador Sun said that problems such as labor could be discussed with the Cambodians, but Zhang interjected that the problem of insufficient food was a bit sensitive because of the ongoing drought and other severe food shortages. The ambassador continued that since the Cambodians had promised to provide training for translators, "we can request however many translators we need. I think we can also request for small tables and chairs." He reiterated that all of these issues could probably be discussed, with the exception of the food problem because it would be a bit awkward.

Discussion moved to personnel problems with the technical team:

> First, some comrades have been here for two years and their families are not having an easy time of it. Second, those who are unable to work should not insist on working. Third, there are some whose thoughts aren't hard enough [*sixiang bu gou yin*]....We want the technical team to increase thought work and management work [*tongshi xiwang jishuzu jiaqiang sixiang guanli gongzuo*]. They should make plans to make sure this is completed on time....Meanwhile, we are creating a lot of difficulties for the Cambodians by being here for too long. Based on these considerations, swiftness should be our top priority....Based on these subjective reasons, these comrades need to "do some work" [*xuyao zuo xie gongzuo*] and the ECD should "do some work," as well. We hope that the ECD will reflect our concerns to the *waijing bu,* and give us the appropriate support based on what is happening on the ground in Cambodia.

An embassy official confirmed that Ambassador Sun would talk to the Cambodians about the issues, which now included seven main points. The first had to do with labor. The Chinese side required 350 laborers, including 200 for construction and another 100 for installation work. They sought older and more technically proficient workers, although this was a tall order, given that many of them had been killed or had taken on new identities as unskilled laborers in order to avoid political reprisals.

The second had to do with the ways in which labor was being organized. Simply put, it wasn't. This did not only make it difficult to decide which Cambodians would work on various aspects of production and installation; it also made it nearly impossible to train the workers for operating the system once it went on line.

The third issue was that of translators. The Chinese needed as many of them as possible, although they were aware of the possibility of offending the Cambodians, so they sought to be "reasonable" with their requests. The fourth concern had to do with the various possible sources of electricity. Like many cadres in DK, the Chinese were confused about the workings of the DK Energy Committee.

A fifth challenge, one of particular importance to the Chinese, had to do with the various procedures of transporting the completed product from the refinery, namely, refined oil, in a timely manner as well as establishing a protocol for storage. As for specific issues, such as with the furnace and the water source, these would be discussed further in China in an interagency setting; once resolved, the Chinese would bring them up with the Cambodians.

The final problem was food shortages, which was a particular sore spot for the Chinese expatriates at the refinery site, who were having problems adjusting to a diet quite different than what they had been used to.

The next day, December 23, 1978, a half-dozen Chinese technicians left for the Mainland, taking with them a letter that included the key points of negotiation. Over the course of the next few days, the delegation briefed various Chinese units on the talking points. When members of the delegation met again with the Cambodian side on December 29—four days after the Vietnamese invaded, an event about which the Chinese seemed to be blissfully ignorant—the DK representative said that these issues should be discussed with various departments on the Cambodian side, including the "*jingji bu*" ("Ministry of Economics," that is, a generic term for a unit that did not exist). Ordinarily, he said, these issues were under the purview of the Industry Committee, but the appropriate official was "out with a fever"—if this was a reference to Vorn Vet, he had, in fact, been very recently executed—and the DK side would "have to get back to" the Chinese. In reply, the Chinese side was diplomatic but businesslike: "Today, we are trying to discuss several major problems. Some of these are just suggestions. Some of the problems do not need to be resolved immediately.... We understand that the Cambodians are very concerned about the progress of the refinery and want to get this done as soon as possible. We want the same thing as well, but would benefit greatly from your help."

Quite early on in the discussions, however, the conversation got bogged down in platitudes, especially on the Cambodian side: "In the past, you have helped us resolve many problems and trained many of our comrades.... Through the oil refinery project, we have learned a lot from the Chinese. Our workers are new workers, and through your training, they have learned a lot and mastered some basic techniques." When the Chinese expressed the hope that the Cambodian workers would become more proficient, the DK side responded with a non sequitur: "The refinery is much larger than it was before." The Chinese side, betraying a hint of exasperation, sought to clarify: "The size of the refinery is larger, but the amount it can process is still the same. This is because the old refinery processed Middle Eastern oil and now it uses Daqing oil, which requires a great deal of new equipment." Using this as a segue, the Chinese side listed the issues the Ministry of Petroleum Industry working group had formulated, adding:

> Domestically, we are very concerned about the progress of the refinery, and have therefore sent inspectors. Based on our understanding, the Cambodian leadership takes this refinery very seriously, and has given the technical team a lot of support in their daily life. The Cambodians have put in a lot of effort, and this can be seen based on the results of the refinery. The construction work is organized by Cambodian comrades, and we are in charge of guidance and leadership. We are happy to be your advisors. We have several issues we would like to bring up, regarding organization, personnel insufficiency, and so on. The problem of electricity supply and oil supply could potentially affect production down the road. We need a strong and steady supply of electricity in oil refinery because we cannot store oil for a long time. We have these issues to bring up, and because of linguistic barriers, we have had difficulties doing so. Because we are "comrades-in-arms" [*zhan you*], we feel that we can bring these issues up in a frank manner. Based on the situation on the ground, we want to finish this in 1980. This gives us a little more than a year, with a lot of work ahead. Most of the work will be done next year, and this can be accomplished if both sides work hard to fulfill this goal. We hope to finish the refinery as soon as possible so it can serve Cambodia's needs, and we hope the Cambodian side can establish a management network.

The Cambodians countered with a list of responses that must have left the Chinese rolling their eyes. On personnel matters, the Cambodians asserted that "there are currently more than 200 workers, and we will look into improving their technical proficiency." They noted that they had already begun addressing the organizational issues raised by the Chinese but did not offer any specifics. They lamented that they could not provide any additional interpreters, at least not for the foreseeable future, conceding that "technical information is difficult to transfer with mere gestures." They promised to check back with the DK authorities on the electricity, food, and transportation: "We wish to build a railway that connects Phnom Penh with Kampong Som."

Less than two weeks later, the Vietnamese army overran Phnom Penh, sending the Khmer Rouge back into the jungle and precipitating the Sino-Vietnamese war of 1979.

Conclusion

The environment in which expatriate Chinese workers in DK found themselves provides the basic context of the three case study chapters that follow. The preceding discussion highlights that, unlike the conventional wisdom, there appears to have been little sense of socialist brotherhood. Rather, Chinese workers appeared to have expected a professional experience in which they might act as mentors to a rising class of technical workers in DK. Second, although these Chinese experts were almost certainly aware that some horrific political violence was afoot— given their own, less lethal but nonetheless highly violent experiences in China, they certainly must have recognized it as such—there was absolutely nothing that they could do about it, except perhaps aid in a modest way by helping the Cambodians with whom they worked when their CPK supervisors were not looking. Finally, while assistance to DK afforded Chinese experts the opportunity to ply their trades, there was always a possibility that organizational and institutional problems would prevent them from doing so. In fact, Chinese foreign assistance projects, then as now, are often at the mercy of institutional constraints among Chinese bureaucracies as well as the state apparatus of the recipient country. As the next three chapters will demonstrate, however, these constraints varied considerably, providing both challenges and opportunities.

DK PUSHBACK AND MILITARY INSTITUTIONAL INTEGRITY

> It will be up to the Cambodian government to decide how the [Chinese] military equipment and supplies are allocated and used. China will not interfere, nor impose any condition, nor demand any privilege.
>
> —Sino-DK Trade Agreement, February 1976[1]

> We have to watch out for China. We certainly owe China a lot, and it is a great country, but it wants to make us its satellite.
>
> —CPK Foreign Ministry cadre, January 1976[2]

Just outside the Cambodian village of Palarng lies the ghostly specter of the vast, unfinished Krang Leav airfield, built by slave laborers, many of whom were murdered upon completing their service. They did not include the disgraced urban bourgeoisie, remnants from the *ancien régime;* rather, they were made up of DK soldiers in varying degrees of political purgatory or disgrace.[3] As Cambodian-Vietnamese relations began to deteriorate from 1977 onwards, the Democratic Kampuchean leadership purged leading and rank-and-file CPK cadres in the Eastern Zone suspected of secretly supporting Hanoi. By some estimates, tens of thousands of former Eastern Zone cadres were rerouted to Kampong Chhnang province and press-ganged into constructing the Krang Leav airfield before their torture and execution in Phnom Penh.[4] Those who could not keep up expired on the spot, were summarily executed, or, according to some reports, were buried alive. Villagers recalled that the smell of the corpses lingered for a decade.[5] Deaths associated with the construction of the airfield help explain why, according to the Documentation Center of Cambodia's 1999 Mapping Project, Kampong Chhnang has the highest "brutality index," calculated by dividing the number of people killed by the local population, in all of DK.[6]

The Krang Leav airfield is noteworthy because its planning and construction took place under the supervision of Chinese managers and technicians sent down by Beijing.[7] To be sure, the laborers were not under direct Chinese control—that responsibility fell under Sou Met, the secretary of Division 502 in charge of the DK air force.[8] But the airfield and surrounding infrastructure could not have been built without Chinese technical expertise.

Today, the airfield remains in remarkably good condition, given the interven-
ing decades of civil war and neglect. Indeed, when the Vietnamese left in 1989,
the only serviceable national road was the one connecting Kampong Chhnang to
Phnom Penh, which itself was an extension of the Krang Leav airfield infrastructure.[9] Ten years later, Dragon Gold Sdn. Bhd., an investment company based in
Malaysia, purchased the rights to the airport and the surrounding land for seventy years, with the goal of transforming the airport into a cargo hub. According
to Dragon Gold's chairman, Iain Gray, "We don't have to spend $600 million to
build an airport.... It's already there."[10] Although Dragon Gold was subsequently
closed down for fraud, this has not stopped plans to expand upon Krang Leav
on an even more ambitious scale.[11]

Krang Leav provides the first of three case studies driving the argument of
this book, namely that Chinese influence was largely insignificant when it came
to shaping DK goals and means of achieving them. But, unlike what we will
see in chapter 5—in which I describe how this inability of Beijing to guide
DK policy was the result of institutional fragmentation and organizational
breakdown—in the case of Krang Leav and military aid more generally, it was a
result of a political and bureaucratic stalemate. In this policy area the two sides
were evenly matched with regard to the respective institutions involved in planning and managing the project, so China was unable to influence Phnom Penh
in terms of DK military policy.

Given the asymmetry of power relations between the two countries, how
was Phnom Penh able to hold the Chinese at arm's length and yet get Beijing
to underwrite DK military goals, even when they differed, at times quite significantly, from Chinese preferences? There are several reasons why this may be so.
The first is a literal reading of Chinese pronouncements that Beijing would not
interfere in DK politics and policy. But this conflates Chinese willingness to affect
policy with its ability to do so, considerably muddying the waters conceptually
and requiring an unwarranted degree of credulity.

Another is that China was so afraid of losing influence in Southeast Asia
with the winding down of the Vietnam War and Hanoi's increasing proximity
to Moscow's orbit that Beijing was willing to give DK whatever it wanted, as long
as it guaranteed China a foothold in Indochina; this is the *Realpolitik* argument.
This is certainly true, so far as it goes, and it provides an overall context for Sino-
DK relations, but, on its own, it is an indeterminate explanation that may explain
Krang Leav but is unable to explain the variation encapsulated in this and the
following two chapters.

The argument that explains such variation in policy outcomes is the dynamic
interactions between the two states' domestic bureaucracies in the transmission
of aid and assistance. According to this argument, as applied to military assis-

tance, the interaction of two strong bureaucracies—the PRC and DK militaries—held China's ability or willingness to shape DK military policy at bay.[12] The sections to follow underscore the two key aspects of this relationship. First, Chinese military aid and assistance to DK was substantial and extended into all areas of defense, including land, sea, and air, and into the manufacture of weapons and the training of pilots and other specialized military units. Second, it shows an emerging pattern in which Chinese proposals were adopted if they served DK interests but were politely but firmly brushed aside by the Cambodians if they did not.

Sino-DK Military-to-Military Relations

No foreign country was more important to DK than China, particularly when it came to military assistance.[13] In addition to weapons, training, and other materiel, the PRC provided many of the basic necessities of communication and surveillance to the Cambodians, assisting the Center's ability to monitor other parts of the country.[14] The Chinese helped with the construction of several broadcasting stations as well as providing DK with teleprinter machines and related training. By the end of 1975, the Chinese proposed building power generators to boost radio communication ability within DK and waited patiently while the CPK decided which roads to repair and expand so that China could arrange the network of cables.[15]

Sino-DK Military Negotiations

At a meeting on October 9, 1975, Pol Pot uncharacteristically deferred to China regarding the content of artillery training for CPK soldiers, and committed a group of some three dozen Cambodians to be sent to China.[16] He emphasized some months later at a Standing Committee meeting on February 22, 1976, that efforts should be concentrated around the infantry as well as the production of weapons, ammunition, mines, and the procurement of tanks. Reports from Ratanakiri, he lamented, told of villages possessing only one gun each. In the next three to four years, there should be as many as two hundred thousand people with semiautomatics, he said. Aircraft can be based in two sites, he continued, not just one—in Ratanakiri and in Mondulkiri, both of which were in the remote northeastern highlands. At that same February meeting, Pol Pot framed gunpowder production as a crucial goal, ordering preparations for the weapons factory, depots to be set up in distant locations, and plans for a brand-new airfield to be constructed near Tmat Porng or in Kampong Chhnang.[17]

At subsequent SC meetings, artillery continued to be a top priority. This was not simply for battle preparations but also for what DK leaders saw as essential defensive fortifications for Cambodia's evolving industrial development infrastructure. To defend against air assault, plans were made to expand DK's 12.7-mm, 20-mm, 37-mm, and 40-mm cannons as well as 75-mm cannons against ships. The leadership decided to explore the use of larger 85-mm and 105-mm guns for the long run and to keep the rest in warehouses in case the ordnance would someday be needed for infantry support. Koh Kong had only BCF guns on the island, so it was decided that 75-mm and 105-mm guns should be placed there and also on Koh Smach and Ch'ov Chopn in order to protect DK fishing operations. Finally, and no less important, was the protection of the oil refinery operations (see chapter 5). These facilities were to be protected by 12.8-mm and 37-mm cannons to protect against naval assault.[18]

In March 1976, the Chinese pledged 4,000 tons of weaponry, 1,300 vehicles, and 100 120-millimeter artillery components. Beijing also agreed to supply men and materiel in the form of anti-aircraft weaponry, radio operations, "four navy escort ships, and four torpedo boats, parts of an army tank and signals regiment and of three artillery regiments, and a fully equipped pontoon regiment." There was also a promise of "130-millimeter artillery and tanks...four more escort ships and four torpedo boats, anti-aircraft batteries for the air force, and radar equipment." China would also send over six jet fighter aircraft and two bombers once the Chinese-built airfield was complete as well as "more tanks and radar equipment, two more navy escort ships, and two more torpedo boats."[19]

Eventually, ambitious plans were drawn up for establishing a military-industrial complex to build up DK's naval functions and maritime defensive capabilities as well as exploration facilities for potential oil deposits on outlying islands in the Gulf of Thailand. The SC decided to construct shipbuilding facilities in 1977 to build twenty high-speed chasing boats because of concerns over conserving and protecting larger boats that would be needed in case of Vietnamese or Thai attacks that the SC fully expected to occur by 1980; toward this end, it was decided to take larger boats out of the water and hide them on concealed dry docks.

Beginning on September 24, 1976, DK officials held a series of meetings with leaders from a Chinese team of artillery experts in Cambodia providing technical training to the DK military. The Chinese opened the meeting by raising several issues: the 1st Technical Training Course with seven classes, which had ended in November, and preparations for the 2nd Technical Training Course; an additional training course focused on lathe vehicles; the scheduling of a live-fire exercise of shells, including 37-mm, 85-mm, 122-mm and 130-mm shells;

trainees for the officer class; and the failure to make lists of equipment and expenses for the training courses.

The Chinese began by discussing the seven training courses planned for early November for the 193 DK trainees. They would focus on 13-mm guns, 37-mm guns, 85-mm guns, 132-mm guns, walkie-talkies, spying, the measurement and surveying of land, and the formulation of aircraft. They elaborated further on the need for training according to Cambodia's actual situation, stressing that the Chinese team's most important goals were to train artillery operators and to provide training to a smaller number of individuals in walkie-talkie use and spying. They also outlined the specifics of the proposed training, suggesting that since interpreters would not be required, the training time could be reduced to two months. The Chinese proposed having four battalions in the first course, with previous trainees as the core. Training time could then be further reduced since cadres rather than combatants would be the trainees, and as such they would not need as much training in walkie-talkie use as they would need in firearms. As the Chinese side emphasized, "Comrades [of Cambodia] can find ways and methodology without being on our trail. Comrades can assign the training based on the real situation of Cambodia." The course would finish with a live-fire exercise, with the number of real shells to be fired already having been agreed upon by the two sides.[20]

Chinese Military Assistance on the Ground

Mai Oeun was a soldier based in Takeo who managed to survive the entire DK period unscathed, serving in the 270th Division along the Cambodia-Vietnam border. In addition to his division, divisions 210 and 230 also had Chinese advisers. These three units all operated along the border and were the only ones, he says, that had PRC advisers. Twenty Chinese advisers, in light green uniforms, worked with his division from 1976 through 1978. He recalls that the Chinese were the only foreigners who interacted with his division, and that they provided medical and "moral" support, military equipment, and training.

Equipment provided by the Chinese included T-54 and T-63 tanks and VPBE patrol boats. The tanks started arriving in 1977. Most of the other equipment started coming in 1975. The Khmer Rouge forces had used M-16s and other American weapons during the civil war, but after 1975, only Chinese weapons were used. These included AK-47s, B-40s, 12-mm guns as well as many other types of artillery. Three DK divisions—132, 136, and 128—possessed anti-aircraft guns, all imported from China. They used "tiny aircraft" made of "paper"—probably balsa wood—as targets during training exercises.[21]

Training included a three-month course in late 1978 near Phnom Thmei and involved about thirty DK soldiers. The Chinese taught courses in martial arts, weapons, and tactics for battle. According to Mai Oeun, "We had a moral obligation to listen to them. They were higher-ranking officers and had come to Cambodia to help us." Nevertheless, this did not extend to when he was in the field. Indeed, the Chinese military advisers never engaged in combat. DK tactics and strategies were based on Chinese advice, which DK officers always followed, but decisions in the field were made by DK officers, while the Chinese advisers always stayed behind at the base. Their input was through training and advice before a given battle began. Chinese advisers never told DK troops how or when to invade along the border or to attack Vietnamese positions.[22]

One former DK soldier noted that a group of Chinese advisers would arrive in two buses and work with his group for a week at a time. The Chinese stayed in Phnom Penh, in separate accommodations from their civilian counterparts.[23] He noted that civilian technicians he saw stayed at the "Blue Hotel," near the Central Market, while military advisers stayed at a guesthouse referred to as "K-7," which appears to have been under Office 870 and not under the Foreign Ministry, B-1. According to him, after breakfast in Phnom Penh, the Chinese would shuttle to the training site to instruct the Cambodians for a few hours and then make sure they were back in Phnom Penh for lunch. He confirmed that what had been discussed at the SC level had materialized on the ground: China provided military equipment including tanks and many types of guns. All the weapons they used for training, he said, were from China.[24]

Loy Unn, who worked for the commerce bureaucracy at the port of Kampong Som, recalled seeing only Chinese vessels among foreign warships at port; there were normally a dozen Chinese patrol boats at the harbor and the surrounding area at any given time. Chinese patrol boats were piloted by DK soldiers, and PRC commercial vessels were piloted by Chinese. On one occasion, he saw approximately two hundred tanks offloaded at Kampong Som, and he also saw ships carrying weapons, such as rifles and artillery. Ships transporting military goods came more frequently in 1977, especially later in the year. By autumn, three to four Chinese vessels were arriving each month with military equipment for DK forces.[25]

Holding China at Arm's Length

One of the first things the Chinese military advisors did was assess the state of Cambodian aviation, as reported at a SC meeting on October 9, 1975. The Chinese examined about one hundred aircraft that had survived the civil war in

Kampong Cham, Battambang, Uddor Meanchey, and elsewhere. They concluded that of these, the U.S. T-28s, a training aircraft used for counterinsurgency during the Vietnam War, were serviceable, while the U.S. C-41s, light training Cessna aircraft, were beyond repair, having effectively been destroyed in the fighting. They also mentioned that there were some U.S. C-47 military transport planes at Uddor Meanchey. Based on this preliminary survey, the Chinese proposed to provide training for DK pilots and the construction of additional runways at Phnom Penh's Pochentong Airport as well as build airfields at Uddor Meanchey and Siem Reap.

Pol Pot agreed to the Chinese proposal to train DK pilots, seeking to send as many as China would be willing to train, emphasizing that they should concentrate on fighter pilot training of C-47s and helicopters. The Cambodians also stipulated that they choose the pool of potential trainees, from which the Chinese would subsequently select candidates for pilot training.[26] As far as the T-28s and C-41s were concerned, Pol Pot said that the Cambodians would figure out how to operate them without Chinese help.

DK Defense Minister Son Sen had, earlier in the meeting, underscored some of the tensions arising from differing DK and Chinese priorities. He had noted the need to build up a radio and communications infrastructure and to set up storage areas for bombs and napalm, with small arms ammunition to be stored in Phnom Penh. Chinese advisers had already conducted an inspection of Chkae Pruh ("Barking Dog") as a possible site to build a naval port and were continuing

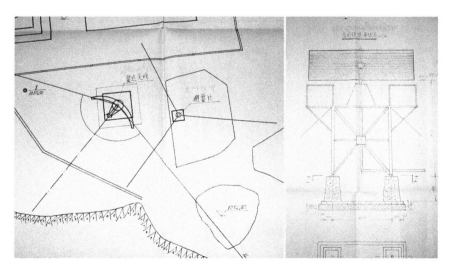

FIGURE 4.1.   Chinese blueprints for radar installations in Democratic Kampuchea. Cambodian National Archives, "China" File 13.

to scout locations throughout the country to build radar facilities, listing Bokor, Koh Rung Saloem, Khmeraphoumin City, Anduang Teuk, Trapaing Run, and Koh Kong as desirable sites. At odds with the Chinese suggestions, Son Sen argued that the CPK leadership consider Tmat Porng, Battambang, and Phnom Traom as proposed air force radar sites instead. China had proposed setting up a station at Kampong Som first and then setting up telephone and telegram links along Highway 3, whereas Son Sen stated that he wanted them to be built on the coast and in Ratanakiri.[27]

Pol Pot threw his support behind Son Sen, arguing that DK should learn from the Chinese in terms of building and repairing radio installations, but only insofar as this would ultimately contribute to Cambodian self-sufficiency.[28] He proposed that there be ten radio installations: three or four sites along land borders—"we should see where the principal nodes of information/communication are and then build them in those sites"—along the border between Ratanakiri to Kratie or between Steung Treng and La Ban Siek. There should also be one or two in the east, he added, as well as one reporting from the bases on the Coastal Zone, in Koh Kong. In addition, he proposed a station in the Northwest for reporting on the military situation along the border, one at Siem Reap, and "absolutely" one at Preah Vihear. Thus, as we will see below with airfields, while the Chinese wanted to set up these stations based on their own international interests and needs, projecting outward in the Gulf of Thailand and, significantly, not along the land border with Vietnam, Pol Pot wanted them located in areas that best served his domestic (security) interests: "There will be four sites along the coast, two in the East and two in the West."

To avoid ruffling Beijing's feathers, Pol Pot said that the matter must be kept quiet.[29] In the meantime, Cambodians would be sent to China to receive training

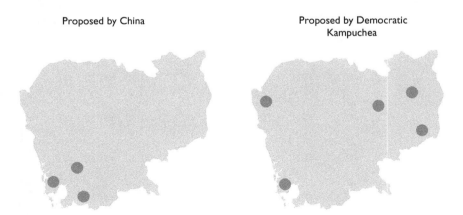

FIGURE 4.2. Proposed radar sites.

so that this network could be expanded in the future. He proposed sending several dozen trainees to China to study the operation of radio equipment.

While Beijing wanted the radio installations to serve naval, commercial, and outward force projection needs, Son Sen pushed for them to be placed within Cambodia's interior, near its borders with Thailand, Laos, and Vietnam, reflecting CPK concerns over current and likely future border skirmishes with Vietnam, Thailand, and Laos and a desire to establish a "Fortress Cambodia."[30]

Pol Pot's discussion of airfield construction and repair further underscored these differences of opinion, during which he asserted in no uncertain terms that the Chinese and CPK "goals are different." For the time being, he argued, they should move ahead with expanding Pochentong Airport. But as far as new airfield construction was concerned, Pol Pot rejected China's proposed site at Uddor Meanchey. Instead, he said, the airfield should be built in Kampong Chhnang.[31]

The Krang Leav "Chinese" Airfield

The Krang Leav airfield was in many ways the jewel in the crown of Chinese military assistance. In the context of the foregoing discussion, it reflects the DK's preferences over those of China in terms of its physical location. Krang Leav is in the center of the country but close to the Vietnamese border, while China's choice of Uddor Meanchey is at the very northernmost part of Cambodia, near the Thai border. After consulting with the Chinese, the DK Standing Committee made the decision during a series of meetings on April 19–21, 1976 to select Kampong Chhnang as the site of a major military airfield.[32] According to one report, "The airstrip would have allowed the Chinese to stage short-range bombing raids over southern Vietnam and its near-completed status, some military analysts have argued...was what Hanoi's leaders feared as well, and was thus likely in Hanoi's thinking and partially responsible for its invasion of Cambodia."[33] Although it is impossible to know what Chinese leaders were thinking, internal DK SC meeting minutes summarizing Sino-DK talks on the matter suggest that Beijing sought to avoid an airfield that was too close to the Cambodia-Vietnam border. Quite apart from the fact that Vietnamese artillery would (and did) have no trouble targeting Krang Leav, the Chinese did not want to appear provocative to Hanoi.

At N 12°14'0", E 104°40'0", the nearly eight-thousand-foot-long Krang Leav airfield is right in the middle of Cambodia, which, in turn, is in the exact center of Southeast Asia. Although a strategically advantageous locale, Kampong Chhnang was virtually indistinguishable, in its utility as a forward base of operations for military activity, from the other proposed site at Uddor Meanchey, which had the

FIGURE 4.3.   The Krang Leav airfield. Photograph by the author, March 2010.

exact same theater-wide strategic value but without the additional vulnerability of Krang Leav's proximity to Vietnam.

The disagreements between China and DK notwithstanding, the key importance of Krang Leav was reflected in the military hardware that China provided DK. In anticipation of the successful construction of the airfield, DK pilots undertook bomber flight training courses in China, upon completion of which, in March 1978, China would donate aircraft to Cambodia. DK requested a "donation" of eight bombers with two more for training purposes after March 1978 and another twelve fighters, plus six for training, after June 1978. According to the agreement, China had already pledged to provide Cambodia with a total of fifty-six aircraft: seventeen bombers for active use and three for training purposes as well as thirty fighter planes for active use and six for training, provided the Chinese were satisfied that the roads had been constructed and repaired so as to prevent damage to aircraft in transport.[34]

The Khmer Rouge Military

As noted in chapter 2, the most powerful DK government ministry was the Ministry of Defense, headed by Son Sen, who was in charge of internal and external security. Son Sen belonged to a Central Committee Military Committee, along with Pol Pot, Nuon Chea, and other ranking cadres such as So Phim and Ta Mok. He was also, as noted earlier, chairman of the General Staff, which was the central commanding unit of the Revolutionary Army of Kampuchea (RAK).

There were three components to the DK military, as mandated by the CPK Constitution: "regular, regional, and guerrilla." "Regular" or "centralized" divisions and regiments were directly under the General Staff. As noted in chapter 2, the RAK, with about sixty thousand troops, was organized into nine divisions (703, 310, 450, 170, 290, 502, 801, 920, and 164), three independent regiments (152, 488, and 377), and several offices (including S-21, M-63, and M-62). Division commanders had weekly meetings as well as occasional one-on-one meetings with Son Sen, who was also the link between the General Staff and the CPK CC Military Committee. Three battalions made up a regiment, and three regiments made up a division. Divisions generally had between five and six thousand troops, while independent regiments had anywhere between eight and eighteen hundred.

The second dimension of the DK military was the regionally based armies of the zone commanders. Although zone commanders had given up some of their forces to constitute the regular, centralized military divisions and regiments, they retained the bulk of the armies that they led during the civil war and the CPK's rise to power. Thus, their power also rested with their ability to control a considerable degree of the DK armed forces. Although this made it difficult for the Center to remove a zone commander when he ran afoul of Office 870, compared to other types of cadres (who were simply rounded up and liquidated), this is in fact what happened to most of them.[35]

The Center was able to remove a zone commander by mobilizing another zone commander to mount a military-style political attack, a regional coup d'état. Ke Pauk provides fascinating insights into how this occurred. He was placed in charge of the newly created Central Zone, controlled by the Center. The Central Zone was divided into three regions: Region 41 included Prey Chhor, Cheung Prey, Kang Meas, and Kampong Siem districts; Region 42 was made up of Tang Kok, Baray, Steung Treng, Chamkar Leu, and Prek Prasap districts; Region 43 had Santuk, Kampong Svay, and Stung districts.

Before the revolution, Ke Pauk had been deputy secretary of the Northern Zone and secretary of the Siem Reap sector. In January 1977, he was called to Phnom Penh under the pretext of an "inspection tour" but was instead taken to meet Pol Pot and Nuon Chea. They designated him acting secretary of the Northern Zone, replacing Koy Thuon, who had been brought to Phnom Penh as minister of commerce. He was also told that there were "traitors" in the Central

Zone, indicating that he would be called upon to assist with their capture, transport to Phnom Penh, and even their execution.

The next month, trucks arrived from Phnom Penh to arrest the leaders of zone-level offices, counterparts to the central functional ministries, including those of agriculture, industry, and social affairs. Later that same year, more trucks arrived from Phnom Penh to arrest "5–6 chiefs of Region 41, 5–6 chiefs of Region 42, and 5–6 chiefs of Region 43." The next wave of arrests targeted the functional region-level "ministries" and the regional commanders-in-chief, followed by a wholesale purge and arrests of district and selected subdistrict-level officials that were completed by June of that year.

According to Ke Pauk, this only marked the "first stage." Once the zone had been thus "softened up," the leaders in Phnom Penh brought in about two hundred cadres from the Southwest Zone to fill all of the newly unoccupied positions throughout the Central Zone.[36] Some Southwest Zone cadres were more "moderate," always a relative term in DK, such as those May Sisopha recalled: "The Southwest meant to do good. They gave the people enough to eat and they killed only the cadre, not the April 17 ["new"] people. They killed maybe 20 to 30 percent of the cadre, very secretly.... They made us work even harder, much, much harder. We worked twenty hours a day and slept four hours. We worked to find water, digging deep in the land for wells and to make canals. But we had a second rice harvest we didn't have before. And we ate good rice."[37]

However, many were quite brutal, in keeping with that zone's reputation for brutality and Zone Commander Ta Mok's moniker as the "Butcher of Takeo." They "added salt" (*thaem ombeul*)—that is to say, they overdid it. Ke Pauk even complained to Son Sen that such actions "had destroyed our fundamental political foundation."[38]

The third and final element of the DK armed forces was the local militias (*chhlop*) at the district level. The militias included children, overlapping with the CPK Communist Youth League. They would monitor the most basic behavior of DK citizens and report any malfeasance to their superiors: "[The] *chhlop* spied on people and reported them. They worked with us and were always watching us. When they found someone guilty, the chief of the informers would take him or her to the group leader to be educated and then the accused would go home. Serious offences carried a prison or death sentence."[39] They would "walk underneath houses to listen to people conversing; if anyone conversed in a foreign language, presumably to try and fool the people who [were] walking under the house, they were pulled out as traitors."[40] This reflected another important political dimension in Cambodia at the time: the central role of youth in DK governance, based on an organizing principle that stipulated youths as the most reliable cadres and shouldering them with considerable responsibility regardless—or, more likely, because—of their inexperience.

Although the militias were the part of the armed forces that most Cambodians came into contact with during the DK era, we are concerned here with the formal command structure, particularly Division 502.

DK Division 502 and Krang Leav

Krang Leav was solely under the jurisdiction of the centralized DK military apparatus and thus did not suffer from the unclear lines of authority that plagued other DK bureaucracies discussed in the chapters to come. The airfield was the responsibility of Division 502, the DK air force, and under the command of Sou Met and under the direct supervision of Ta Lvey, the third-ranking cadre in Division 502 (who, according to surviving witnesses, was distinguished by his "enormous pot belly"), Ta Thuok (Lvey's personal secretary), and Group Chairman Yerng.[41] Division 502 was established not long after the fall of Phnom Penh and was responsible for radar installations in places like Bokor and Pochentong, anti-aircraft batteries, and for air traffic monitoring over Cambodia, Vietnam, and Thailand. Division 502 also operated an anti-aircraft technical school at Pochentong and a related detachment nearby at Wat Chom Chao and Wat Kok Anhchanh. The division also provided security in some parts of Phnom Penh; its areas of operations in the city were concentrated around Tuol Sleng.

Division 502 reported directly to the General Staff. Sou Met was regarded as Defense Minister Son Sen's de facto "number two." While most divisions were made up of three regiments each containing three battalions, 502 appears to have been made up of "at least" fifteen battalions organized around two regiments. Estimates of 502's size range from 5,500 and 6,400 personnel. The ranks of Division 502 were filled by soldiers from other units who were distinguished by their "good" backgrounds.

RAK members with "questionable" backgrounds were identified, arrested, and purged as "traitors," accused of "theft, sabotage, attempting to evade military duties, not following orders, or having liberal tendencies... [engaging in] activities that challenged CPK ideologies and policies such as questioning authority, not complying with ideals of revolution, and spreading discontent." They were also eliminated for simple guilt by association with others who had already been purged, whether relatives or unit commanders. These purges were handled by the GS and senior division and independent regiment officers.[42] DK soldiers from divisions 310 and 11 and the Northern Zone were commandeered to work on Krang Leav in 1977, which meant that they were "absorbed" into Division 502.[43]

As we will see, by 1978 huge numbers of cadres and children from the suspect Eastern Zone under disgraced Zone Commander So Phim came to work on the airfield. According to the co-prosecutors of the Extraordinary Chambers in the Courts of Cambodia (ECCC):

> [Airfield] workers were subject to execution at any time. Those who did not work to satisfaction of the guards were often executed in the forest just west of the airfield site. Hundreds of workers may have been executed there. In addition, workers were continually "sent away" for execution, often being taken in trucks to S-21 or other prisons. Many of those to be killed were taken to the District 14 Security Office in Toek Phos, at Krasang Doh Laoeng in Kbal Toek village. Soldiers at Prey Sar (S-24) observed recently-arrived Kampong Chhnang airfield workers being sent by truck to S-21 to be killed. Mass executions occurred as the Vietnamese approached the airfield construction site in 1979 and prisoners were removed from the site by the truckload. In particular, workers from the East Zone were killed en masse with the arrival of the Vietnamese.[44]

Division 502 was a particularly oppressive institution, even by DK standards. Sou Met was a vigorous and enthusiastic enforcer of doctrine and regularly cleansed the ranks in his division, sending scores of subordinates to their deaths via "processing" at Tuol Sleng (S-21). In addition, 502 operated its own security (*santebal*) center, S-22, where lower-ranking 502 personnel were sent if they were accused of treason. Prisoners were routinely beaten and given meager rations while incarcerated at S-22.[45]

The Chinese Military and Engineering Corps

On an official organization chart, China's Ministry of National Defense (*guofang bu*) appears as one of the principal bureaucracies in the foreign assistance cluster (*xitong*). But this is misleading, as the ministry of defense is a government bureaucracy, and China's military reports to the Chinese Communist Party, not to the government. For this reason, the actual dynamics of military assistance are murky at best. David Shambaugh describes the ministry of defense as "a relatively hollow shell," with its main functions since the 1950s focusing on matters of protocol, specifically the execution of foreign military exchanges. Although the ministry of defense has a Military Attaché Bureau, Shambaugh cautions that "there should be no misunderstanding about the [Chinese ministry of defense] having principal authority over its military attaches abroad. The attaché offices, their personnel, and funding all come directly from the Second Department of the General Staff Department, because their principal job overseas is to collect intelligence." The Military Attaché Department (*juncan chu*) at Chinese embassies probably also provided the main node of contact on military aid and assistance, including engineering.[46] Classified military volumes on China's air force and missile program describe several examples of Chinese military engineering corps that were quite likely to be similar to those at Krang Leav. Although there is some variation among them because of specialization, one common thread is their direct, centralized reporting relationship to the unit commander (*silingyuan*).[47]

One of my sources guessed there were about a hundred Chinese experts at the site at a given time; others suggest twice that number.[48] Unlike their counterparts at the oil refinery at Kampong Som discussed in chapter 5, the Chinese who worked on the airfield were exclusively engineers, not a combination of engineers and skilled workers. They lived in a dedicated building for foreign experts about two miles east of the airfield, just outside of the city of Kampong Chhnang, and not far from the field kitchen and barracks housing the Cambodian labor pool.[49] The residence was visible from the control tower at the airfield.

The Chinese would arrive every morning at seven. A minibus with seats for twenty passengers would show up, depositing five Chinese, with the other Chinese on the bus moving on to other parts of the site. One worker I interviewed recalled that five Chinese experts, including a rare Chinese interpreter, were assigned to his unit, where they remained for the duration of the project. The Chinese did not spend all their time with any single unit; they would show up from time to time, see how things were going, and then move on to another unit. The Chinese met regularly with the Cambodian group leaders of a given task. The Cambodian group leaders had a lower status than the Chinese; the former were simply regular workers who had been assigned a little more responsibility. The Chinese would communicate their instructions to the group leaders, who would then order the workers to do whatever needed to be done.[50]

One group leader recalled that the Chinese were actually quite nice, that they would have a good time talking and hanging out, and that they offered him cigarettes. The Chinese never gave absolute orders and never scolded the workers. They were also willing to get their hands dirty and to undertake some of the manual labor in order to show how things should be done. Unlike the CPK cadres, he said, they actually set a good example. Three Chinese had been assigned to his unit. Later on, he was selected with two other Cambodians to work as assistants to hold tape measures and various other minor tasks. Each of the Chinese demonstrated a particular type of expertise.[51]

The Chinese would leave in the afternoon and did not stay at the site overnight. During our interview, I asked him how old the Chinese were; he pointed at me, then clarified by saying that they were in their thirties and forties. By his account, the Chinese knew how hard the Cambodians were working, but they had only a vague idea how little the Cambodians ate or the state of their living conditions. Given their proximity to the site and their own modest accommodations, however, it is perhaps not surprising that the Chinese were very lenient with the Cambodian workers. If somebody made a mistake, they would not punish them but would simply have them try again.[52]

Still another worker at Kampong Chhnang recalls that his interactions with the Chinese were almost completely taken up with mundane technical matters. There did not appear to be any fraternizing in his experience, although he, too, remembers the Chinese as being sympathetic, letting the Cambodians rest from time to time and desisting from making critical comments about the Cambodian workers.[53]

The brutality and the humanity of the CPK cadres and Chinese engineers, respectively, threaten to obscure what the two sets of management cadres had in common, that they were embedded within bureaucracies with a clear command-and-control authority structure. From a completely amoral efficiency perspective, it is not surprising that the Krang Leav airfield and surrounding complexes, although still unfinished at the time of the Vietnamese invasion, remain the most successful and durable legacy of Chinese assistance to DK.

Construction of the Airfield

Krang Leav was built in the former location of the village of Bat Lang, which had been evacuated after 1975. Construction began in 1977 and was slated for completion by the end of 1978. Laborers who were mobilized during the early stages of the airfield construction appear to have been under a political cloud, but they were treated far better than the workers who were later sent from the Eastern Zone purges, as we shall see. In fact, this initial wave of workers recalls the tempering facilities where they had initially been sent after being demobilized after the fall of Phnom Penh as being worse than their experience at Krang Leav. One recalls having worked outside the capital, in Anlong Knagn, where he was sent to dig canals. He remembers many people being selected to "to study" who were never seen again. At the site, the workers' food consisted of rice gruel instead of the actual rice—however meager—at Krang Leav, and there was an additional work shift from 6:00 to 11:00 p.m. One morning at around 1:00 a.m., he was loaded onto a convoy of three trucks and unceremoniously taken to Krang Leav. Another worker notes that he was called to a meeting at Wat Phnom, where he listened to a broadcast of his division commander confessing to treason, after which he was sent to Kampong Chhnang.[54]

When these workers first arrived, the future airfield was nothing more than a village. Upon arrival, each soldier was given a hoe, an axe, a knife, and a bushel basket. He worked from 7:00 to 11:00 a.m. and then again from 1:00 to 5:00 in the afternoon. If the workers in a unit completed their goal early during the morning session, they could rest for an extra hour before starting up again in the afternoon; if they finished their goal early in the afternoon, they could take the rest of the afternoon off, but they were forbidden to leave the site. But if they did not meet the goal at hand, they would have to work overtime. If it was raining, they would typically have to wait it out and make up for the lost hours.[55]

The first year was devoted to uprooting trees, flattening hills, and evening out the land. One informant recalled that the most difficult work he faced was uprooting the ubiquitous sugar palm trees, as they have very deep roots, often twelve feet or so. His unit worked on about one-third of the total area of the airfield, from which they removed about four hundred trees. They also leveled around a hundred hillocks of roughly fifteen feet in diameter, each of which would take around two days. The rest of the year was taken up with excavating soil, laying the sand, and smoothing out the surface. Before pouring the sand, they had to make sure that the earth was uniformly hard. If there were soft patches, they would have to remove the softer earth and replace it with harder earth from elsewhere. They did this by hand, by tractor, and, on occasion, by bulldozer.

In addition to the airfield itself, there was a control tower, fuel tanks, storage facilities, a garage, a paved road to and from Kampong Chhnang, a testing ground for assessing the correct pressure for the concrete, a control center for airfield leaders, and radar installations. Construction was also under way for a weapons workshop and a secret strategic arsenal for concealing specialized aircraft, bombs, and other materiel from a hollowed-out mountain in the vicinity of Sdok Ach Romeas ("Rhinoceros Shit"). In a nearby hill (Phnom Touch, "Little Hill") the Chinese constructed an underground bunker and command center about two miles to the southeast of the airfield. Although it remains unfinished, it is impressive in scope: built into the rock, it extends hundreds of feet into the hillside. The height of the ceiling is easily twenty feet in places, with passages carved out above and below the walkways for drainage pipes, ventilation, and electricity. The more finished corridors are narrow, barely allowing two people to walk side by side comfortably, and connect to several office-sized chambers as well as to large rooms, some easily measuring fifty feet across. A longer, hollowed-out hill was to be a hangar for airplanes. Another hill was being used to store a radar unit. Like the rest of the Krang Leav airfield area, it is a notable and complicated feat of engineering and excavation that would have been impossible without Chinese technical assistance.[56]

FIGURE 4.4. Corridor in underground command center, Kampong Chhnang. Photograph by the author, March 2010.

The surrounding areas contain a large stone quarry where many Cambodian workers reportedly died. Although it had been used before 1975, it was active through the DK period and remains in use today. There is also a series of water tanks a few miles from the airstrip in what appear to be the ruins of a cluster of small buildings and a courtyard area. Nearby, a huge tank easily four stories tall and a hundred feet across has been built into the hillside.[57] According to a worker assigned to constructing the control tower, the Chinese told him that in addition to the concrete runway, there was also a dirt landing strip that would be used if an airplane had to make an emergency landing.

Beginning in 1978, workers began putting rocks and pebbles into the area to be used for the runway and then began pouring the concrete. The rocks came from elsewhere, and he would take them by hand and carry them to the runway site. They would first place larger rocks, then a layer of smaller ones about the size of a person's forearm, and then sprinkle pebbles. The rock layer was eighteen inches thick, and the cement was another eighteen inches thick.

The final stage was the pouring of cement. This coincided with the uptick in hostilities with Vietnam along the border not far away, which had the effect of intensifying the work schedule. This period of "hot work" (*kangea kdao*) included an additional shift from six to ten at night. The Chinese would help to advise the exact proportion of sand and other materials they needed to make the cement. Workers were told that they would be killed if their supervisors saw a single blade of grass growing in the cracks of the cement.[58] The end result was such a hard surface that when in 1979 a bomb from the Vietnamese landed on the airstrip, it was, according to one of the former Cambodian soldiers press-ganged to work on the airstrip, "like a chicken pecking the runway" (*doch mean kay dei*).[59] Even in 2018, one would be hard-pressed to find a single blade of grass on the runway.

Deterioration of Conditions

Things got much worse later in 1977 and worse yet in 1978. As noted above, many of the original workers were demobilized soldiers whose biographies contained elements the CPK deemed suspicious. During the establishment of the centralized armed forces just after the fall of Phnom Penh, they were sent to "tempering" sites like Anlong Knagn, Tuol Sangke, and Baset, where they were forced to dig canals and work on the rice fields before being sent to Kampong Chhnang.[60] As the political situation took a sharp downturn in 1977–1978, conditions at Krang Leav deteriorated even further. The two principal causes are interrelated: increased frictions on the Cambodian-Vietnamese border and the purge of Eastern Zone Commander So Phim and those subordinate to him.

So Phim had commanded the zone before 1975, in which capacity he continued after the establishment of DK; he was also on the CPK Standing Committee. He was not at all unfamiliar with the ultra-Machiavellian nature of DK politics, having himself overseen a massive purge of a thousand Eastern Zone cadres before 1977. However, as relations deteriorated between DK and Vietnam, border skirmishes increased, and it soon became clear to the top leadership that the zone army was unable to hold its own against the Vietnamese. As a result, the entire Eastern Zone political framework fell under suspicion.[61]

So Phim had been successful before 1975 in managing CPK relations with its Vietnamese allies before relations between the two began to sour. According to Becker, So Phim "reaped the immediate benefits of the Vietnamese army fighting the war for the Khmer Rouge. The Vietnamese passed on captured weapons and gave the Eastern Zone the time to build up its forces."[62] Despite So Phim's demonstrated loyalty to the Center, the DK military losses to Vietnam pointed to only one conceivable conclusion, as far as Pol Pot was concerned: So Phim had gone over to the Vietnamese side:

> Thus began, on 25 May 1978, the massive conventional suppression campaign, known in the East since then as "the coup" (*rot praha*). Eastern Zone resistance to this Centre imposition of control provoked the enormous massacres of the eastern population in the second half of 1978. The Centre described the entire population of the Zone as having "Khmer bodies with Vietnamese minds" (*khluon khmaer kuo kbal yuon*) and set about eliminating it either through mass evacuation or mass murder.[63]

As with the purge of the Central Zone discussed earlier in this chapter, Ta Mok's Southwest Zone army was sent into action, this time taking over the Eastern Zone, killing many, sending others to be tortured in Phnom Penh—So Phim committed suicide rather than face torture and execution—and press-ganging many of the rest into working on the Krang Leav airfield, still under Division 502.[64]

Conditions for these purged Eastern Zone cadres were as brutal as any imaginable in DK, and thousands died under the harsh conditions or were taken away and killed. Once the Vietnamese invaded, Eastern Zone cadres working on the airfield were arrested and taken to designated killing sites. One of these was at Kampong Speu.[65] Another was at Thnàl Bèmbèk, to which possibly thousands of Eastern Zone cadres were sent under the pretext of "going to fight the Vietnamese."[66] Others, on the day the Chinese experts were evacuated from Krang Leav, were instructed to collect their belongings and retreat to Om Leong, where the Southwestern troops continued to carry out mass executions through February 1979.[67]

Conclusion

In this chapter, I have argued that Krang Leav illustrates several important dimensions of my overall argument. First, the decision to place the airfield in Kampong Chhnang is just one of many instances where DK preferences won out over Chinese ones. This is perhaps not terribly surprising, but it stands in sharp contrast to the case of commerce, which will be examined in chapter 6. The second point underscored in this chapter is that even if China wanted to, it was unable to influence DK in the implementation of policy—except in the narrowest, most technical sense—because the bureaucracy in charge of the airfield, the RAK's Division 502, was among the strongest and most centralized in the country. As a result, Krang Leav is a rare instance in which a major Chinese assistance project in DK was an unqualified success; indeed, the Vietnamese invasion of Cambodia in December 1978 was the only thing that prevented the airfield from becoming fully operational. In the next chapter we will see China's inability to influence DK policy play out in a completely different way. Unlike Krang Leav, where stalemate was the result of two strong bureaucracies going up against each other, China was unable to shape the processes and outcomes at the petroleum refinery at Kampong Som because of the degree of fragmentation of both the Chinese and the DK bureaucracies in charge. This is where we now turn.

THE FAILURE OF THE KAMPONG SOM PETROLEUM REFINERY PROJECT

We need principles for these foreign aid projects. We look pathetic.

—Chinese worker at Kampong Som

Working here is like fighting a war on the bottom of the ocean.

—Chinese worker at Kampong Som[1]

The port of Kampong Som boasts a history far more colorful than its sleepy environs would indicate. It was the site of one of the last great infrastructure developments of the Sangkum era of Norodom Sihanouk, the petroleum refinery, which began operations at the end of 1968. The port was the final act of a bizarre mutiny, the first on a U.S. ship in 150 years, of the SS *Columbia Eagle*, which was carrying napalm and war materiel to Thailand for use by American forces in Vietnam, by two idealistic but misguided young crewmembers, Clyde McKay and Alvin Glatkowski. Assuming that they would be welcomed by the left-leaning Sihanouk, they arrived just in time for the March 1970 action that deposed the prince and brought into power the pro-U.S. Khmer Republic under Lon Nol and were promptly imprisoned. Glatkowski was eventually extradited to the United States, while McKay escaped, sought refuge with the Khmer Rouge, and was never seen again. During the civil war, Kampong Som was one of the key locations where war materiel from China was offloaded to be taken to the pro-Hanoi guerillas in South Vietnam. Just a month after the fall of Phnom Penh, Kampong Som briefly gained notoriety once again when U.S. bombers strafed the petroleum refinery in the fiery conclusion of the *Mayaguez* incident, an invasion of Cambodia by U.S. Marines to free a container vessel that had been impounded by the Khmer Rouge, the last battle of the U.S. war in Indochina.[2] In this chapter, I argue that Kampong Som is also the site of one of the most spectacular failures of Chinese assistance to Democratic Kampuchea, the repair and refitting of the Kampong Som petroleum refinery.

China was unable to shape the DK policy area of infrastructure development for two reasons. First, as indicated in chapter 2 and argued at length below, DK institutions were simply incapable of managing the complex tasks assigned to them, particularly once the internal political purges began. Skilled

Cambodians had either been killed during the early stages of the revolution or were hiding their identities in order to avoid such a fate. Thus, the majority of managers as well as laborers at Kampong Som were Cambodian children, aged eight to fifteen; they referred to the Chinese who were in their thirties or early forties as "grandfather" (as much because of the age difference as for according formal respect to the latter). One Chinese expert recalled declining his only opportunity to visit Angkor Wat because he found out that his pilot was only seventeen![3] Even those in positions of authority, such as the managers of the oil refinery, were only eighteen or nineteen, with just a secondary school education, if that.[4]

The second reason has to do with the fact that the Chinese institutions were themselves fragmented and incapable of effectively planning and coordinating the various technical and managerial dimensions of the project, let alone of exploiting DK institutional weakness, however modestly, to influence DK policy. The sheer number of contracting and subcontracting parties soon became unmanageable, especially when combined with the similarly chaotic DK workforce; by 1978 it became clear that only a miracle would result in the completion of the project at all, let alone by the scheduled date of 1980.

Some may argue that a focus on institutions is beside the point, that military aid was more important to Phnom Penh than was trade or an improved energy infrastructure. But when we take into account the types of aid that would make DK more dependent on China, a different calculus emerges. The Krang Leav airfield would have helped Chinese force projection capabilities but was not something that would necessarily lock in Cambodian dependence on China. The Chinese-retrofitted petroleum refinery in Kampong Som, by contrast, would have made DK rely on crude oil from China, rather than from the Middle East, which would have brought DK into China's orbit as much as did the Krang Leav airfield, if not more so. It is all the more stunning, therefore, that the project failed as spectacularly as it did.

The Historical Context

In the late 1960s, the French company Elf Aquitaine concluded a joint venture agreement with the Royal Government of Cambodia on an oil refinery at what was then called Sihanoukville, in southwest Cambodia.[5] The refinery opened on November 14, 1968, and began processing petroleum by the end of the year. On January 3, 1969, the first shipments of refined oil were sent to Phnom Penh along National Highway Number 4; later the Sihanoukville-Kampot railway line was used.[6]

After Sihanouk was deposed, the name of the town reverted back to Kampong Som, and the oil refinery became a target for Khmer Rouge and Vietnamese communist insurgents fighting the Khmer Republic. The refinery was vulnerable on two sides: it could be easily attacked from the sea, but because it was located on the edge of the jungle—some distance from the nearest urban area—it was an obvious target for land attacks as well. Rather than undertake repairs at the time, the French decided that they would wait until the political situation stabilized, dismantling the machines and storing them against the oppressive humidity.[7] The Khmer Republic was responsible for maintaining the security of the facilities, but as with many other aspects of its rule, it failed: "What remained of the refinery, supposed to be protected by the army, was disassembled and left in pieces for shipment to Thailand: electronic material, copper, and the driving screws of the pumps."[8]

The State of the Petroleum Facility in 1975

The facilities lay unused until the CPK victory in 1975. During the DK era, the site took on a somewhat unique character beyond a simple DK commitment to the successful recovery, repair, and refitting of the petroleum refinery. According to Henri Locard:

> The entire peninsula of Kampong Som (now Sihanoukville), the country's high sea harbour, was something of haven of near normality in a sea of misery in this particularly wretched Southeast region. This had to be so for the visiting Chinese sailors or other foreign visitors. The Chinese built a long pier and warehouses, while the oil refinery, burnt by the Khmer Rouge in the early days of the civil war, was being repaired by Chinese experts, and was planned to reopen in 1980. Food was plentiful and no one knew of the excruciating living conditions a few miles north in Prey Nup district. Still no freedom of movement was allowed outside the peninsula. If you were caught trying to escape towards Thailand in a motor boat, the only punishment was death. All technicians who were denounced as suspicious elements would be taken to the local prison in one of the pagodas that dominated the city.[9]

In August and December 1975, the two countries signed economic agreements that entailed aid projects, including the oil refinery. On June 9, 1976, a Chinese investigation group (*kaocha zu*) of technicians was sent to Kampong Som to start drawing up plans for the oil refinery.[10] China would renovate and expand the refinery and provide all equipment and facilities for its construction (*chengtao shebei*), which was slated to be finished by 1980. The estimated cost was 38.8 million yuan. In addition to building the refinery, there were arrangements made for the training of Cambodian interns in China. Eighty-four Cambodians would be sent to Lanzhou, and another twenty-two would go to Yumen (both in Gansu province). The facilities at Yumen, which were not large, were deemed a suitable "teaching refinery" for the Cambodians. In terms of manpower, the original plan was to send around 450 Chinese to Cambodia to work on the project. It was intended that they would be mostly managers or technical experts, but they also had to send laborers.[11]

A Chinese technician who had worked at Kampong Som said that the project was important, but in terms of the scale it was not an overwhelming operation: they did not have to build it from the ground up but were instead only refitting an existing refinery, although Moeung Sonn and Locard argue little more than the foundation remained. In any case, the expansion of the facilities required extra equipment for catalytic cracking (*cuihua liehua*), because they were also switching the technology away from processing crude oil from Qatar to refining equipment that could process oil from China's Daqing oil fields. Although China officially claimed this as Chinese technology, it actually came from Cuba. The Cubans had somehow obtained blueprints of the original facility from the Americans, and since they had an extra set, they decided to share one with the Chinese. The Chinese followed the blueprints diligently in producing the equipment.[12]

As noted in chapter 3, the Ministry of Foreign Economic Relations was the lead agency that interfaced with its Cambodian counterparts (the Ministry of Commerce and the Commerce Committee) as well as the coordinating organization in China. Once a project had been specified, the Ministry of Foreign Economic Relations would contact the appropriate ministries, working primarily with these ministries' foreign affairs bureaus. The leading cadre of the project group in the foreign affairs bureaus of the participating ministries would then outsource the project through various enterprises and institutes to undertake the design, construction, and operation of the project.[13]

The Chinese official in charge of this project acted as a liaison, coordinating the foreign assistance departments at the construction unit in Cangzhou (*Cangzhou shisan huajian*), the production unit in Lanzhou (*Lanzhou lianyou chang*), and the planning unit in Luoyang (*Luoyang lianyou chang shejiyuan*). Although none of these units was physically located in Beijing, they were nonetheless under the direct control of the Ministry of Petroleum. It was the ministry and not the local governments where the units were located that handled the personnel and budgetary allocations for the three units. At each of these units, there was a leader who would be in charge of the specific oil refinery project. The person in Lanzhou, for example, was simultaneously the assistant to the minister

FIGURE 5.1. Chinese schematic for the Kampong Som refinery. Cambodian National Archives, "China" File 7.

of petroleum (*buzhang zhuli*) and the factory manager (*changzhang*) of the oil refinery in Lanzhou. Despite being physically located at the site of the subordinate units, that individual was part of the national Ministry of Petroleum.

Each of these departments, in turn, would coordinate manpower and resources. The Luoyang Design Institute would first inspect the existing facilities to see what needed to be done and then undertake a preliminary design. This design required the approval of experts, such as those in the Bureau of Machine Building (*jijian ju*) and other units in the Ministry of Petroleum. Following this meeting, they would come up with the final blueprint for construction design (*shigong tu*), which would again require approval from the experts at the Ministry of Petroleum.[14] In addition, specialty items had to be ordered from other work units from locales ranging from Shenyang to Tianjin to Wuhan.

The vast configuration of bureaucratic units mobilized for this project was vast, but, as we will see, in practice it became impossibly unwieldy.

Problems at the Site Originating from DK

An on-site worker summed up the situation at the oil refinery in somewhat brusque and dire—but accurate—terms that matched the general mood of workers who had been assigned to the project on a long term basis:

It has been three years since we have been working on this refinery...but there have been so many problems, especially with electricity. Also, the supply chain from China to here has simply been disconnected. The Cambodian side seems to refuse to learn about what we are doing. We also need to train translators. The Cambodians who should be in charge of production are poorly educated, and too young. The techniques and methods of operation for the oil refinery are unique, and workers need a basic industrial knowledge base.[15]

This provides just an inkling of the many problems plaguing the oil refinery project at Kampong Som. In fact, it seems all but certain that even if Vietnam had not invaded DK that the oil refinery would not have been completed on schedule.

The Quality of the Cambodian Workers

One of the most difficult challenges faced by the Chinese on site had to do with the quantity and quality of the Cambodian workers. Because of the brutal CPK policy toward educated people, the overwhelming majority of those who had not fled the country by 1975 had either been killed or had changed their identities and were passing themselves off as peasants or unskilled workers. DK policy was particularly dismissive of scientific knowledge and formal training. During a 1976 meeting of secretaries and vice secretaries of military divisions and regiments they were instructed: "It is also imperative to push study in all fields of technical expertise, but this must be premised on politics, ideology and the Party's organizational principles. *Don't make technical expertise paramount over politics.*"[16]

Compounding the lack of emphasis on technical ability, the surviving Cambodian workers, soldiers, and officials, beset with the survival mechanism of mute shock, interacted as little as possible with the Chinese on the assumption that the Cambodians were constantly being watched. This frustrated the Chinese no end.

In addition to the issue of quality, there was an insufficient number of workers at the refinery. The Chinese had initially assigned 380 people to work on recovering the facility and construction as well as 55 people for production, but these numbers were not being met because of the high rate of absenteeism on the Cambodian side. The Cambodian workers that did show up for work did not inspire confidence. The frustration of one Chinese worker was palpable: "After being in Cambodia for a year, we have no clue what we have to do. We just mend roads, dig dirt, and we have no idea if we should be doing any of this because no one tells us anything. We have been digging a warehouse of dimensions 1.7 by 3.724 meters, and as we dig in the pits, the Cambodians are up there laughing at us."[17] Another worker complained that the Cambodians didn't seem to be worried about completing the project even remotely on time, that "they seem to have their own thoughts and ideas that make little sense to us" (*Jianfang bu zhaoji, yinwei ta you ta de xiangfa zan ye bu qingchu*).[18] Another Chinese worker argued that the Cambodian workers were unmanageable (*Jianfang renyuan buneng duli guanli*), adding that there were no staff members in charge of supply planning (*meiyou gongying jihua renyuan*) and that many of the on-site physical resources were broken and in disarray.[19] Yet another worker complained that the Cambodians were misusing equipment: "The three generators that arrived on February 4, 1977, are being used to recover production. We will try our best to fix the small one. The big one was to be used only from 8:00 a.m. to 10:30 a.m., but the Cambodians are using [that is, overusing] it until 12:30. Let us try and protect these machines, because if they operate as normal, they should continue to work."[20]

Furthermore, the Chinese regarded the Cambodian site leadership as "not very capable" (*wuneng de*) because they could not keep up with the Chinese on technical matters. Even worse, according to their Chinese colleagues, they did not take the project particularly seriously, to the point of not caring about mundane technical aspects of the project. One exasperated Chinese worker complained: "There is even a problem with gloves. How come some people aren't wearing their gloves? There's an issue with safety here. What if someone fell down at the work site, got hurt or died? What would happen? Don't labor safety laws count for anything? Even basic ones?"[21] If such an assessment had not been so insulting to the particularly face-conscious Cambodians—or if the punishment meted out to Cambodians for criticizing DK had not been the death penalty—they might well have agreed.

One of the biggest problems had to do with the dearth of interpreters. Given the technical nature of the project, simply employing bilingual ethnic Chinese Cambodians was insufficient to the task. According to an embassy official, "Because [the project] concerns technical issues, even a normal translator might not be up to the task."[22] A former technician recalls a Comrade Hu who was responsible for acting as translator between the Chinese experts and the higher-level Democratic Kampuchean leadership. Hu was the principal conduit between the Cambodians and the Chinese, tasked with translating directions from the Chinese experts and workers. There were weekly meetings, during which the Cambodians would present their list of requests (*tichu yaoqiu*). These requests reflected the pressure they were under to finish the project on time since they mostly centered around the status of the refinery. But they also included requests for basic goods that were unavailable in DK but to which the Chinese had access, such as brooms, toothpaste, towels, soap, and rubber slippers. In addition, there was a Comrade

FIGURE 5.2. Chinese experts and their Cambodian counterparts at Kampong Som. Photographs in the author's possession.

Zhang, an ethnic Chinese who provided basic medical care to the Cambodians when they fell ill; she would ask the Chinese for extra medicine they might be willing to give her. Finally, Hu's wife was in charge of managing the warehouse attached to the refinery in which materials sent by China were stored to be used later. Although she had only a rudimentary education, she could communicate directly with the Chinese as well.[23]

Lastly, there were problems with the supply chain of materials provided by the Cambodian side. Even the very basic items that the DK side had been tasked with providing were not available. This was an outcome of the purges that were rocking the various DK ministries to their foundations.

The Implosion of the Committee on Public Works

The committee that interfaced the most with the Chinese on the project, at least initially, was the Public Works Committee (S-8) in the Ministry of Commerce, run by Tauch Pheaun (a.k.a. Phion) until his arrest on January 26, 1977. After the fall of Phnom Penh, Tauch recruited several people he had worked with in the past and placed his wife Chhim Sophon (a.k.a. Touch) in charge of the S-8 administrative office. The staff of S-8 at the time came predominantly from Region 25, the Eastern Zone, and the Southwest Zone.[24] Offices included the Irrigation Technical Section, the Road Construction Group, the Water Tank Unit, the Russey Keo Technical School, the Support and Design Unit, the Electricity Section, the Railroad Construction Section, the Trapaing Krâloeng Quarry Section, and the Hydroelectricity Committee. Although it was placed under the Ministry of Commerce with a large workforce of as many as three thousand, the Public Works Committee supervised public works projects that were largely under the direct control of local leaders including power plants, roads, water pumping stations, as well as the Steung Meanchey Cooperative Palm Juice Producing Station, the Chamkar Mon Drinking Water Factory, and many others.[25]

The State of Affairs before the Purges

A March 10, 1976 meeting on public works provides a useful example of the process as well as the elite atmospherics. As minister of public works, Tauch Pheaun presented a report to Pol Pot on the state of affairs at the ministry. He began with a discussion of its core personnel: CPK members, Youth League members, the administrative staff, and the "mass section." He then presented updates on the construction of the Kirirom Dam and the Chroy Changvar Bridge. The pillars for the dam have already been built, he said, and rope installation and the requisite forest clearing were almost complete. However, a number of problems remained: nearly half of the water pipes were damaged; stones could only be crushed manually; the nuts necessary for the construction had not yet arrived, and so on. With regard to the Chroy Changvar Bridge, he reported, progress appeared slow because of a lack of pebbles, which would not be available until May or June. In addition, the project lacked a crane capable of lifting more than 100 tons of materials, necessary because each part of the bridge to be installed was to weigh more than 110 tons. The cranes currently in use could lift only 60 tons. Finally, he reported a request for additional mechanics from the Southwest.

In the areas of water and electricity, he requested an immediate delivery of raw materials, as the electricity section had run out of spare parts at all of its three locations. Moreover, the water section's stocks of chloride would be depleted within three months, and its supplies of aluminum could last for only two more months. Tauch Pheaun also reported an appeal for improved supervision of electrical technicians, citing difficulties in work operations to date.

He concluded his report with an update on National Roads Numbers 4 and 5. He reported requests to Pol Pot to arrange for the repair of bridges along these major roads in order to bring them up to standard, thereby ensuring that they would be sufficiently durable and would not require further repairs in the future.

In light of subsequent events, it is remarkable that Tauch Pheaun was comfortable reporting this long litany of problems to the top leadership as candidly as he did. Unfortunately, although Pol Pot's response was both spirited and characteristically specific to the point of micromanagement, it was not terribly helpful given the lack of resources and talent within the DK institutional ranks. Based on previous work reviews, he said, it was possible for the ministry's various sectors to fulfill their duties. With regard to electricity, for example, he claimed that the ministry, despite its limited capital, could perform well with regard to the production of wires and utility poles. Production of other types of cables was also possible, he asserted. In the future, the ministry could master wire installation and arrangement "using machines." Citing the example of a glass manufacturing factory that succeeded in producing insulators, he exhorted, "We must try harder. We must try to produce by ourselves anything that we can produce."

Next, Pol Pot imposed a de facto merger on the public works and industry Party committees, stating that Comrades Vorn, An, Phin, Say, and Kmào "must cooperate with one another." In doing so, the research that had been undertaken by the Public Works Committee could be shared with the industrial section, which lacked a think tank and the personnel responsible for planning and executing its projects. He continued by calling on technical officers to obtain materials for project setup and planning, perform industry modeling, and carry out further experimentation in the chemical industry. He emphasized the importance of organization and mobilization, stating, "Only when we assign tasks in this way can we operate our work. If mobilization is to be done now, it is not possible because we lack manpower. Nevertheless, mobilization must be done in the future" in order to expand existing roads and bridges. He noted that experimentation and on-site learning during the construction of the Kirirom Dam offered an opportunity to learn how to master such projects in the future. Building upon experiences at Kirirom, he asserted that Cambodia would operate 100-, 500-, 1000-, and 2000-kilowatt dams in the future. "For this reason," he underscored, "We must try our best to study."

Pol Pot concluded with a series of directives on water and electricity, roads and bridges, manpower reinforcement, and housing for technicians. For water and electricity production, Cambodia would buy spare parts itself, he said. Aluminum and chloride must be purchased, but only after first checking with the Commerce Committee to inquire whether they had any in storage. He also ordered water to be shut down overnight in order to conserve it. In the area of road and bridge maintenance and construction, he authorized borrowing labor from Southwest Zone Commander Ta Mok. Teams then had to be organized and plans drawn up for Cambodia to maintain roads, build bridges, and make sewage pipes by itself. To reinforce the available manpower, he ordered Minister of Commerce Soeu Vasy to contact and bring in people from outside so that they could carry out design and experimentation work in the Technical Department. Attention should also be paid to administering additional political education, he said. Finally, Pol Pot ordered that the houses in which the foreign experts were staying be supplied with water, electricity, and toilets, noting, "This is also politics."[26]

The Cratering of DK Organizational Integrity

Within a year, however, this structure and process of supervision, reporting, policymaking, and policy implementation would be rocked to its foundations by internal purges and the neglect of the procedural imperatives that inevitably occurred in their wake. The purges described in chapter 4 that targeted regional and local leaders also extended to functional leaders at the Center, including the ministers and their staffs. Much of the slack was taken up by Nuon Chea.

Nuon Chea, or "Brother Number Two," was a full-rights member of the CPK Central Committee, of which he was also deputy secretary. He was also a full-rights member of the Standing Committee of the CPK and a member of the Central Committee Military Committee with an active role in military decision-making alongside Pol Pot and Son Sen. The key institutional power base for Nuon Chea was his direction of the CPK Organization Committee, which recruited new Party members and supervised existing ones. This power of appointment ranged from CPK cadres in offices and ministries to that of zone and sector CPK committee leaders, particularly of sectors 105 and 103. Moreover, Nuon Chea assumed responsibility for "party work, social welfare, culture, propaganda and formal education," effectively giving him oversight over three ministries: Propaganda, Education, and Social Affairs. Nuon Chea was given this responsibility because the ministers of these units were not full-rights members of the Central Committee. What this meant in practice was that these ministers "did not have the decision making power to eliminate people," according to Duch, adding that "everything had to pass through Nuon Chea."[27]

By late 1978, this appears to have included the commercial and industrial portfolios as well. In December, Vorn Vet had joined earlier disgraced ministers Koy Thuon and Hu Nim for "processing" (torture, confession, and execution) at S-21. According to Kiernan, the normally serene Pol Pot, in an uncharacteristic fit of personal violence, set upon Vorn Vet, supposedly breaking his leg.[28]

> [Up to that time] the Ministry of Industry led [by] Vorn Vet, controlled several Phnom Penh ministry workforces in industry, agriculture, electricity, public works and railways. Vorn Vet had the authority to appoint and remove the leaders of major units under his control....Around the beginning of the 4th quarter of 1975, Vorn Vet announced the appointment of [Phion] as Chairman and Chon Vice Chairman of the Public Works Ministry, and removed Sok, Mon and Saeng, transferring them to the General Staff. Vorn Vet also controlled lower echelon leadership in sub-units of ministries under his leadership, [appointing] a new chairman of the Steung Chral Electricity Plant, part of the Ministry of Electricity, after a previous chairman had been arrested by the Organization.[29]

These political machinations simply deepened the void of bureaucratic accountability and institutional communication, which directly affected the Chinese. On December 12, a few weeks before Vorn Vet was arrested, there was meeting at Kampong Som during which a Chinese embassy official made a remarkable—even startling—admission: "Since we are not sure who is in charge of operating the refinery [*shi gongye weiyuanhui haishi dongli weiyuanhui guanli*], perhaps we should really try and find out."[30] That is, three years after the project had started, the Chinese Embassy was unclear about whether it was the DK Industrial Committee or the DK Power and Public Works committees that had jurisdiction over the oil refinery. Further complicating the picture was the fact that Kampong Som, with its direct, centralized authority relationship with Phnom Penh, did not pass through the zone leadership.[31]

The reasons for needing to know who was in charge on the Cambodian side are both obvious and manifold. As summarized at a December 13, 1978, meeting among technicians:

> Cambodian leaders are starting to take up a leadership role in managing the refinery. Based on the agreement, this is what is supposed to be done, since Cambodia is the country that owns the refinery. Therefore, they should take more steps to cultivate talent in this area, because it would set a good foundation for the proper management of this refinery in future. We are currently only training a few individuals. This is not working. Without a proper mechanism, we don't have a permanent set of workers to train, and linguistic differences make training difficult. This would make future production even more complicated. Oil refining techniques, tests, equipment and measurement are all complicated. The Cambodian side needs to come up with a leadership system, and we would be happy to assist and act as consultants. Next year, according to the [1976] agreement, work on the refinery will reach its peak. The Cambodian side needs to invest more people in this operation.[32]

The only dedicated management team that the Chinese identified by name was a Comrade "Yi Te," the DK cadre in charge of the refinery. He was assisted by a Comrade "Gai," Yi Te's "right hand" (*diyi bashou*) cadre. In addition, there was a Comrade "Luo," who was vice director of the refinery in charge of production, and a Comrade "Jia Mei," who was the vice director in charge of supplies and the day-to-day operations.[33] But the real problem was how to link these individuals to an ever-changing functional leadership structure in Phnom Penh. According to another Chinese technician, "Originally, leaders would come once a month. Now, we don't have translators and don't know what attitudes the leaders have towards the refinery. There is also a big problem with labor. There are ten people who are supposed to grind the dirt, but they just sit there. Can we bring this to the attention of the [DK] Energy Committee?"[34] Things were not much better at the site level:

> We need to talk about the following issues with the Cambodians. First, the Cambodian workforce may have 400 people. However, they are not physically capable, they are mainly girls, and ... the labor force is not stable and often fluctuates. Our people often have to do all the work. The Cambodians must also have leadership, an organizational hierarchy for the installation work. They need a person to be the leader, and we can be the advisors. There has to be planning and management. Without a strict organization, we cannot complete this project. In order to learn

techniques and management skills, we also need translators. We are also worried about whether the Cambodians can guarantee the provision of local materials for construction. Next year is the peak of construction, so they need to make sure they supply enough materials.[35]

This was echoed by another Chinese expatriate: "The biggest problem is that of leadership on the Cambodian side. They have no command system.... There is also transportation where the equipment or materials would arrive at the port but wouldn't get to the refinery until a month later because of ground transportation issues."[36] What he did not mention was that there were also considerable coordination problems that had nothing to do with the Cambodians, problems that emanated from China.

Problems Originating from China

The coordination problems inherent in China's planned economy became particularly acute when more moving parts were added to a given project. Kampong Som had many more of these problems than comparable projects for which technical plans and blueprints are available. Indeed, even though the actual work at Kampong Som was not terribly ambitious, the complexity of coordinating supplies and expertise from the vast network of bureaucracies in China was significantly higher than was the case with other Chinese-sponsored aid projects in DK. To appreciate this, it is helpful to look at the evolution of the petroleum bureaucracy in China and the challenges that emerged in its ability to manage projects within its institutional mandate.

Background (1949–1975)

Immediately after the establishment of the PRC in 1949, China faced a dearth of experts, particularly those trained in petroleum-related areas of engineering and design.[37] The Petroleum Management General Bureau (*shiyou guanli zongju*) within the Ministry of Fuel Industry (*shiyou gongye bu*) recommended that a training facility (*Suzhou gaoji gongye xueyuan*) be established in Suzhou, in Jiangsu province. Potential recruits were enticed by the free tuition and the guarantee of a job upon graduation at the Petroleum Management General Bureau. Nevertheless, because of the difficulty of the work, the lack of ideal resources—textbooks were in English, for instance—and the scarcity of experts able to teach these subjects (one teacher from Beijing and one teacher from Shanghai would commute to the institute every week), enrollment was initially quite low. In 1951, there were forty graduates; but the following year, there were eighty.

Among the class that graduated in 1952, ten were sent to Beijing to learn
Russian for three years. Another ten were sent to Shenyang to learn Russian for
two years. Still more were sent to tinker with the antiquated oil refineries the
Japanese had left behind. This was before the discovery of oil at Daqing, when
China was considered an oil-poor country.[38] Most of the refineries at that time
were designed to produce synthetic oil (*renzao shiyou*). Four of these—refineries
One through Four—were in Fushun, Liaoning province, and used *yetan*, which
contains between 5 and 10 percent oil. Refinery Five was in Jinxi, and Number Six,
which had been built and run by the Japanese navy before 1945, was in Jinzhou.
The Number Seven refinery in Dalian processed natural oil. Refineries Eight and
Nine were in Xiping. The only refinery not built by the Japanese was located
in Yumen.[39]

Between 1954 and 1958, a huge oil refinery that would produce one million
tons of oil was constructed in Maoming in Guangdong province. This was the
first synthetic petroleum refinery ever built in China; oil would be extracted from
a layer of rock on top of coals to make *yetan*. Because there was a shortage of
experts in the various dispersed petroleum institutes at the time, they were combined and consolidated in Beijing, and a planning institute was established in
Fushun in 1956.[40] Following the disastrous Great Leap Forward (1958–1961), in
which China attempted to accelerate the transition to socialism by undertaking
agricultural and industrial reform in both the cities and the countryside, and in
which a famine caused by inflated reporting and economic bottlenecks killed 30
million people, the next massive scale economic project was the Third Front construction. The Third Front was China's attempt to clone or transport its entire
military-industrial complex deeper into China in order to protect it from possible attack from the Soviet Union and from potential escalation and spillover of
the U.S.-sponsored war in Vietnam.[41] As Mao himself put it:

> We must grasp the Third Front construction to buy time against the
> imperialists and the revisionists....I once said when the atom bombs
> would explode, even if half of the human race is extinguished, it is only
> half. [Edgar] Snow once asked me why I didn't discredit this idea, but
> I stood firm. I once said when the war will break out, half the people
> will die...but there is an even worse scenario. There is an American film
> that describes it even more starkly! Khrushchev spoke much more about
> this topic than I have. He said that there are weapons that can destroy the
> entire human race....The Third Front construction will develop steel,
> iron, national defense, machinery, chemical industry, oil, railways; [once
> accomplished] we will have nothing to be afraid of....What you do with
> your war is up to you, I am only interested in construction.

As the Third Front construction project supplanted the original Third Five Year Plan, however, the institute in Fushun was ordered to move inland in order to protect it better from Soviet attack by hiding these facilities within mountainous areas. Luoyang, in Henan province—probably the easternmost point on the Third Front—became the new site of the Fushun design institute. The plan was to build a five-million-ton refinery six miles long and two miles wide, even though the standard at the time was half that capacity. It was hard to find a location in Luoyang that could accommodate such a large project without destroying or displacing items that had significant cultural or historical significance. In the end, they decided on a large tract of land close to the Yellow River. With a supply of water like that, they could produce ten million tons of oil.

Work at this time was very difficult. Some technicians were placed in the ramshackle homes of local peasants. Others were tasked with carving out living spaces in caves—a throwback to the days of Yan'an—where they constructed their own "mod cons," including doors, electrical networks, and heaters. These actually seemed to work quite well; grass began to grow inside the heated caves. They were engineers, after all![42] Eventually, Luoyang became an important epicenter for engineering design, particularly for petroleum-related industrial projects, both in China and for Chinese assistance projects targeted overseas.

The twists and turns described above were equaled, and most likely surpassed, by the bureaucratic and other political convulsions that shook the institutional home of the design facilities, the subject of the next section.

The Chinese Bureaucratic Politics of Petroleum

At the end of 1949, the top government unit charged with petroleum (as well as the chemical and coal industries) was the then Ministry of Fuel Industry (*ranliao gongye bu*) under the Finance and Economics Commission (*caizheng jingji weiyuanhui*). This consolidation reflected the early stage of state-building as well as the underdevelopment of these key industries at the time.[43] By 1955, coal and petroleum were divided up into separate ministries; chemicals were folded into the new Ministry of Petroleum Industry (*shiyou gongye bu*).[44] A year later, the Ministry of Chemical Industry (*huaxue gongye bu*) had also been established.[45] In 1970, in line with the imperatives of the Third Front, the coal, petroleum, and chemical industries were combined into the newly-formed Ministry of Fuel and Chemical Industry *(ranliao huaxue gongye bu)*, where they remained until 1975.[46]

Although there were certainly rational, organizational reasons for this evolution, such as fine-tuning based on the growing complexities of the policy area, these ministries did have an inordinate number of highly educated and skilled engineers and technicians who, starting with the 1957–1958 Anti-Rightist

Campaign that inordinately targeted China's intellectuals, came under increasing suspicion as political class backgrounds became more important than talent and expertise in judging Chinese ministry employees. By the time of the Cultural Revolution (1966–1977), for example, the superior-subordinate relationship between the Petroleum Design Institute, hitherto the superior unit, and the Number One Petroleum and Chemical Construction Company was reversed because the former was represented by the intellectual class, by that time referred to as the "stinking ninth category" *(chou lao jiu)*, while the latter, as a company run by the state, was represented by workers. Not surprisingly, during this period, none of the experts could be called *shejishi* ("designers"); they had to sign official documents as *fuwuyuan* ("attendants").[47]

Of course, bureaucratic politics played a role as well. The Ministries of Petroleum and Chemical Industry often suffered from "contradictions" (*maodun*), a result of competing overlapping jurisdictions and organizational mandates. Moreover, as various new properties of oil were discovered, the previous scientific knowledge that had been the foundation for the decisions on organizational structure had to be revised, necessitating reorganization of the relevant policy institutions but leading to organizational confusion as well. For example, petroleum production and refining produces chemical byproducts as well as synthetic fibers and fertilizers; each of these could theoretically fall under the jurisdictions of multiple ministries. These "contradictions" were not simply the result of aggressive attempts to capture new jurisdictional spaces; they would also occur when no agency would be willing to pick up the slack in less exalted policy areas, so many tasks would remain undone.[48] As work units at the mercy of the bureaucratic chart, the institutes in Luoyang, Lanzhou, and Cangzhou had to amend their design plans constantly. When China slowly began moving toward a post–Cultural Revolution phase in politics by 1975, this system had not seen reform in quite some time, so it is not surprising that some of the biggest obstacles toward successful policy completion were due to China's institutional disorganization.[49]

As noted in chapter 3, on December 22, 1978, three days before the Vietnamese invaded Cambodia, a group of Chinese technical leaders presented a report based on more than a month of survey work at the refinery site:

> When it comes to the supply of materials, it has been lax. The work that needs to be done now needs to be done mostly by the Chinese. Therefore, when the supplies do not arrive on time, or if they are incompatible, we cannot do our job properly.... Please tell the superiors back home [*gei guonei zuo gongzuo*].... The commerce unit has already stamped this request, and the *waijing bu* wrote back and said that the Embassy

needed to send a full request. At present we only have a small jeep and it is not able to do the trip. In addition, there is a lack of water bottles. Please try and solve these problems for us.[50]

Arguments over the scarcity of resources as well as the seemingly unequal distribution of production inputs began to dominate the conversation. A Comrade Fan seemed to have an animus directed at one or more individuals (in particular, a Comrade Yang) from the Lanzhou team.[51]

> There were problems when we tested the pressure. We first used the method that Lanzhou had suggested, but it didn't work. When we were using the boiler, Lanzhou said that [a certain type would function, but that is not true]. When we need to use pipes, we can't find them. When I need personnel, Yang claims that there aren't any available. I don't know what to do with him. Our water pump was also taken away by him. When he borrows our equipment, he doesn't actually use it. I am extremely annoyed.[52]

After looking at these issues, the leader of the visiting technical team attended a "sit-down meeting" (*zuotan hui*) that included representatives from various work units (Lanzhou, Cangzhou, Yumen, and the Foreign Languages College). The conversation underscores the institutional and bureaucratic fragmentation and inefficiencies in the planning and execution of a project involving a great many discrete bureaucratic actors: "The companies that send people have no idea how to organize and manage these people. The Cangzhou Thirteen Huajian Company certainly has no clue. So much has been invested that this is clearly not a joke. It seems more like a war, but a war that we're losing. The mission is simply not clear.... We have no clue what is going on and what we have to do."[53]

Discussion also pointed to problems with the quality of the technicians and skilled workers sent from China, suggesting that it was not necessarily the best or the brightest that were being sent to Democratic Kampuchea.

> Those sent from the Mainland were not sent according to national standards, and therefore the quality of people is quite low. We're not going to give specific examples, but...everyone knows this is the case too. In order to finish this mission, the Ministry [of Petroleum] does not know what is going on, the Ministry of Foreign Trade doesn't know what is going on or if they should be sending technical teams or actual workers. Now, even those who are in charge of the project have no idea how to fight this war.[54]

The result was a kind of surreal state of suspended animation in which there was no clear line of responsibility and where nothing seemed to function properly, if at all.

> People come but don't have critical equipment like a water pump. The cars come and break down after a month. When we work, we just surround the bulldozer, clueless as to what to do. We can't construct this way or that because the responsibilities are not clearly delineated, whether from within or from the outside. There are so many difficulties in building this refinery. There are 200 or so people from Thirteen Huajian, but the work is not coordinated at all....We need to be clear about who needs to do what, and when the equipment comes, we need to get our act together.[55]

Adding to the growing bonfire of discontent, another Chinese expert chimed in:

> Machines, equipment and small tools should have arrived, like rulers and pencils. When we have no pencils, we just have to use nails instead. Even when the equipment was coming in, we didn't even have an oil pump. We should really work on finishing this project properly. Otherwise, we are not going to get a return on our investment. As far as bread-and-butter issues of daily living, the design people [from Luoyang] requested that the Mainland send some pickled vegetables. No more fish, please! They want *vegetables*.[56]

These complaints about bureaucratic politics even extended to entertainment: The chorus of disaffection extended to the distribution of water and the selection of movies, with some grumbling that team leaders should not have veto power over what movies are brought over from China. There were also complaints that the interpreters were not able to translate anything beyond generalities, and the people from the Lanzhou design units were also upset because they lacked rubbing alcohol for medical purposes while workers from the Cangzhou units did have access to it.[57]

Endgame

If politics in DK were not so horrifically brutal, the petroleum refinery might be seen as a comedy of errors. It provides the perfect storm in which all of the institutional weaknesses of the two regimes collided and reinforced one another, to the point that any prospect of eventual success seemed to get ever more remote. Placing this chapter in the context of the overall argument of this book, it seems absurd to contemplate whether and how China might have better influenced this situation to its advantage, given that the coordination problems it faced in China were almost as great as—and in some cases, greater than—those they faced from the Cambodian side. Ultimately, Chinese attempts to refurbish the refinery were overtaken by events, primarily the Vietnamese invasion of Cambodia in 1978.

The paranoia that led to the continually shifting purges of various zones and ministries in DK affected the Kampong Som refinery both directly and indirectly. The folding of the economics portfolio into the authority of Nuon Chea created coordination problems that plagued the refinery project up to the very end. Indirectly, the purges in the Eastern Zone undermined its ability to deter or repel a Vietnamese invasion, which put an end to the DK regime as well as the infrastructure projects it was pursuing.

After the invasion, Kampong Som became noteworthy not as the centerpiece of Chinese aid and assistance but as site of the disorganized and panic-ridden retreat of the Chinese.[58] News from Radio Kampuchea downplayed events—the Chinese radio broadcasts actually announced the defeat of Vietnam—but after hearing rumors from their Cambodian workers and listening to the BBC on a shortwave radio, the Chinese realized that all was not well. When informed that the Chinese Embassy in Phnom Penh had been "relocated" to Thailand and that their passports had been deliberately destroyed along the way, the Chinese technicians became truly alarmed. Injured Chinese advisors who had fled from hospitals in Phnom Penh reported that as many as two hundred other immobile and wounded Chinese were unable to leave and had become de facto prisoners of war. Refugee Chinese advisors trucked overland from Krang Leav joined the throng.

Only two hours after they sent a desperate telegram to the Chinese Ministry of Foreign Economic Relations, they received an emergency response from the State Council instructing them to return to China by way of the cargo ships *Xianghong* and *Lianghu* docked at Kampong Som.[59] These plans were delayed when Cambodian Minister of Foreign Affairs Ieng Sary ordered that all off-loaded goods, including boxed components for four airplanes, several hundred cannons, ten thousand missiles, and containers of diesel fuel, be reloaded onto the ship before it could leave port.[60] For the next two days, the Chinese assisted in loading the cargo before the more than five hundred of them were allowed to leave Cambodian waters. After ten days at sea, living on canned goods and with no more beer left on board, the ship arrived in the port of Guangzhou, where the exhausted evacuees were met by a receiving line of officials from the Chinese Foreign Ministry and provincial officials from Guangdong.[61]

Other Chinese fled to Thailand but reentered Cambodian territory to link up with the Khmer Rouge in the *maquis* and to maintain the legitimacy of the just-deposed regime by having the Chinese Embassy to Democratic Kampuchea follow the retreating Khmer Rouge cadres into the malaria-infested jungles. This continued for a few weeks until even the most ideologically fervent Chinese could no longer deny the absurdity of the situation. To paraphrase *Macbeth:* nothing became the doomed Kampong Som refinery project more than the leaving of it.

CHINA'S DEVELOPMENT OF
DEMOCRATIC KAMPUCHEAN TRADE

We have no assistance from outside for industry or agriculture. North Vietnam, after liberation in 1954, was greatly assisted by China and Russia.... China and [North] Korea, after liberation, were greatly assisted by Russia. Broadly speaking, other [socialist] countries were greatly assisted by foreign capital after liberation. For us, at present, there is some Chinese aid, but there isn't very much.... This is our Party's policy. If we go and beg for help we would certainly obtain some, but this would affect our political line.... This is because, if we asked help from them, a little or a lot, there would be political conditions imposed on us without fail.

—The Party's Four Year Plan to Build Socialism in All Fields, 1977–1980[1]

Hong Kong's Happy Valley, Pao Ma Di in Chinese, is an upper-middle-income section of Hong Kong Island sandwiched between the neighborhoods of Wan Chai and Causeway Bay. It is the site of various roads and tunnels that lead to the southern part of the island, the famous horseracing track, and, for a time, the place where CPK cadres running Democratic Kampuchea's import-export trading company made their home, at 39 Village Road.

Their leader was Van Rith, who came to resemble China's own "red capitalist" of the 1970s and 1980s, Rong Yiren. Van Rith's political education came early, having been imprisoned in 1952 for criticizing Princess Monique—now Queen Monineath (then Paule-Monique Izzi)—for winning a beauty contest in which she was the only contestant as well as other perceived slights against the royal family. Not long after his release, having been rehabilitated, he joined the army reserve, during which period he reported on progressives while he worked at the Sangkum Ministry of Finance. But in 1968, he was arrested again, and this time he was severely tortured. As relieved as he may have been by Sihanouk's overthrow, Van Rith, not feeling at ease with the establishment of the new Khmer Republic in 1970, fled to the *maquis* the following year. There he was reunited with Vorn Vet, whom he knew from the 1955 elections and who became Van Rith's sponsor, introducing him to people in the upper echelons and exploiting his capacity as an intellectual to work as a political commissar with the KR militia; at one point

Vorn Vet protected him from arrest. After 1975, Van Rith moved into the policy area of commerce.

The Village Road apartment was a short streetcar or taxi ride to 242 Des Voeux Road in Hong Kong's Central Business District, where the import-export company Ren Fung (Ying Feng in the Mandarin transliteration) was located. Ren Fung illustrates the tensions and contradictions within the DK while also symbolizing how China was able to shape the structure and process of DK government institutions in commerce and trade.

In military and infrastructure assistance, the policy areas discussed in chapters 4 and 5, respectively, Chinese aid ostensibly came with "no strings attached." Of course, no aid is truly unconditional, but the degree of such "nonconditionality" can itself be negotiated. In the case of defense, Beijing's attempts to influence DK decision-making came to nothing because the Cambodian bureaucracy in charge was one of the strongest DK institutions. In the case of the petroleum refinery in Kampong Som—the jewel in the crown of Chinese aid—Chinese influence was undermined by the bureaucratic fragmentation in China as well as in Cambodia. In this chapter, I look at trade and commerce as the one area where China was able to shape DK practices significantly—as well as the institutions involved. This was because Chinese commercial institutions did not suffer from the degree of fragmentation and lack of coordination documented in chapter 5 and because DK's Ministry of Commerce, although by no means a weak institution like the Ministry of Social Affairs, for example, was nonetheless institutionally complex and fragmented. This allowed China to colonize the institution structurally and especially procedurally in ways unimaginable in the case of military assistance.

Like much that was being constructed and initiated at the time, this commercial infrastructure was modest in scale, and it was cut short by the Vietnamese invasion of 1978. Yet it appears to have been a viable forum for the exchange of ideas and expertise, one that could have been developed into an important asset in terms of creating revenue and maintaining informal contacts with a wider range of international actors than was willing to admit public dealings with the Phnom Penh regime. Most important for this book, it was the single policy area where hina was able to obtain some return on its considerable investment in the DK regime.

Shipping and Receiving

Within days of the fall of Phnom Penh in April 1975, Chinese ships bearing emergency food aid had docked at Kampong Som. Just three days after the Khmer Rouge entered Phnom Penh, the first shipment from China arrived in the form of the *Hongqi 153*, which, according to Kiernan, off-loaded 202 tons of salt.[2] On May 15, the *Hongqi 153* came again to Kampong Som with nearly thirty thousand sacks of rice, nine containers of chloroquine, 141 boxes of medicine, and 833 pieces of cloth.[3] Although in June, there were no shipments from China, in July there were seven (see table 6.1).

Loy Unn, a Cambodian worker at the Kampong Som port from 1975 to 1977, was in charge of recording and controlling the lists of goods imported

Table 6.1 Early Chinese aid shipments to Democratic Kampuchea (in metric tons)

	HONGQI 155 JULY 6, 1975	DAQING 25 JULY 9, 1975	ZHEJIANG JULY 16, 1975	HONGGUANG JULY 17, 1975	YONGCHUN JULY 20, 1975	TIANSHUI JULY 26, 1975	FUNG'E JULY 31, 1975
Rice	–	–	–	10,126.97	3,535.25	5,045.06	–
Salt	–	–	–	–	–	–	–
Chloroquine	–	–	–	–	–	–	–
Medicine	–	–	–	21.62	–	–	–
Cloth	–	–	–	–	–	611.94	1,551.74
Camera equipment	–	–	–	.277	–	–	–
Sewing machines	–	–	–	12.20	–	–	–
Machine oil	–	–	196.00	–	–	–	–
Gasoline	–	2,367.57	–	–	–	–	–
Gasoline L65	–	–	368.98	–	–	–	–
Diesel	–	1,596.42	–	–	–	–	–
Diesel LO	–	–	1,650.72	–	–	–	–
Gasoline L66	–	–	464.55	–	–	–	–
Gasoline L70	–	–	774.25	–	–	–	–
Diesel generators	–	–	–	–	–	–	1.59
Hemp	–	–	19.25	–	–	–	140.42
Cotton	–	–	–	–	–	–	11.75
Raw cotton	–	–	–	–	–	–	187.53
Shovels	–	–	–	–	–	–	192.38
Hoes	–	–	76.00	–	–	–	136.62
Plowshares	–	–	–	–	2.60	–	–
Agricultural tools	–	–	–	–	–	197.07	–
Trucks	–	–	–	–	140.80	316.80	–
Food, supplies for embassies	–	–	–	–	–	Amount not specified	–
Train parts	6,646.60	–	–	–	–	–	1,323.81
Railroad spikes	–	–	–	–	–	–	3,780.00
Military items	–	–	–	–	3,063.07	–	–

Source: The Complete Register of Imports from China in 1975, Ministry of Commerce, Cambodian National Archives, File B-1, Number 2, December 30, 1975, pp. 2–4, 6, 14, 15, and 18.

from overseas, managing a team of twelve. He recalls that most of the goods he processed from China were agricultural products, medicine, machinery, bicycles, and other light industrial goods, while most Cambodian exports were generally agricultural products or exotic commodities. Since he was in the commercial section, he did not receive any military hardware. On average, there were three Chinese shipping vessels that docked there every month, usually in the first half of the month, providing between thirty and sixty thousand tons of goods. The heaviest shipments arrived in January/February and July/August. He estimates that up to 80 percent of imports came from China; North Korea was the second-largest exporter to DK.[4]

The institution in which Loy Unn found himself was the DK Ministry of Commerce. As noted in chapter 2, it was one of the more expansive DK ministries, along with Foreign Affairs and Defense, but also the most complicated and fragmented. It was unique in that it housed a growing number of other ministries and committees, some of which, like rubber plantations and water transport, appear to have been fairly competent in executing their responsibilities, while others were barely functional, most notably the public works and energy committees (see chapter 5). The DK Ministry of Commerce was the node through which scarce resources in the form of imports were distributed among the other ministries and regional governments, as indicated in table 2.1. This was a source of power, but it was also symptomatic of its unwieldy and amoebic nature, which provided the "policy spaces" necessary for China to exploit and shape outcomes.[5]

At the top of this bureaucracy was Vorn Vet, deputy prime minister with portfolio for the economy who was appointed in March 1976. Below him was Koy Thuon, who was transferred from his former position of Northern Zone secretary to become the minister of commerce. After Koy Thuon's arrest and execution the following year, he was succeeded by Commerce Committee Chairman Soeu Vasy (a.k.a. Doeun) as commerce minister. After Doeun himself was arrested, the authority for the department fell to the position of the chairman of the Commerce Committee, then filled by Van Rith. Although Van Rith was not even on the Central Committee, he appears to have been quite instrumental in working with the Chinese to shape the institution. He was fortunate to have escaped the political suspicion that killed his predecessors, dying of natural causes in 2008.

In 1976, China and DK started to deepen and extend the contours of bilateral trade. In early 1976 Foreign Trade Minister Li Qiang led a Chinese trade delegation to DK to forge a set of bilateral aid and commercial agreements. The DK side requested a loan of 140 million yuan and US$20 million. Van Rith was responsible for the spending of these funds.[6] It was at this point that aid was combined with trade and commerce between the two countries and third parties under Chinese tutelage.

A bilateral protocol from March 10, 1976 stated:

• Article 1: From 1976 to 1977, China will provide Democratic Kampuchea materials which are registered in [a] list accompanying this protocol. The above accompanying list cannot be separated from this protocol....

• Article 2: The cost of products provided to Democratic Kampuchea as stated in Article 1, will be refunded to China in the amount of 140 million yuan which is notified in the agreement of economic cooperation between "Democratic Kampuchea and the People Republic China" signed in Phnom Penh on March 10, 1976."

• Article 3: According to the notification of this protocol, the cost of products which China provides to Democratic Kampuchea must be negotiated by the organizations of commerce of the two countries in order to find a steady price which is based on the international market while yuan is considered as the basic currency.

• Article 4: Committees of Commerce of Democratic Kampuchea and the Foreign Trade Ministry of the People's Republic of China are the only parties who implement this protocol while Organizations of Commerce which each country has assigned are the only signatory parties.

Following the meetings with the Chinese, Foreign Minister Ieng Sary and Commerce Minister Koy Thuon each presented reports to the Standing Committee on March 13, 1976. The Standing Committee then formed a separate working group to review merchandise to be purchased from China; it was led by Koy Thuon and included Khieu Samphan and, as consulting members, Ieng Sary, Vorn Vet, and the DK Ministry of Commerce Secretary Doeun (Soeu Vasy). The working group was charged with reviewing the CPK's requests for merchandise from abroad as well as recommending future purchases.[7]

After four days, the working group submitted its recommendations: the request by the Ministry of Railways for additional spare parts for trucks was to be removed from the trade balance sheet because they were already included in the Chinese aid package. The working group emphasized that greater coordination was necessary when purchasing weaving machines along with more than a dozen additional recommendations in amending earlier proposed purchases.

The March 13 meeting's emphasis that imports from China needed to be speeded up and the March 17 committee recommendations were codified in June after negotiations between the Chinese Ministry of Foreign Trade and the DK Ministry of Commerce (the DK delegation was led by Koy Thuon and included, among others, Sar Kimlomouth, who would soon become deputy director of the not-yet-established DK bank).[8]

In addition to the boilerplate statements of revolutionary solidarity, a June 25, 1976 letter from Vorn Vet to Foreign Trade Minister Li Qiang contained some important contours of the relationship, including the establishment of a financing institution that had been urged by China.[9] Goods coming into DK were then distributed to the various ministries and zones, as shown in table 2.1 in chapter 2, all of which passed through the DK Ministry of Commerce and the network of warehouses under its jurisdiction.

Inevitably, with the increase in goods to be off-loaded, it became clear that the port facilities were not up to the task. There were problems lifting the goods from the docked ships, and the cranes at the dock were sometimes stretched to their limit by individual loads of over three tons. The derricks on the ships posed additional problems: derricks on the Chinese and in particular the North Korean ships were inadequate to the tasks of lifting heavier loads. In some cases, the aging Chinese fleet had derricks that were broken or otherwise inoperable. In other cases, tensions arose because the DK workers dared not stop during periods of rain, or during the regularly scheduled breaks taken by the Chinese, even while Chinese crews were afraid that the precipitation would damage the derricks if used during the heavy rains.

The docking facilities also created bottlenecks with the distribution of commodities for storage. Oftentimes, the docks would be full of trucks that, having received goods, were unable to depart, forcing the cranes and the derricks to be idle while empty trucks waited to receive merchandise just outside of the port. At other times, the trucks and the warehouses were poorly equipped to receive and store merchandise. The Chinese themselves were skittish because of the negative experiences they had had in Vietnam, where they tended to be interrogated by the police when on shore leave. They were unclear about how to interact with DK security forces and customs officers over things like water and electricity expenses. There were shortages of fresh water for replenishing the ships' stocks, and the facilities for housing Chinese and other foreign crews were regarded as unclean.[10]

Shaping the Ministry of Commerce Structure and Process

The ongoing trade talks between the two countries created a system in which the CPK, through the DK Ministry of Commerce, would incorporate in its organizational structure specific Chinese suggestions even though they ran counter to Pol Pot's very literal interpretation of Marxist political economy. The main Chinese units that were involved were the Ministry of Foreign Trade; the Ministry of Foreign Economic Relations (*duiwai jingji lianluo bu*), for foreign assistance and aid; and the Ministry of Communications, for infrastructure and shipping. They negotiated with their DK counterparts, the Ministry of Foreign Affairs, in the person of Ieng Sary, and the Ministry of Commerce, often directly with Vorn Vet. The principal node of the relationship was the DK Ministry of Commerce. Although the DK Ministry of Commerce was a complex and over-extended bureaucracy because of the multiple subordinate units (called "committees" [denoting direct CPK management] or "ministries" [denoting a given unit's functional responsibilities]) it contained, the Ministry of Commerce itself had enough institutional integrity and representation among the top leadership that it could function as a trading unit, the liquidation of several commerce ministers notwithstanding.

For their part, the Chinese bureaucracies had clear functional delineations of responsibility, compared to the chaos described in chapter 5; they were able to handle disputes within China—that is, that did not play out on Cambodian soil—and they did not have to rely on technical institutes or a constellation of subordinate units. So there was a relatively coherent Chinese partner that worked together with a somewhat viable DK institution that—uncharacteristically for the regime—was not averse to learning how to undertake a new set of state functions, even as these very functions aroused suspicions among the more hardline leaders. As a result, China was able to make significant headway in shaping the process and even some of the structure of DK trade and commerce.

The Ren Fung Company (HK) Limited

In October 1976, to facilitate trade with a growing number of potential trading partners, which grew to include China, North Korea, Japan, Singapore, and Yugoslavia, DK established with direct Chinese assistance the Ren Fung Company Limited, with its office in the Central District of Hong Kong. As noted above, the director, Van Rith, was a veteran of the Cambodian revolutionary struggle.[11] After the CPK victory, Van Rith worked in the commerce sector, visiting Vietnam on a commercial delegation that year as well as helping establish warehouses for state commodities. On April 4, 1976, he embarked on a week-long trip to China and Hong Kong to discuss Cambodia's needs with Chinese leaders and to explore the possibility of opening of an office in Hong Kong. While in the territory, a Chinese company helped introduce Van Rith to local businessmen.[12] In May 1976, the CPK Standing Committee decided to send Van Rith to Hong Kong in order to set up the framework for operations there.[13] Ren Fung was incorporated on October 19, 1976, with the legal representation of Ford, Kwan & Co.[14]

Capitalized at 1.5 million Hong Kong Dollars, the 15,000 shares were divided among the staff: Van Rith, General Manager So Chea, Deputy General Manager San Sok (4,000 shares each), and First Secretary Honat (3,000 shares).[15]

The purpose of Ren Fung was to facilitate imports into and exports from DK with countries that did not wish to be associated with the regime or had trade restrictions leveled at Phnom Penh. Startup funds provided by China were in the form of loans, with the accounts held in Chinese banks. The 140 million yuan negotiated with Li Qiang earlier that year was split between two accounts. The A account was reserved for purchasing Chinese goods to be imported to Cambodia "with all the paperwork done by the Chinese." The B funds were credits for Cambodian exports to China at that time such as timber and coconuts. Van Rith maintained that funds set aside for commerce not be used for the purchase of weapons; arms and military equipment were negotiated in separate agreements with the Chinese.[16]

Accordingly, a bank was established to facilitate imports and exports—the Overseas Commercial Bank of Cambodia, ostensibly under the Commerce Committee. Again, this was instigated by the Chinese. According to Sar Kimlomouth, who was appointed deputy director of the bank, he was told by Vorn Vet that somebody with banking experience was needed in preparation for meeting with a Chinese trade delegation and that he should prepare "civilian" (that is, Western) clothing to wear at the meeting.

The bank, such as it was, was located in the Ministry of Commerce compound, now the site of the Ministry of Defense. It was not part of the ministry, however, but organizationally separate or, more accurately, isolated. Preteen messengers from the Central Communication Office would drop off documents to and from the upper echelon for the deputy director to sign. But ultimately, the bank itself was mainly for show and acted more as a notary than anything else. According to Sar Kimlomouth, there was no actual money in the bank, and transactions were handled by the Commerce Committee, as the bank lacked any form of accounting system.[17] He simply compiled selective lists of goods that were imported and exported. Van Rith concurred, saying that only he and Ieng Sary handled the actual money and that Sar Kimlomouth "knew nothing about Democratic Kampuchea finances."[18]

With Van Rith at the helm, Ren Fung appeared to be thriving, as trade continued to expand. By 1978, in addition to the considerable trade with China, DK's trading partners included Singapore, Japan, Bangladesh, Madagascar, North Korea, Yugoslavia, and even France. By 1978, plans were afoot to establish another import/export company in Singapore.[19] It is important to underscore, once again, how alien this was to the top leadership, with the possible exception of Ieng Sary, as well as the considerable role that China played in establishing the commercial infrastructure, from the bank to Ren Fung, that was necessary for trade to proceed. In addition to these more "macro" level institutions, China was also critical in providing "micro" level assistance. No example is more illustrative and substantively important than the *Yong Kang* container vessel.

The *Yong Kang* and Creation of a Trading Protocol for DK

By late 1976, it was becoming clear that DK needed up to ten 100-, 200-, or 300-ton transport vessels to handle the growing volume of international trade.[20] DK's ship-building operations were focused on military crafts, so on June 26, 1977, DK and Chinese officials from the Chinese Ministry of Communications entered into serious talks over the leasing of a Chinese commercial vessel to DK. DK was represented by Foreign Minister Ieng Sary, Minister of Industry Cheng An, and Van Rith. The Chinese opened the meeting by proposing three items for the agenda: protocol, management of trading activities, and training for crews.

The Chinese side went into excruciating detail over the myriad technicalities involved, underscoring the vast distance that the DK side was behind China in terms of the knowledge and resources necessary to make such a venture work on their own. These included certification, pricing structures, shipping fees, insurance, crew member salaries, and documentation. The Chinese went on to say that that telegraph, telephone, and mail should all be used to maintain frequent contact, with a dedicated Chinese state-owned company serving as the point body for communication. The Chinese called on the DK government to designate a parallel organization for facilitating communication, explaining that "the ship shall sail for one year, allowing us to consolidate all our knowledge so that we can better understand the situation."[21] Both sides would need to communicate frequently about shipping routes, to ensure that all documents were agreed upon, and to deal with any problems that might arise. The DK Maritime Navigation Company linked with the DK Ministry of Commerce would serve as the Cambodian organization charged with supervising the *Yong Kang*, a cargo ship that China leased to DK.

The Chinese also underscored the importance of Ren Fung as a locus of bilateral communication concerning the *Yong Kang*. Although the DK side clearly felt more comfortable with limiting communication through their respective embassies, particularly on issues that were still awaiting resolution, the Chinese delegation insisted that meeting annually would suffice and that additional meetings should be held only if special issues arose. In fact, as available DK telegrams make clear, Ren Fung, and not the diplomatic infrastructure, became the locus of trade and commerce.

Somewhat counterintuitively, there were extensive discussions over earn- ings and revenue. The two sides declared that the *Yong Kang* was "a production tool" and that "every single minute is profit."[22] Since the vessel accrued daily costs of US$1,552 when idle, the *Yong Kang* had to operate, fully loaded, on a constant basis and avoid docking at too many ports in order to minimize or spread out docking fees. For instance, it cost the *Yong Kang* US$18,624 to dock at Huangpu for twelve days and US$20,176 to dock at Kobe for thirteen days. The Chinese delegation stressed the importance of making financial cal- culations that balanced docking costs with potential profits from loading and unloading goods, emphasizing that it was critical to consider the amount of goods before loading them at port, especially Japanese ports. As for payment, the Chinese charged 3 percent of its profit, on the low end of China's typical 3 to 5 percent scale.

The two sides ultimately agreed that the *Yong Kang* alone would be inad- equate to serve all requests for Cambodia's foreign trade and that it would be necessary to add other vessels. In a July 22, 1977 telegram, Phnom Penh was already checking with Ren Fung about the possibility of leasing other ships for regular circuits between Hong Kong and DK as well as other, larger vessels that could make the voyage to countries like Albania, which were exporting tar to DK.[23]

The Expansion of Trade, 1977–1978

Around the same time, after the DK Ministry of Commerce made its recom- mendations to the top leadership regarding further imports from China, the CPK Standing Committee made several decisions. Agreeing with the ministry, the SC confirmed the increase of processed rubber exports from 40,000 to 45,000 tons, calling attention to the need to maintain the highest quality of rubber and standards of rubber cultivation. The leadership also agreed to test the market for high-quality timber and, in order to avoid having to be coordinated by the Ministry of Commerce, to coordinate directly with local authorities to devote manpower to this pursuit.

Acknowledging its comparative advantage in exotic flora and fauna, the lead- ership emphasized exporting commodities like coffee, frangipani flowers, kapok, arica, soy and soy products, and lotus. Rare animal skins, pelts, and other body parts were to be collected from Preah Vihear, Kampong Thom, Kratie, Zone 31, and Zone 32. Pigs and smoked fish were to be collected from each zone on a quarterly basis.[24] The leadership emphasized that the Chinese market would be the main priority, with the North Korean market second. They stated that there was no reason to purchase big machines, as they were included in the Chinese aid package. They also began to think about establishing trade with Yugoslavia for tractors and other durables.[25]

In addition, imports were continuing apace, both through commercial activity at Ren Fung, as described above, and from China as well. This expansion of trade—as well as a complete unawareness of the impending Vietnamese invasion of DK—is reflected in the last set of trade talks between the two countries.

The Final Trade Negotiations with China

By the end of 1978, DK imports and exports had been increasing annually, and commercial activity had doubled from the year before. The improvement of international telecommunications between Cambodia and China in 1978 had enhanced trade activities, and the DK and Chinese banks were now able to work together smoothly. Although there were still hiccups, especially with regard to the quality of some DK exports, China had been largely forgiving about this. China had provided machinery and mechanical equipment, had dispatched Chinese technicians, and had even set the prices of Cambodia's exported products to conform to international market prices. In this context—blissfully ignorant of the Vietnamese plans to invade only weeks away—the two sides sat down to discuss commerce and trade for 1979.

At 5:00 p.m. on December 2, 1978, DK Minister of Foreign Affairs Ieng Sary, accompanied by Van Rith, Sar Kimlomouth, and others from the DK Ministry of Commerce, met with Chinese trade officials, Ambassador Sun Hao, and other commercial delegates and embassy personnel. Vorn Vet had already been arrested. The hour-long meeting opened with a standard exchange of well wishes between the two sides; both parties concurred that the previous Chinese delegation led by CCP Vice Chairman Wang Dongxing had strengthened their fraternal revolutionary outlook and strategic solidarity.

Ieng Sary stressed that Cambodia and China were approaching the trade tasks at hand on the basis of friendship: "We trust China. Only China understands us in the present situation. These discussions will set the agenda for the following years." He noted that DK officials had previously met with Chinese Deputy Prime Minister Li Xiannian to discuss implementation of Cambodia's commercial contracts with China following two of the most devastating floods in the previous seventy years. The Chinese were sympathetic: "Kampuchea is defending itself against the invasion of Vietnam, and yet it was devastated by two destructive floods. Should there be changes in the contracts, it would only be natural."

The DK foreign minister next struck a pragmatic chord, noting that Cambodia assumed the signing of the bilateral trade agreement was about both politics and technology but that Cambodia was happy to have it nonetheless. "We are pleased to have the commercial agreement," he said, because "we cannot be in debt to the equipment manufacturers, but we can do so with the banks." The agreement would help Cambodia learn more about trade, he added. To that end, the Chinese delegation called on Cambodia to set its own prices for its exported products in future contracts. China also pledged to assist Cambodia with any problems with quality control and packaging of exports.[26]

What Might Have Been

Few CPK cadres ever knew much about the technical aspects of applied economics in the real world. None had the experience of individuals like Van Rith or even Sar Kimlomouth, who were spared liquidation during the initial purges and were put to work in the service of the regime. But even they—particularly Sar Kimlomouth—were constrained in their ability to take the initiative and put their knowledge into practice. The Chinese filled this void, essentially teaching DK, from the top CPK cadres down to the actual trainees, how to engage in viable commercial activity. Issues such as economic efficiency and profit, fees and insurance, quality control and distribution were as alien as Adam Smith or David Ricardo to Cambodian communism. Yet it was China that impressed upon DK the understanding that such activity was vital to the survival of the state. The degree to which these things became internalized within the DK government are suggested by a March 13, 1978 letter to San Sok at Ren Fung, which deserves to be quoted at length:

Dear Comrade Sok;

Regarding our letter No.016/HK/78 February 3, 1978, point number 7 on exporting goods to sell on the free market....

It is clear to us that large Japanese companies are trying to sell as much as possible to us, without buying our goods....Perhaps we should look into using Hong Kong trading companies rather than shipping directly to Japan....

As far as the Hong Kong market, large, medium and small trading companies have been inundating us with requests to sell our agriculture and forest products to them along with paying commissions to them. For instance, the Chung Ji Company has made a number of contacts with us and they want to sell our rubber exports on our behalf (for a commission)....The Union

Company (William Leon) wants to buy a lot of our agricultural products (red corn, beans, dried fish, etc.) for the Singapore market....Yat To Company, [with] whom we discussed leasing shipping vessels, wants to buy products from us as well (cows, water buffalos, etc.)....

These and other Hong Kong traders not mentioned above have enjoyed a long relationship with us, and we should build up our relationships with them rather than with the Japanese...

Wishing you health and success.

Highest warm revolutionary respects,

March 13, 1978
[DK] Commerce Committee[27]

Although things were cut short by the Vietnamese invasion on December 25, 1978, all indications suggest that DK was on an upward trajectory with regard to international trade and commerce, which, thanks to China, would have only continued to grow into the future.

WHAT IS PAST IS PRESENT

I have realized that the past and future are real illusions, that they exist in the present, which is what there is and all there is.

—Alan Wilson Watts

In *The God Delusion*, Richard Dawkins discusses the cult on the island of Tanna in Vanuatu, which reveres a possibly apocryphal figure named John Frum, who, among other things, was said to have claimed to be the "King of America." After American troops arrived to recruit workers for a U.S. base on nearby Éfaté Island during the Second World War, Tannans by the hundreds cleared off an area in the middle of the island so that John Frum's own plane could land:

> The airstrip had a bamboo control tower with "air traffic controllers" wearing dummy headphones made of wood. There were dummy planes on the "runway" to act as decoys, designed to lure down John Frum's plane...[The "radio"] consisted of an old woman with an electric wire around her waist who would fall into a trance and talk gibberish, which [the local high priest] interpreted as the words of John Frum.[1]

When I first laid eyes on Krang Leav, it initially evoked subconscious early memories of the David Attenborough footage of Tanna I had seen on television as a child. Yet the Krang Leav airfield carries precisely the opposite image and meaning of this and other "cargo cults." Unlike the denizens of Tanna, the local Cambodians do not engage in rituals in order to facilitate the return of the Chinese engineers, much less the CPK regime. And unlike Tanna, where models of airplanes and other physical elements were lovingly constructed out of local materials to guide John Frum safely back, Krang Leav sits idle, while much of the surrounding infrastructure, constructed from Chinese imports, was allowed to rust and decay.

I was simultaneously struck by the magnitude and the durability of the project, on the one hand, and by the "forgotten" nature of it, on the other. The very physical presence of Krang Leav compelled me to set aside the book project on which I was then working in order to seek out an answer to a set of questions that kept nagging me: What exactly were the Chinese doing here?

How and why were they doing it? How did they feel about it? What does this tell us about the present? While I do not claim to have many answers, I have attempted to provide some suggestions for how we might go about thinking of them.

Much of the analysis contained herein can be understood as being grounded in history; however, I am not trained as a historian, nor do I claim any contributions to historiography. Rather, as a political scientist, as a student of government and politics, my primary challenge is to demonstrate a degree of variation among the phenomena I am studying as well as associated variation among the explanatory mechanisms I identify as being the principal causes of these phenomena. This has been the subject of the preceding three empirical chapters. In this conclusion, I seek to meet a second challenge of such a historically grounded project: assessing its value in explaining contemporary China and, to a lesser degree, Cambodia.

China's engagement with the developing and developed worlds over the past decade has been nothing short of breathtaking. China has shaped agricultural and commodity markets in Africa, and its demand for Brazilian agricultural products, particularly soy, and Australian ore have in great measure protected those countries from the economic crisis that began in 2008. Chinese demand for oil has transformed from a node by which to criticize Chinese support for petroleum-exporting autocracies like Sudan to a serious discussion about competition over energy, bringing about closer relations between China and Russia under Xi Jinping and ramping up China's regionally unpopular claims over the Senkaku/Diaoyu Islands. Indeed, Cambodia's current willingness to support the Chinese position in its capacity of a member of ASEAN has contributed to the vast amounts of aid from Beijing to Phnom Penh.

There is a growing amount of Chinese aid concentrated around infrastructure projects in Cambodia, including the construction of several hydropower projects, such as the 194-megawatt Kamchey hydropower plant in Kampot, the first large-scale hydropower plant in the history of the country. In addition, the China National Heavy Machinery Corporation is building the 246-megawatt Stung Tatay hydropower plant in Koh Kong province at a cost of US$540 million, and the China Huadian Corporation is building the 338-megawatt Stung Russey Chrum Krom hydropower plant at a cost of US$495.7 million. What was implied during the Sino-DK era is now explicit, however: the Chinese companies will operate the plants for decades into the future—in the case of the Stung Tatay, thirty-seven years.[2] It is important to note, as I have written elsewhere, that one of the keys to understanding Chinese hydropower politics is the endemic bureaucratic fragmentation in which policy—including but by no means limited to hydropower—is embedded.[3]

Chinese military assistance is also consistent with past practice. In the early 2000s, Chinese military aid to Cambodia hovered around 40 million yuan: "Projects have included building the High Command Headquarters on National Highway 4, developing the Combined Arms Officer School Thlok Tasek near the town of Pich Nil in Kampong Speu province and constructing a five-story building at Preah Ket Melea military hospital, which was recently completed."[4] Since then, according to sources sympathetic to China, it has conservatively grown to five million dollars annually: "Since 1997, China has [become] the biggest source of military aid to Cambodia, contributing more than 5 million U.S. dollars a year. A large sum by the Cambodian standard [*sic*]. China also . . . commissioned a [number of] other military projects. China also sponsors 40 Cambodian officers to study in China on a yearly basis."[5] Most recently, China and Cambodia signed a memorandum of understanding in which China will provide Cambodia almost US$20 million for military aid as well as to train Cambodian officers.[6]

The benefits to China are straightforward. On the economic front, the relationship helps manage current challenges to China's export manufacturing base; it creates opportunities to sell and service massive technical projects, particularly in energy generation and infrastructure development; and it provides investment opportunities for China's increasing pool of mobile capital. Militarily, such aid provides much of the same benefits as it did during the DK era: a check on Vietnam's power and on the diminution of China's regional influence vis-à-vis ASEAN and of Beijing's pursuit of its maritime claims.

Politically, the unconditional nature of the aid pointedly denies any quid pro quo in the form of domestic political liberalization, something the current Hun Sen regime in Cambodia appreciates. However, it has already provided clear benefits in the international arena for Beijing: Cambodia's derecognition of Taiwan in 1997, the forced repatriation of ethnic Uyghur to China in 2009, and, as noted, support for China's claims in the South China Sea.

Chinese aid is thus different from "conditional" Western aid, which centers around the transparency and accountability of donor agencies as well as aid effectiveness, measured in metrics like impact on growth, poverty reduction, and institutional development. In offering export credits and nonconcessional state loans, China offers developing countries alternatives to "Western" development assistance that comes with no overt strings attached. Moreover, the form and substance of Chinese aid has also been far more consistent over time, from the Cold War era to the present day:

> China's aid and economic cooperation differ, both in their content and in the norms of aid practice. The content of Chinese assistance

is considerably simpler, and it has changed far less often. Influenced mainly by their own experience of development and by the requests of recipient countries, the Chinese aid and economic cooperation programs emphasized infrastructure, production, and university scholarships at a time when the traditional donors downplayed all of these. Chinese loans for infrastructure were intended to reduce the high costs of production (although contracts were tied to Chinese firms and the bidding was not very transparent). Subsidies for productive joint ventures were supposed to create employment, local capacity, and demand for Chinese machinery and equipment. Preferential loans for buyers of Chinese goods, and tariff-free access for commodities…emphasized trade over aid. Popular rotating health teams staffed local hospitals again and again, for decades.[7]

For recipient countries, Chinese nonconditionality provides an alternative aid regime that is particularly desirable to authoritarian regimes which tend to see Western demands for greater transparency and political liberalization as direct threats to the continuity of their rule. As Dan O'Neill has cogently argued, China's outward foreign economic policy offers benefits to the foreign state's executive—primarily by enhancing his grip on power—thus shaping the incentives faced by the leader in the recipient country to constrain predatory actions against Chinese firms.[8] Sophal Ear emphasizes the costs to other groups in the recipient country.[9]

Given this spate of activity and particularly the seductiveness of China's "no strings attached" approach to foreign aid, many scholars, policymakers, and commentators have been confronted with the question of how we are to respond to China's inevitable and inexorable rise.

The research presented in this book suggests that we take a step back, along with a few deep breaths. China's contemporary policymaking structure and process as it pertains to Beijing's "Belt and Road" policy (*yidai yilu*) of increased international economic integration remains opaque at best and in some areas and along certain dimensions is still best characterized as a "black box." But as Graham Allison noted more than forty years ago, we can leverage our knowledge of structure and process and even mitigate the "blackness" of the box itself by looking at bureaucratic politics and organizational process, as opposed to working inductively backwards from outcomes.[10] Although much of this remains murky with regard to contemporary China, I suggest that historical experience can also work to fill in some of these gaps in data and the accumulation of "unknowns" in Beijing's foreign assistance regime. In other words, China's experience in the past can illuminate some of the gaps in our ability to understand what is occurring in real time today.

Using the Past to Illuminate the Present: Institutional Fragmentation

This claim rests on an important assumption, at least as far as the approach in this book is concerned, that the fragmented bureaucratic structure that implements and manages China's foreign aid is at least as fragmented as it was during the period under review here. Perhaps the most durable approach to Chinese policymaking and policy implementation is the notion of "fragmented authoritarianism," a term coined by Kenneth Lieberthal and Michel Oksenberg and anticipated by and built upon by David M. Lampton. The initial research that led Lieberthal and Oksenberg to the formulation of this framework was based on the energy bureaucracy in China. Their report and subsequent book, *Policy Making in China,* was about Chinese energy policy in the late 1970s and early to mid-1980s, coinciding with the period I study here.[11] Their thesis, that policy outcomes are shaped by the institutional fragmentation of the system rather than by power relations or rational decision-making, is borne out by the analysis in this book, particularly by the Kampong Som refinery. How credible is the notion that the fragmentation of the energy bureaucracy from 1975 to 1979 matches the contemporary institutional landscape of energy policy in China?

The Chinese Energy Sector

The short answer is: *very.* Recent groundbreaking work by Kjeld Erik Brødsgaard and by Nis Grünberg shows an energy bureaucracy that, rather than having consolidated, has in fact become fragmented along dimensions beyond even those documented by Lieberthal and Oksenberg. In part as a response to the type of fragmentation described in chapter 5, China established a National Energy Commission in 1980 in order to control the various ministries involved in energy policy, which, as a higher-ranking commission, it theoretically had the power to do. This experiment ended in failure two years later. In 1988, the Ministry of Energy absorbed the Ministry of Coal, the Ministry of Nuclear Industry, and the Ministry of Water Resources but was hobbled by its dependence on the State Planning Commission and its successor incarnations, the State Development and Planning Commission (1993–2003) and the National Development and Reform Commission (2003–present). In 1993, the Ministry of Coal and the Ministry of Electric Power were folded into the State Economic and Trade Commission before the entire SETC was transformed into the NDRC a decade later. Finally, in 2005, China created the Energy Bureau within the NDRC, upgrading it to vice-ministerial rank and renaming it the National Energy Administration three years later.[12]

But, as Grünberg has cogently argued:

> All comprehensive organs in the energy sector, such as the 1980 NEC and the 1988 MoE, and even the Energy Leading Group under (then) Premier Wen, failed to assume authority against their competitors in [the] bureaucracy and industry, especially against the high-ranking commissions and administrative organs....In light of this, the more recent intentions to push for a "super ministry reform" (*da bu zhi gaige*), with ministries powerful enough to overcome the current fragmentation of authorities, seems to be a strategic path of reform chosen by the central administration. Even so, after three rounds of reforms to form "super ministries" there still remains a significant degree of fragmentation of authority in the system, and the NEC was prone to fall short in influence against the other players in energy governance from the start. So far, path-dependence and the resulting difficulty to reassign real authority to new, less integrated and less established institutions has reinforced the static nature of bureaucratic authority.[13]

In addition, there has been substantial restructuring of China's energy-related state-owned enterprises (SOEs), further complicating the picture:

> After the abolishing of the Ministries of Energy (1993), Coal, and Electric Power (1997), the State Power Corporation was formed in 1997 as a ministry-level organization in charge of overseeing electricity generation and grid operation. This professionalization of energy industries away from industrial ministries was already initiated in the oil sector in 1982, with the creation of China National Offshore Oil Corporation (CNOOC), and one year later China Petro-Chemical Corporation (restructured in 1998 to form the present day China Petrochemical Corporation, or Sinopec Group; parent of the Sinopec Corporation established in 2000). The third "oil champion" China National Petroleum Corporation (CNPC) was established in 1988, with its main subsidiary PetroChina carved out in late 1999. By restructuring of ministries into large SOEs, Beijing extended the general SOE reform of 1997...into the energy sector. This effort was further deepened with the landmark reforms of 2002/03, when transmission and generation were separated, and five "energy giants" and two grid companies were carved out of the State Power Corporation (Huaneng, Guodian, Huadian, Datang, and China Power Investment Corp.; State Grid and Southern Grid).[14]

In an attempt to rein in the various competing interests, the State Council in January 2010 established the National Energy Commission, directly under the authority of the State Council but managed by the vice-ministerial National Energy Administration, which was responsible for coordinating more than twenty higher-ranking ministerial units. Initial skepticism about the NEA's prospects seem to have been proven correct by subsequent events: "One of the central reasons for the weakness of the NEC vis-à-vis other institutions, appears to be the result of the very problem it was meant to resolve: the fragmented authority over energy issues between established bureaucratic *xitong* [clusters of policy-related bureaucracies], which are reluctant to share or cede their authority over energy."[15]

As far as the thesis of this book is concerned, Grünberg's masterful mapping of the energy bureaucracy demonstrates that the energy sector is at least as fragmented today as it was back in the DK era. It is, therefore, just as likely, if not more so, to experience the type of bureaucratic infighting and institutional fragmentation that drove much of the failure at Kampong Som and other energy-based overseas assistance to the developing world.

China's Military

The black box of China's military allows in precious little light, thus necessitating that observers rely inordinately on policy inputs and outputs to infer the processes and structures contained therein. Nevertheless, it appears that the Chinese People's Liberation Army is more fragmented now than it was in the late 1970s.

In January 2011, China tested its new J-20 stealth fighter jet just hours before President Hu Jintao was preparing to meet with U.S. Secretary of Defense Robert Gates. Ordinarily, this would have been interpreted as Beijing flexing its muscles in front of a captive foreign audience. The problem with this interpretation is that by all accounts the news surprised Hu every bit as much as it did Gates. Indeed, the Chinese civilian leadership, apparently unaware of such a test, scrambled to get in front of the story in full view of the nonplussed U.S. defense secretary.[16] Particularly germane to this discussion is that President Hu's ignorance of the test was hardly an anomaly; indeed, this was quasi-standard practice. According to Michael Swaine, "Even though senior party leaders in all likelihood formally approve all major military-related policies and programs...such individuals simply do not possess the political clout, knowledge of military issues, or personal influence and charisma to ensure control over the details of military activities in many areas that pose implications for foreign policy."[17] And this is particularly true of the lower level: "PLA [People's Liberation Army] actions can certainly play an important role in precipitating and shaping the course of a crisis in ways unintended by the senior civilian leadership. This is largely because local PLA entities are not necessarily under the close direction of the senior civilian or perhaps even military leadership and thus can at times take actions that run counter to the overall intent and strategy behind PRC foreign policy."[18]

In fact, the Gates incident was the culmination of a number of such events. On March 7, 2009, two days after coming into contact with a PLA Navy frigate and subsequent flyovers by a Chinese Y-12 plane, a Chinese intelligence vessel contacted the USS *Impeccable,* which was monitoring submarine activity in the area, to the effect that it would "suffer consequences" if it did not leave. The next day, the *Impeccable* was met by five Chinese boats, two of which were representing civilian agencies, which ordered it to leave the area. After spraying the nearest ship with water, the *Impeccable* radioed the Chinese boats to let them know it was leaving the area and requested safe passage. As it was leaving, crew from the Chinese boats dropped wood in the water directly in path of the *Impeccable,* while two Chinese vessels forced the *Impeccable* to make an emergency stop by maneuvering directly in front of it. As the *Impeccable* started away again, Chinese crews from one of the boats attempted to snag the ship's sonar array. After an unsuccessful attempt to resolve the issue diplomatically, the United States sent the USS *Chung-Hoon,* a guided missile destroyer, to protect the *Impeccable* while in the South China Sea.[19]

On September 7, 2010, after encountering the Chinese trawler *Minjinyu 5179* traveling within ten miles of the Senkaku/Diaoyu Islands, the Japanese coast guard vessel *Mizuki* ordered it to stop in order to be inspected. The *Minjinyu 5179* fled the scene and collided with several Japanese boats that were in pursuit. The next day, the *Minjinyu 5179* was stopped, and the captain and crew were detained. In the meantime, a YouTube video of the incident had gone viral. Eventually the crew and then the captain were released, and the incident was seen as a victory in China and a defeat in Japan.[20]

This points to perhaps the greatest irony of the Chinese system. In an environment in which everything is bureaucratized, the one entity missing (until 2013) was a Chinese version of the U.S. National Security Council, a dedicated organization that performs effective interagency coordination to supply the executive with the information necessary to make the most informed decisions on security matters in a timely fashion. The result was a situation in which "the absence of integrated intelligence, the presence of direct lines of communication to the [Politburo Standing Committee], and the existence of personal advisers to the party general secretary mean that lower-level units and individuals can exert a disproportionate influence over crisis assessments and decisions made at the top."[21] In such a way, China's leaders would be overwhelmed with underevaluated, possibly biased, and even inaccurate information with no way to manage and appraise it. Although it is risky to make conclusions before all the facts are in, it certainly appears that the computer hacking scandal traced to Chinese

PLA Unit 61398, housed in a nondescript suburb of Shanghai, is merely one example of this.[22]

For the purposes of generalizing the analysis of this book, it would be overstating the case to equate this degree of fragmentation with that plaguing the energy sector. At the same time, it makes China's ability to strong-arm client states—as well as respond to any overseas transgressions—a far more complicated process, particularly as such incidents increasingly make it into the news and thus bring attention to the fragmentation within China's military. In other words, while recent Chinese military-grounded foreign policy behavior is consistent with the story presented in this book, it may, in fact, point to a potentially less unified authority and reporting structure within the military than that which existed in the mid- to late 1970s. This, in turn, suggests that China might be even less able to influence policy of client states in the military arena than was demonstrated in chapter 4. Developments under Xi Jinping may further complicate the situation.

Chinese Trade and Commerce

The restructuring of the commercial sector is more of a mixed bag. On the one hand, as has been pointed out, the institutions within this functional bureaucratic system, or *xitong,* have been streamlined to some degree, given the combination of the centrality of trade to China's economic development program and its adaptability to the trade processes themselves.[23] On the other hand, the Chinese trade policymaking umbrella has since 1990 included a rapidly-growing number of bureaucratic actors that increasingly makes both trade policymaking and policy implementation a challenge.[24]

It appears that the current Chinese ministry handling trade, the Ministry of Commerce, is a fairly effective coordinating mechanism for these various competing interests, especially when it comes to managing trade at the national level. That said, as Chinese investment continues to grow in the developing world and as Chinese SOEs and their national and local government representatives and associates in China find themselves involved in the actual implementation of such policy far away from Beijing and in the sovereign borders of recipient countries, Beijing's ability to control such behavior becomes less certain or, at the very least, open to manipulation. While it does seem likely that commerce remains the area where Chinese leverage is most likely to succeed, the picture here too is more complex than in 1978.

The overall conclusion, then, is that, rather than getting better, bureaucratic fragmentation since the time frame covered in this book has actually gotten worse, deepening along traditional cleavages while extending into new ones. As a result, we are likely to see less variation today than we have across the three cases in this book. Indeed, what we might see is a situation in which all three policy areas—to varying degrees—actually begin to approach the case of Kampong Som documented in chapter 5, rather than the other way around. The import of this from a policy perspective is tantalizing: rather than representing a juggernaut that will set the terms of trade for the foreseeable future by engaging and locking in the developing world, thus creating a new economic order, Beijing's overseas experiment might better be conceptualized as an extension of its fragmented domestic structure outward, onto its foreign aid and assistance regime. The result is a very different picture from the conventional wisdom of an ever-powerful China increasing its economic muscle on the international stage; instead what we may be seeing is a fragile and vulnerable China that may be unable to force its priorities onto its new developing "client" states and is ill equipped to handle sudden or complicated crises, especially once China's domestic audience catches wind of it.

Cambodia Then and Now

It is, perhaps, more difficult to trace a connection between Cambodia's past and present. Although the Kingdom of Cambodia today contains the nominal trappings of an electoral democracy, authority is tightly controlled by Cambodia's leader, Hun Sen. Much has been said about the fact that Hun Sen was a Khmer Rouge commander in the Eastern Zone who defected to Vietnam only when he believed his own life was threatened. In power since 1985, Hun Sen's longevity and sheer political skill, shown in his ability to outmaneuver Sihanouk, Pol Pot, and the entire United Nations Transitional Authority in Cambodia (UNTAC) apparatus, and his legendary patronage networks, which have corrupted much of the system, make it very difficult to analyze and evaluate Cambodia's governing apparatus in a way that eschews a personalist approach.

That said, based on the analysis in chapter 2, one can make a few careful, tentative observations. Much like during the DK period, a great deal of national and local authority relations appears to conform to a dynamic that can be described as "fluid but never quite jelling." That is, while authority at the very top of the system is unambiguous and absolute, below this level authority relations remain in flux. This seems to be due more to Hun Sen's ability to keep any potential competitors for power on an unstable footing rather than the regime itself not having had the time to "mature," as was the case in DK. Like Pol Pot, Hun Sen appears to be a micromanager famous for keeping long hours into the night. However, unlike the DK era, there appears to be less emphasis placed on symbolic or revolutionary-based political capital among officials; rather, the wheels of authority are embedded within a breathtaking network of corruption and political patronage. And, of course, although there is no shortage of political repression in contemporary Cambodia, equating or even comparing it to the DK period dilutes and devalues the suffering of the Cambodian people under the Khmer Rouge as well as misunderstands the dynamics of contemporary political subjugation in Hun Sen's Cambodia.

So, if such a comparison on the national level fails along some important dimensions, can the experience of bureaucratic politics under the CPK tell us anything about Cambodia today or possibly tomorrow? There are two nodes where such a comparison may provide better conceptual leverage: in a future, post–Hun Sen regime and today at the subnational level. Hun Sen's sheer political genius is something that happens fairly rarely, and the successor to a personage with such power seldom enjoys the same degree of authority. Part of this is because when authority becomes personalized, it undermines institutional integrity. When such a leader passes from the scene, we are left with a vacuum that is quickly filled by political repertoire-based standard operating procedures that draw from experience in past political environments. Such would also be true of the DK period.

Second, even today there are many former Khmer Rouge officials in positions of power and authority, either as active members of the ruling class or as retired but engaged patrons. These are the individuals who make news every now and again; Ieng Sary's son is vice governor of Pailin province; Sou Met remained active in politics until his death in 2013. So did Meas Mut, if largely symbolically.[25] More generally, a very large number of individuals at the local levels draw from the skills they forged as officials during DK—as well as before 1975 when they experimented with governance in the *maquis* and after 1979 when Khmer Rouge–controlled areas emerged along the Thai-Cambodian border in places like Anlong Veng and Pailin—and they continue to use them as local bureaucrats to this day.

Indeed, several of the former Khmer Rouge officials I interviewed for this project retain official roles in various ramshackle government offices far from Phnom Penh. How they approach their tasks, how they navigate the bureaucracy, and how they solve problems in an environment of scarcity all depend on the repertoires they developed as functionaries within DK. Moreover, when we understand that these officials were not involved in security—but rather in communications, commerce, and other politically "secular" areas of DK governance—the potential utility of chapter 2's institutional mapping of DK for understanding bureaucratic dynamics in Cambodia today becomes apparent.

So one might cautiously draw in part from the basic contours of the DK state apparatus described in detail in chapter 2 to draw inferences about contemporary Cambodian administrative behavior while substituting the positive incentives of corruption for the negative one of fear. Of course, much work remains to be done in this area, work that combines the richness of history with the systematic rigor of the social sciences.

In recent years the field of political science in the United States has discounted the role of area studies and history in explaining political processes and outcomes. This arises from a genuine desire to achieve a degree of precision, elegance, and predictability that many of the natural sciences take for granted. It is also a completely appropriate and necessary response to the unsystematic, undisciplined, and impressionistic approaches to understanding political behavior a generation or so ago. There is often, however, a tendency in the discipline to take such a striving for the scientific method literally—to establish laws in the social sciences that are akin to those of chemistry or physics—when in fact, the scientific method can be at best only a metaphor to which the social sciences can aspire, because fundamentally human beings—the very center of social phenomena—possess agency. Oftentimes, this prevailing view privileges less messy, less complicated, and—dare I say—less *political* phenomena as topics for study in the pursuit of parsimony and precision.

There is evidence that students of politics are starting to take history seriously again. This is a welcome trend, one in which an appreciation of historical analysis is not simply a contextualizing ornament or a necessary bookend to understanding concepts like historical institutionalism or path dependency. History can serve a far simpler and more fundamental role as a venue for data collection, thereby enhancing, (re)animating, and legitimizing moribund or otherwise impossibly under-specified research agendas while also necessarily complicating hitherto "settled" questions. It is only by engaging in a fuller understanding of the past, combined with a more systematic approach to documenting it, that our ability to shape the present can be accurate and informative. But because potential informants die of old age, archives disintegrate, and historical artifacts go missing, this is an imperative as much as it is a cliché.

Notes

CHAPTER 1

1. Stephen R. Heder, "Khmer Rouge Opposition to Pol Pot: Pro-Vietnamese or Pro-Chinese," presentation at Australian National University, Canberra, August 28, 1990, p. 12.

2. Kong Sothanarith, "China Played No Role in Khmer Rouge Politics: Ambassador," *Voice of America* Khmer, January 22, 2010, available at http://www.voanews.com/khmer/2010-01-22-voa1.cfm, accessed March 24, 2010.

3. http://www.globaltimes.cn/content/735647.shtml (accessed October 4, 2012).

4. The photograph is not dated, but Ichinose was killed by the Khmer Rouge near Angkor in November 1973. The photograph is reprinted here with the generous permission of the Taizo Ichinose estate.

5. Horst Faas, Tim Page, and David Halberstam, *Requiem: By the Photographers Who Died in Vietnam and Indochina* (New York: Random House, 1997), pp. 312–313.

6. For the remainder of this book, I use the term "Khmer Rouge" more or less interchangeably with the Communist Party of Kampuchea (CPK) and refer to Democratic Kampuchea (DK) as the country ruled by the CPK until January 9, 1979. Although some may object to this usage, likening it to referring to the PRC as "Red China," it is the commonly used term used by most Cambodia experts.

7. Sophie Richardson, *China, Cambodia, and the Five Principles of Peaceful Coexistence* (New York: Columbia University Press, 2009), pp. 70–71.

8. Adam Nossiter and Bree Feng, "Ghana Arrests Chinese in Gold Mines," *New York Times,* June 6, 2013, available at http://www.nytimes.com/2013/06/07/world/africa/ghana-arrests-chinese-in-gold-mining-regions.html?_r=0, accessed August 10, 2013.

9. A minority are more balanced in their assessments. See, for example, Deborah Bräutigam, *The Dragon's Gift: The Real Story of China in Africa* (New York: Oxford University Press, 2011).

10. See Kenneth M. Quinn, "Explaining the Terror," in *Cambodia 1975–1978: Rendezvous with Death,* ed. Karl D. Jackson (Princeton NJ: Princeton University Press, 1989), p. 219. See also Henri Locard, "Le Réseau Carcéral des Khmers Rouges," *Communisme* 95/96 (2008): 37–41. On Kang Sheng, see John Byron and Robert Pack, *The Claws of the Dragon: Kang Sheng, the Evil Genius Behind Mao and His Legacy of Terror in People's China* (New York: Simon & Schuster, 1992).

11. See, among others, Nayan Chanda, *Brother Enemy: The War after the War* (New York: Harcourt, 1986); Odd Arne Westad and Sophie Quinn-Judge, eds., *The Third Indochina War: Conflict between China, Vietnam, and Cambodia, 1972–1979* (London: Routledge, 2006); and Robert S. Ross, *The Indochina Tangle: China's Vietnam Policy, 1975–1979* (New York: Columbia University Press, 1988).

12. Richardson, *China, Cambodia, and the Five Principles of Peaceful Coexistence.*

13. "Indochina: Each to His Own," *Far Eastern Economic Review,* June 13, 1975, p. 25; and Ian Dunbar with Edith Lenart, "Following Peking's Revolutionary Model," *Far Eastern Economic Review,* May 23, 1975, pp. 22–23; cited in John D. Ciorciari, "China and the Pol Pot Regime," *Cold War History* (2013), DOI: 10.1080/14682745.2013.808624: 5.

14. Richardson, *China, Cambodia, and the Five Principles of Peaceful Coexistence*, p. 70; Zhongguo gongchandang zuzhi shi zi ke huibian, lingdao jigou yange he chengyuan minglu [*Compilation of the Chinese Communist Party organizational history: Leaders, units, evolution, and membership lists*], Beijing: *Zhonggong zhongyang dangxiao chubanshe*, 1995, p. 1120. I use the terms "vice" and "deputy" interchangeably throughout the book.

15. Interviews 12PP01A and 12PP01B, Phnom Penh, December 30 and 31, 2012. Interview designations are compiled as follows: the first two digits denote the year, the last two digits denote the chronological order of the interview within a given locale (indicated by the first and second, and sometimes, third, letter in the interview designation). When the interviewee was interviewed more than once, the letters A, B, C, etc. round up the interview designation. So, for example, Interview 12KC02 indicates that it was a one-time interview with the second person I met in Kampong Cham in 2012; Interview 12PP01B indicates that it was a second meeting with the first interviewee I met with in Phnom Penh in 2012. All interview designations are followed by the actual location and date of the interview.

16. *Le Monde* has called this the "largest aid package that China had ever given to one country." *Le Monde*, September 13, 1975, cited in Ciorciari, "China and the Pol Pot Regime": 6.

17. Interviews 12PP01A and 12PP01B, Phnom Penh, December 30 and 31, 2012.

18. Norodom Sihanouk, *War and Hope: The Case for Cambodia* (New York: Pantheon, 1980), p. 86; and Philip Short, *Pol Pot: Anatomy of a Nightmare* (New York: Macmillan, 2005), p. 301. See also Ciorciari, "China and the Pol Pot Regime": 7.

19. It is unlikely that Sihanouk was even aware of the existence of the CPK, let alone the various factions within it, or who was in charge. He referred to them collectively as *les Khmers rouges*.

20. Meeting Minutes of the Standing Committee of the Communist Party of Kampuchea, March 13, 1976, Documentation Center of Cambodia (hereafter referred to as DC-CAM), Documents D00690 and D00691. As this suggests, they were also fearful of how China ("some adults") might react, given that Beijing's support for Sihanouk predated and exceeded Beijing's support for the Khmer Rouge.

Becker implies that Sihanouk was unceremoniously "retired" in 1976, possibly against his will; in fact, Sihanouk demanded that he be allowed to do so, and the CPK reluctantly agreed. Becker, *When the War Was Over: Cambodia and the Khmer Rouge Revolution,* revised edition (New York: PublicAffairs, 1998). Short also minimizes this event, suggesting that it did not hamper long-term relations with China and that it was consistent with Pol Pot's desire to get Sihanouk out of the way altogether. Short, *Pol Pot.* While Short is correct, it is equally clear that at the time, Sihanouk's actions caused the otherwise unflappable CPK leadership to convene a hasty set of meetings to resolve the issue.

21. I am grateful to Xu Xin for providing this insight.

22. Interview 12PP01B, Phnom Penh, December 31, 2012.

23. Ben Kiernan, *The Pol Pot Regime: Race, Power, and Genocide in Cambodia under the Khmer Rouge, 1975–79* (New Haven, CT: Yale University Press, 1996), p. 136.

24. "Dear Brother Khieu and Brother Tom," DC-CAM, Catalogue No. L01291, cited in Ciorciari, "China and the Pol Pot Regime": 10.

25. Ben Kiernan, "Conflict in the Kampuchean Communist Movement," *Journal of Contemporary Asia* 10:1–2 (1980): 57, cited in Ciorciari, "China and the Pol Pot Regime": 16.

26. Interview 12PP01B, Phnom Penh, December 31, 2012.

27. Ibid.

28. Chanda, *Brother Enemy,* pp. 98–102.

29. Interview 13AV01, Anlong Veng, January 3, 2013.

30. Interview 12PP01B, Phnom Penh, December 31, 2012.

31. Cultural and informational exchanges increased as well: in the fall of 1978, two journalists from Hong Kong representing the *Wen Wei Po* and *Ta Kung Pao* newspapers toured the country for three weeks; on November 10, 1978, a delegation from the PLA's acrobatic troupe, led by Cheng Zemin, deputy director of the Political Department of the Shenyang Military Region, visited the country; and on December 22, 1978, Ieng Sary received a group of reporters from Xinhua led by Li Nan, deputy director of Xinhua's International Department. This mirrored a DK policy of minimally opening up to the outside world through a series of carefully stage-managed tours. Interview 12PP01B, Phnom Penh, December 31, 2012.

32. "Translations on Telecommunications Policy, Research and Development," U.S. Joint Publications Research Service, November 9, 1977, available at www.dtic.mil/dtic/tr/fulltext/u2/a375644.pdf, accessed April 1, 2013; and Interview 12PP01B, Phnom Penh, December 31, 2012. Thanks to Fu Liangyu.

33. Timothy Carney, "The Organization of Power," in Karl Jackson, ed., *Cambodia, 1975–1978: Rendezvous with Death* (Princeton, NJ: Princeton University Press, 1989), p. 104.

34. Interview 11LY01C, Luoyang, November 16, 2011.

35. Interview 12PP01B, Phnom Penh, December 31, 2012.

36. Keng Piao, "Report on the Situation on the Indochinese Peninsula," *Issues and Studies* 17, no. 1 (1981): 83, cited in Ciorciari, "China and the Pol Pot Regime": 20; Interview 12PP01B, Phnom Penh, December 31, 2012.

37. See, among others, Andrew Mertha, "China's 'Soft' Centralization: Shifting *Tiao/Kuai* Authority Relations," *China Quarterly* 184 (December 2005): 791–810.

38. Socheat Nhean, *Democratic Kampuchea: Chain of Command and Sociopolitical Structure of the Southwest Zone,* Master's thesis, Northern Illinois University Department of Anthropology, 2010.

39. Kiernan, *Pol Pot Regime,* pp. 87–88.

40. Socheat Nhean, *Democratic Kampuchea;* David Chandler, *Voices from S-21: Terror and History in Pol Pot's Secret Prison* (Berkeley: University of California Press, 1999); and Sara Colm and Sim Sorya, *Khmer Rouge Purges in the Mondul Kiri Highlands, Region 105,* (Phnom Penh: DC-CAM Documentation Series no. 14, 2009), p. 64.

41. Chandler, *Voices from S-21,* pp. 61–63.

42. Ke Pauk, "Ke Pauk's Autobiography from 1949–1985," document on file with DC-CAM, available at www.d.dccam.org/Archives/Documents/Biography/Biographies_Autography_Ke_Pauk.htm, accessed November 8, 2012.

43. It should be noted that very few countries can claim to be innocent of directly or indirectly assisting the Khmer Rouge, including, most notably, the United States after 1979. In this respect, Beijing's support of DK might charitably be seen as less cynical than that of Washington.

44. One diary by a particularly meticulous, high-ranking cadre on the Kampong Som petroleum refinery project provided a wealth of information on meetings, day-to-day activities and challenges, and the general atmospherics of the project. It provides many key pieces of information in chapter 5.

45. Unfortunately, I have been unable to locate any Chinese who worked on the Krang Leav airfield; all recollections are from Cambodian workers mobilized for the project.

46. Ieng Sary died on March 14, 2013.

47. The one exception seems to be Kaing Guek Eev [a.k.a. Duch]; see www.cambodia-tribunal.org/sites/default/files/resources/e159_10_en.pdf, accessed April 1, 2013.

48. Frederick C. Teiwes, *Politics and Purges in China: Rectification and the Decline of Party Norms, 1950–1965* (Armonk, NY: M.E. Sharpe), 1997.

49. See, among others, Noam Chomsky and Edward Herman, "Distortions at Fourth Hand," *The Nation,* June 25, 1977; and Malcolm Caldwell and Lek Tan, *Cambodia in the Southeast Asian War* (New York: Monthly Review Press, 1973).

50. Henry Kissinger, *White House Years* (Boston: Little, Brown, 1979), p. 1085.

CHAPTER 2

1. Henri Locard, *Pol Pot's Little Red Book: The Sayings of Angkar* (Bangkok: Silkworm Books, 2004), p. 112.

2. Ibid., p. 113.

3. Hannah Arendt, *The Origins of Totalitarianism* (New York: Schocken, 2004); Carl Friedrich and Zbigniew Brzezinski, *Totalitarian Dictatorship and Democracy* (New York: Praeger, 1966).

4. Benito Mussolini and Giovanni Gentile, quoted in Anne Applebaum, *Iron Curtain: The Crushing of Eastern Europe, 1944–1956* (New York: Doubleday, 2012), p. xxi.

5. Ith Sarin, *Sranoh prolong Khmer* [Regrets of the Khmer soul], partially translated in Tim Carney, "Communist Party Power in Kampuchea (Cambodia): Documents and Discussion," Data Paper: Number 106, Southeast Asia Program, Department of Asian Studies, Cornell University, Ithaca, New York, January 1977: pp. 34–55; Kuong Lumphon, *Report on the Communist Party of Cambodia, May 8,* 1973, David Chandler Cambodia Collection, Series 3: Unpublished Reports and Documents (Inventory of files), box 6, available at www.lib.monash.edu.au/matheson/asrc/inventories/cambodia-collection/series-3.html, accessed June 24, 2013. See also David Chandler, *The Tragedy of Cambodian History: Politics, War, and Revolution since 1945* (New Haven, CT: Yale University Press, 1991), pp. 218–220.

6. See also Kenneth Quinn, "The Khmer *Krahom* [Khmer Rouge] Program to Create a Communist Society in Southern Cambodia," U.S. Department of State Airgram A-8 from Consulate Can Tho, February 20, 1974. There are other firsthand accounts that are somewhat less systematic in their approach. See François Bizot, *The Gate* (London: Harvill Press, 2000); Richard Dudman, *Forty Days with the Enemy* (New York: Liveright, 1971); for a more benign view, see Serge Thion, "Cambodia 1972: Within the Khmer Rouge," in *Watching Cambodia* (Bangkok: White Lotus, 1993), pp. 1–19. For an extended discussion of the factionalism within the CPK, see Craig Etcheson, *The Rise and Demise of Democratic Kampuchea* (Boulder, CO: Westview Press, 1986); and Michael Vickery, *Cambodia, 1975–1982* (Bangkok: Silkworm Books, 1984).

7. Vickery, *Cambodia, 1975–1982,* p. 74, citing Steve Heder, "From Pol Pot to Pen Sovan to the Villages," paper presented at the International Conference on Indochina and Problems of Security in Southeast Asia, Chulalongkorn University, June 1980, pp. 7–9; and Ben Kiernan, "Conflict in the Kampuchean Communist Movement," 51, respectively.

8. See, among others, Laurence Picq, *Beyond the Horizon: Five Years with the Khmer Rouge* (New York: St. Martin's, 1989), p. 45.

9. Meeting Minutes of the Standing Committee of the Communist Party of Kampuchea, October 9, 1975, DC-CAM, Document D00677.

10. Chandler, *Voices from S-21,* p. 16.

11. DC-CAM, Document TSL 4787/D13627; ECCC Testimony of Witness Oeun Tan, June 13 and 14, 2012, available at www.eccc.gov.kh/en/witness-expert-civil-party/mr-oeun-tan, accessed November 8, 2012; Interview 11PP01, Phnom Penh, January 25, 2011; and ECCC Document D2/15 – The Etcheson Report. On this last source, according to the September 23, 2009, "Order on Request for Exclusion of the Report of Mr. Craig Etcheson," footnote 2, page 2, the Written Record of Analysis, July 18, 2007, D2/15 (hereafter referred to as "Etcheson Report") "is in the public domain as it is part of the Public Case File in *Prosecutor v. Kaing Guek Eev alias Duch,* Case File 001," available at www.cambodiatribunal.org/sites/default/files/resources/d192_2_en.pdf, accessed November 27, 2011.

12. Khmer Rouge cadres had several aliases, and were often referred to by a single name, a nom de guerre which they continued to use after 1975. To maintain consistency with my sources, I use them here except where noted.

13. "K," or *gaa,* refers to the first consonant of the Khmer alphabet. Some assert that the "K" stands for "Kandal," the location of the Center.

14. Interview 12SL01, Samlaut, October 7, 2012.

15. Military meetings were held at the Olympic Stadium. These included military leaders from all of the zones. Battalion, regiment, and division leaders and others attended the meeting, between fifty and sixty in all. The meetings took place twice a year with Pol Pot chairing and Son Sen participating.

16. Etcheson Report, p. 4.

17. Extraordinary Chambers in the Courts of Cambodia, Closing Order of Case File No. 002/19-09-2007-ECCC-OCIJ, pp. 19–20.

18. Interview 12SL01, Samlaut, October 7, 2012.

19. Ibid.

20. Etcheson Report, p. 7.

21. Justin Corfield and Laura Summers, *Historical Dictionary of Cambodia* (Lanham: Scarecrow Press, 2002), pp. 51, 70.

22. Further complicating the picture, there was a distinction between the candidate and "reserve" (*samachek bomrung*) members of the CC. There was a lower-ranking fourth level, members of which were called "assistants" to the CC (*chumnuoykar kanak kammathekar machchhem*). "Closing Order of Co-Investigating Judges You Bunleng and Marcel Lemonde," September 15, 2010, available at www.sophanseng.info/2011/05/khmer-rouge-tribunal-cases-001-002-003-and-004/, accessed September 28, 2011.

23. Assistant members "enjoyed a status similar to some form of membership, to the extent that they could participate alongside full-rights and candidate members in political training organized at the Party Centre level," "Closing Order of Co-Investigating Judges You Bunleng and Marcel Lemonde."

24. This included specifying the dimensions of sharpened spikes to be placed in covered pits along the border: the "height of a person's foot sole, instep and shin, and up to the stomach." Meeting of the CPK Standing Committee, August 20–25, 1975, DC-CAM, Document N0001022.

25. Etcheson Report, pp. 5–6.

26. Extraordinary Chambers in the Courts of Cambodia, Closing Order of Case File No. 002/19-09-2007-ECCC-OCIJ, p. 18.

27. Vickery, *Cambodia, 1975–1982*, p. 76.

28. Huy Vannak, *The Khmer Rouge Division 703: From Victory to Self-Destruction* (Phnom Penh: DC-CAM, Documentation Series no. 3, 2003), p. 27.

29. According to Chandler, the date was April 23. Chandler, *Brother Number One: A Political Biography of Pol Pot* (Boulder, CO: Westview Press, 1992), p. 109. Vickery places the date at April 24, while Kiernan puts it at April 20. Vickery, *Cambodia, 1975–1982*, p. 76. See also Kiernan, *Pol Pot Regime*, pp. 32–44, 54; Vickery, *Cambodia, 1975–1982*, pp. 77–80; Short, *Pol Pot*, pp. 272–276.

30. Kiernan, *Pol Pot Regime*, p. 32.

31. Moeung Sonn with Henri Locard, *Prisoner of the Khmer Rouge* (Editions Funan, 2007), pp. 49–64; Henri Locard, "Siem Reap-Angkor during the War (1970–1975) and Democratic Kampuchea (1975–1979): From Violence to Totalitarianism," *Siksacakr* 10 (2008): 26.

32. Kiernan, *Pol Pot Regime*, p. 50.

33. Locard, "Siem Reap-Angkor during the War," 26.

34. See, for example, Kiernan, *Pol Pot Regime*; and Vickery, *Cambodia, 1975–1982*, especially pp. 74–88.

35. Chandler, *Voices from S-21*, pp. 57–58, 68–71; Sara Colm and Sorya Sim, "Anatomy of an Interrogation: The Torture of Comrade Ya at S-21," *Phnom Penh Post* 16/22, November 2–15, 2007.

36. Vickery, *Cambodia, 1975–1982*, p. 140.

37. Extraordinary Chambers in the Courts of Cambodia, Closing Order of Case File No. 002/19-09-2007-ECCC-OCIJ, pp. 23–24.

38. Corfield and Summers, *Historical Dictionary of Cambodia*, p. 3.

39. North (divided to include a new Central) Zone (regions 41, 42, 43, 103, and special region 106), Northeast Zone (regions 101, 102, 104, 105, and possibly 107), Eastern Zone (regions 20, 21, 22, 23, and 24); Southwest Zone (regions 13, 25, 33, and 35); Western Zone (regions 11, 15, 31, 32, 37); Northwest (regions 1, 2, 3, 4, 5, and 6). Vickery, *Cambodia, 1975–1982*, pp. 94–148.

40. Meng-Try Ea, *The Chain of Terror: The Khmer Rouge Southwest Zone Security System* (Phnom Penh: DC-CAM, Documentation Series no. 7, 2005).

41. Etcheson Report, p. 6.

42. Ke Pauk, "Ke Pauk's Autobiography from 1949–1985."

43. Very little of which survives today, having been deliberately destroyed, carted off by Vietnamese forces, or left to rot in the unforgiving temperature of Cambodia; Extraordinary Chambers in the Courts of Cambodia, Closing Order of Case File No. 002/19-09-2007-ECCC-OCIJ, pp. 29–30.

44. "Note on the Decisions of the Central Party on Miscellaneous Matters," DC-CAM, Document D00693, cited in Ea, *Chain of Terror*, p. 16.

45. Interview 13BTB01, Battambang, January 5, 2013.

46. Extraordinary Chambers in the Courts of Cambodia, Closing Order of Case File No. 002/19-09-2007-ECCC-OCIJ, p. 27.

47. Interview of Net Savat, DC-CAM, Document D24373, Peam Chimeat Village, Nang Khy Loek sub-district, Koh Nhek district, Mondulkiri, December 17–19, 1999, pp. 78–79.

48. Interview 13BTB01, Battambang, January 5, 2013.

49. Distinctions among ministries, committees, and sections appear to have had far less meaning in DK than did the corresponding hairsplitting of bureaucratic rank in China. This is largely because Office 870 was so intent on micromanaging all the details of policy; it was so unambiguously powerful that ministerial units simply did what they were told. Too much, even a little, interbureaucratic squabbling risked incurring costs so prohibitive that they tended not to arise in the first place, making issues of horizontal or even vertical authority relations (that is, apart from 870) irrelevant. Because some of the units, especially those involved with economics, were sometimes referred to as ministries and sometimes not and because rank ordering between them was largely a nonissue, I retain the more ambiguous term of "ministerial unit" for those offices that were not clearly designated formal "ministries."

50. One explanation is that in 1975, the political line was not very strong, so there was some leniency. These individuals were allowed to take these posts even though they were not on the Standing Committee because they were Party members of long standing. Interview 11PP01, Phnom Penh, January 25, 2011.

51. In 1975, the Standing Committee proposed that hospitals and medical workers be put to work, but only gradually. See Meeting Minutes of the CPK Standing Committee, August 20–24, 1975, DC-CAM, Document N0001022.

52. Ibid.

53. Minutes of the March 8, 1976 Meeting on Base Work, DC-CAM, Document D00684.

54. Extraordinary Chambers in the Courts of Cambodia, Closing Order of Case File No. 002/19-09-2007-ECCC-OCIJ, p. 17.

55. There were other institutions such as the People's Representative Assembly that were largely for show or for information dissemination purposes. There was the security apparatus under the direct control of 870 as well as a more regionally defined military apparatus led by the various zone commanders.

56. "B," or *baa*, refers to the twenty-first consonant of the Khmer alphabet.

57. His brain trust provides one of the most unique characteristics of B-1: it was staffed by some of the most respected CPK revolutionaries and intellectuals ("key people" of the

revolution, the best minds). In fact, in 1977, Pol Pot reportedly sought to put B-1 in charge of managing the civil affairs of the capital, Phnom Penh. But this never came to fruition, as there was a tremendous amount of opposition and pushback from the military. Interview 12PP01A, Phnom Penh, December 30, 2012.

58. Ibid.; and Interview 12TK01A, Takeo, October 24, 2012.

59. Interview 13PL01, Pailin, January 4, 2013.

60. Extraordinary Chambers in the Courts of Cambodia, Closing Order of Case File No. 002/19-09-2007-ECCC-OCIJ, pp. 24–25.

61. Etcheson Report, p. 4.

62. Ibid., pp. 5–6.

63. An exception to this is the centralized procurement of food for the various central ministries. As one staff member recalled: "there was at least one region or zone assigned to produce food for each of the ministries. …Each ministry also assigned some people to grow vegetables in [Chraing Chamreh]." Interview with Rochoem Tun (a.k.a. Phi Puon, a.k.a. Chiem), DC-CAM, Documentation Center of Cambodia Promoting Accountability Project, December 19, 2010, p. 13, available at http://d.dccam.org/Archives/Interviews/Sample_Interviews/Former_Kh_Rouge/Phi_Phuon.pdf, accessed September 30, 2011.

64. Corfield and Summers, *Historical Dictionary of Cambodia,* p. 168.

65. Jan Ovesen and Ing-Britt Trankell, *Cambodians and Their Doctors: A Medical Anthropology of Colonial and Post-Colonial Cambodia* (Denmark: Nordic Institute of Asian Studies Press Monograph 117, 2010), p. 87.

66. "P," or *bou,* refers to the twenty-third consonant of the Khmer alphabet.

67. "Ph," or *phaa,* refers to the twenty-second consonant of the Khmer alphabet.

68. Craig Etcheson, personal communication, September 21, 2012. I am extremely grateful for his generosity in sharing his insights with me. For a detailed description, see Ovesen and Trankell, *Cambodians and Their Doctors,* pp. 107–108.

69. See, among others, Marie Alexandrine Martin, "L'Industrie Dans le Kampuchea Démocratique (1975–1978)," *Études Rurales,* nos. 89/91 (Jan.–Sep. 1983): 77–110.

70. Laurence Picq, the French wife of a Khmer foreign ministry official, describes her work in the foreign ministry "agriculture support unit" in detail. See Picq, *Beyond the Horizon.*

71. Ovesen and Trankell, *Cambodians and Their Doctors,* p. 93.

72. Ibid., pp. 95–96.

73. Ibid., p. 97.

74. Ibid., p. 99.

75. Becker, *When the War Was Over,* pp. 247–253; Kiernan, *Pol Pot Regime,* p. 417.

76. Interview 12PL01, Pailin, October 8, 2012.

77. Ibid.

78. Extraordinary Chambers in the Courts of Cambodia, Closing Order of Case File No. 002/19-09-2007-ECCC-OCIJ, p. 31.

79. Formally, the two ministries remained separate, but in terms of authority relations, they were both unambiguously under Yun Yat. Interview 13PL01, Pailin, January 4, 2013.

80. Extraordinary Chambers in the Courts of Cambodia, Transcript of Trial Proceedings, Case File No. 002/19-09-2007-ECCC/TC, March 29, 2012, p. 10.

81. Extraordinary Chambers in the Courts of Cambodia, Closing Order of Case File No. 002/19-09-2007-ECCC-OCIJ, pp. 32–33.

82. Interview 12PL01, Pailin, October 8, 2012.

83. Extraordinary Chambers in the Courts of Cambodia, Closing Order of Case File No. 002/19-09-2007-ECCC-OCIJ, p. 92.

84. "D," or *daa,* refers to the eleventh consonant of the Khmer alphabet.

85. "Y," or *you,* refers to the twenty-sixth consonant of the Khmer alphabet.

86. Extraordinary Chambers in the Courts of Cambodia, Closing Order of Case File No. 002/19-09-2007-ECCC-OCIJ, p. 92.

87. "T," or *da*, refers to the sixteenth consonant of the Khmer alphabet.

88. Extraordinary Chambers in the Courts of Cambodia, Closing Order of Case File No. 002/19-09-2007-ECCC-OCIJ, p. 92.; Martin, "L'Industrie Dans le Kampuchea Démocratique," 83.

89. Ibid., 88; Gunnar Bergström, *Living Hell: Democratic Kampuchea, August 1978* (Phnom Penh: DC-CAM, 2008). It is important to note that this source draws exclusively from a friendship delegation tour of DK, and the factories Bergström visited may have been Potemkin showpieces, as he belatedly acknowledges.

90. Martin, "L'Industrie Dans le Kampuchea Démocratique," 92.

91. Ibid., 103.

92. Ibid., 94.

93. Interview 13PL02, Pailin, January 5, 2013.

94. Interview 12PP01B, Phnom Penh, January 31, 2012; interview with Rochoem Tun (a.k.a. Phi Puon, Chiem), DC-CAM, Promoting Accountability Project, December 19, 2010.

95. Gold was sent directly to 870.

96. Interview 13AV02, Anlong Veng, January 3, 2013.

97. Interview 13PL02, Pailin, January 5, 2013.

98. Interview 13AV02, Anlong Veng, January 3, 2013.

99. Marie Alexandrine Martin, "Le Problème des Transports sous le Régime des Khmers Rouges," *Études Rurales*, No. 103/104 (Jul.–Dec. 1986): 209.

100. Ibid., 207.

101. Ibid.

102. Interview 10PP02A, Phnom Penh, March 13, 2010.

103. There is still some ambiguity surrounding the Ministry of Public Works and railway construction. From an organizational standpoint, it makes more sense to place it under Industry because it was a more centralized operation than many Public Works projects.

104. Interview 12PL01, Pailin, October 8, 2012.

105. Martin, "Le Problème des Transports," 215.

106. DC-CAM/TSL nos. 1555, 2685, 5230, 6872, 7528, 7548, 9726, 2759, 3193, 11911.

107. "S," or *saa*, refers to the thirtieth consonant of the Khmer alphabet.

108. Corfield and Summers, *Historical Dictionary of Cambodia*, p. 432; Interview 12PL01, Pailin, October 8, 2012.

109. Craig Etcheson, personal communication, September 21, 2012.

110. Kiernan, *Pol Pot Regime*, p. 437.

111. Ibid., p. 327.

112. Ke Pauk, "Ke Pauk's Autobiography from 1949–1985."

CHAPTER 3

1. Becker, *When the War Was Over*, p. 285.

2. Document associated with November 2011 interviews in China.

3. This demographic is beautifully represented in Xinran, "Pioneers of China's Oil: A Distinguished Husband and Wife," in *China Witness: Voices from a Silent Generation* (New York: Pantheon, 2008). It provides an excellent representation of this group of people; I thank William Willmott for bringing this to my attention.

4. Interview 11LY02, Luoyang, November 15, 2011.

5. Interview 11BJ01A, Beijing, October 16, 2011.

6. Chandler, *Voices from S-21*, p. 139.

7. Interviews 12KC01–12KC03, Kampong Cham, January 4, 2012.

8. Interview 11BJ01C, Beijing, November 12, 2011.

9. Helen Grant Ross and Darryl Leon Collins, *Building Cambodia: "New Khmer Architecture,"* *1953–1970* (Bangkok: Key, 2006).

10. Interview 10PP02A, Phnom Penh, March 13, 2010.

11. Interview 12KC02, Kampong Cham, January 4, 2012.

12. Interview 13PP01, Phnom Penh, January 1, 2013.

13. Interview 11BJ01C, Beijing, November 12, 2011.

14. Interview 11LY01B, Luoyang, November 15, 2001, and associated documents.

15. Interview 12PP01B, Phnom Penh, December 31, 2012.

16. Interview with Van Rith in Khpop commune, S'ang district, Kandal province, February 20, 2003, by Youk Chhang, DC-CAM, available at http://www.d.dccam.org/Archives/Interviews/Sample_Interviews/Former_Kh_Rouge/Van_Rith.htm, accessed August 10, 2013.

17. Short, *Pol Pot*, pp. 301–302, citing a document from the Vietnamese archives, Document 32 (N442/T8300).

18 Meeting Minutes of the Standing Committee of the Communist Party of Kampuchea, February 28, 1976, DC-CAM, Documents D00690 and D00683.

19. Part of this has to do with the perennial Chinese practice of splitting up, merging, and then splitting up again and reconfiguring bureaucracies over time. In the period examined here, the foreign relations ministries were being reshuffled after having been separated out from one another (and, then, subsequently, they would be combined again). Today, these include the Ministry of Commerce, the Ministry of Foreign Affairs, the Ministry of Finance, the Export-Import Bank (Eximbank), the Ministry of Transportation, the Ministry of Health, the Ministry of Education, the Ministry of Agriculture, the Ministry of Culture, the State Administration of Radio Film and Telecom, the Ministry of Science and Technology, and the China Development Bank.

20. See Barry Naughton, "The Third Front: Defence Industrialization in the Chinese Interior," *China Quarterly* 115 (September 1988): 351–386.

21. Files 6 and 17, National Archives of Cambodia. Chinese-language documents remain uncatalogued at the National Archives of Cambodia. I list the number of the box in which the document is housed in order to provide some degree of identification. In all, there are, at my last count, thirty-two boxes of primarily Chinese-language materials, almost all of which are devoted to blueprints and shipping documents in the service of civilian and some military infrastructure projects during the DK period. Although they are extremely technical in nature, requiring considerable expertise to translate and to understand, their sheer volume alone attests to the substantial amount of Chinese assistance to the DK regime.

22. Interview by John Ciorciari of Saom, Popeay village, Kampong Thom province, March 20, 2003. Audio transcript available at DC-CAM.

23. Ibid.

24. Interview 12TKM01, Ta Khmau, December 30, 2012.

25. Interview by John Ciorciari of Sao Yon, Samnanh village, Kandal province, March 27, 2003. Audio transcript available at DC-CAM.

26. Interview 11LY01C, Luoyang, November 16, 2011.

27. Martin, "L'Industrie Dans le Kampuchea Démocratique," 87.

28. Interview by John Ciorciari of Kan, Trach village, Kampong Thom province, March 21, 2003. Audio transcript available at DC-CAM.

29. Throughout the history of the PRC, the foreign economic relations bureaucracy and the foreign trade bureaucracies have intermittently been separated from or folded into one another. From June 1970 until March 1982, the Ministry of Foreign Economic

Relations was separate from the MoFT. After March 1982, they were combined into Ministry of Foreign Economic Relations and Trade, now Ministry of Commerce. Both of these were—and remain—separate from the MoFA (Ministry of Foreign Affairs).

30. Interview 11BJ01B, Beijing, October 21, 2011. Of course, a more prosaic reason might be that the facilities were damaged or operating only at partial capacity. China exported eight thousand tons of diesel fuel from Dalian, some of which was used to power these electric plants. The DK Ministry of Commerce decided how to distribute the imported diesel.

31. On *chuizhi guanli,* see Andrew C. Mertha, "China's "Soft" Centralization."

32. Interview 11LY02B, Luoyang, November 15, 2011.

33. They are now combined into a single body called the Economics and Trade Department (*jingshang chu*). Interview 11BJ01D, Beijing, November 19, 2011.

34. Interview 11LY01C, Luoyang, November 16, 2011.

35. Interview 11BJ01D, Beijing, November 19, 2011.

36. Interview 11LY01C, Luoyang, November 16, 2011.

37. These matters were far more commonly parsed together through indirect means, such as the showing of previously banned movies like the *Dream of the Red Chamber.* Movies flown in weekly from China were the primary form of entertainment for Chinese workers and embassy staff.

38. Diary of Chinese technician, "Meeting of the Chinese Communist Party Committee of the Kampong Som Technical Team," December 1, 1978. In author's possession.

39. Because of the lack of skilled Cambodian workers, China had to send its own skilled worker corps as well as technicians to Democratic Kampuchea (Interview 11LY01C, Luoyang, November 16, 2011).

40. Interview 11LY01B, Luoyang, November 15, 2001.

41. The remainder of this section relies on documents associated with Interviews 11BJ01A–D, Beijing, October–November, 2011.

42. All the names of the Chinese workers on the Kampong Som project have been changed.

CHAPTER 4

1. Short, *Pol Pot,* pp. 301–302, citing a document from the Vietnamese archives, Doc 32 (N442/T8300).

2. Picq, *Beyond the Horizon,* p. 46.

3. Interview 10PP02A, Phnom Penh, March 13, 2010.

4. Not all of these purged Eastern Zone cadres would be taken to S-21 for interrogation and torture. Sometimes there was so much going on at S-21 that there was literally no room for these new prisoners; in such cases they were sent directly to be executed at the killing grounds at Choeung Ek. See Chandler, *Voices from S-21.*

5. Thomas Fuller, "Khmer Rouge Killing Field Now a Projected Cargo Hub: In Cambodia, a Runway Forever Awash in Blood," *New York Times,* June 18, 1999, available at www.nytimes.com/1999/06/18/news/18iht-phnom.2.t_0.html, accessed April 9, 2010.

6. "'The Number'—Quantifying Crimes against Humanity in Cambodia," DC-CAM, available at www.mekong.net/cambodia/toll.htm#fn11, accessed April 9, 2010.

7. During 1976, the situation was quite different: the privileged Khmer Rouge soldiers who made up the work force lived alongside the Chinese management team. Interview 10PP02C, Phnom Penh, June 13, 2010.

8. Interview 10PP02A, Phnom Penh, March 13, 2010; and Cambodia Tribunal Monitor, available at www.cambodiatribunal.org/index.php?option=com_content&view=artic le&id=8&Itemid=9, accessed March 24, 2010.

9. Interview 10PP02A, Phnom Penh, March 13, 2010.

10. Fuller, "Khmer Rouge Killing."

11. "Investor Alert: List of Unauthorised Websites / Investment Products / Companies / Individuals," Securities Commission Malaysia, available at www.sc.com.my/main.asp?pageid=1032&menuid=272&newsid=&linkid=&type=, accessed February 15, 2012; "Board of Directors site visit at Kampong Chhnang Airport (Jan 19, 2010)," Kampong Chhnang Int'l Airport website, available at http://kciairport.weebly.com/index.html, accessed February 15, 2012.

12. Of course, one can argue that DK policy privileged the military, which was reflected in Pol Pot's strong negotiating position, thereby explaining part of this variation. But, as will become clear in chapter 5, the Kampong Som refinery was the keystone of Sino-DK projects, reflecting Pol Pot's (and China's) goals for the country, and it was allowed to atrophy. Thus, elite interests alone do not provide a persuasive explanation.

13. Richardson, *China, Cambodia, and the Five Principles of Peaceful Coexistence*, p. 87.

14. Blueprint for the Buguoshan Radar Site, August 1976, Cambodian National Archives, "China" File 13.

15. Meeting Minutes on Propaganda Work, June 1, 1976, in author's possession; Meeting Minutes of the Standing Committee of the Communist Party of Kampuchea, October 9, 1975, DC-CAM, Document D00677.

16. Meeting Minutes of the Standing Committee of the Communist Party of Kampuchea, October 9, 1975, DC-CAM, Document D00677.

17. Meeting Minutes of the Standing Committee of the Communist Party of Kampuchea, February 28, 1976, DC-CAM, Documents D00690 and D00683.

18. Meeting Minutes of the Standing Committee of the Communist Party of Kampuchea, August 3, 1976, DC-CAM, Document N0001374.

19. Kiernan, *Pol Pot Regime,* pp. 132–133.

20. Meeting Minutes of the Discussions with Team of Chinese Military Experts, September 24, 1976, DC-CAM, Document L01514.

21. Interview by Phan Sochea and Ea Meng Try of Sreng Thi, DC-CAM, October 24, 2003, p. 3.

22. Interview by John Ciorciari of Mai Oeun, Chamkar Tanget village, Kandal province March 27, 2003. Audio transcript available at DC-CAM.

23. This interviewee also pointedly noted that whenever the Chinese military advisers arrived at the airport, for example, there were never any Chinese embassy representatives, only Cambodians. Interview 13PP01, Phnom Penh, January 1, 2013.

24. Ibid.

25. Interview by John Ciorciari of Loy Unn, Trach village, Kampong Thom province, March 21, 2003. Audio transcript available at DC-CAM.

26. Interview by Phan Sochea and Ea Meng Try of Sreng Thi, DC-CAM, October 24, 2003, p. 13.

27. Meeting Minutes of the Standing Committee of the Communist Party of Kampuchea, October 9, 1975. DC-CAM, Document D00677.

28. Further extending this into military shipyard construction, Pol Pot said that DK should send people to learn every aspect of port construction and maintenance and even granted them about five months to do so but, once again invoking Cambodian self-sufficiency, insisted that they should quietly pilot back boats from China without bringing any Chinese technicians with them.

29. Meeting Minutes of the Standing Committee of the Communist Party of Kampuchea, October 9, 1975, DC-CAM, Document D00677.

30. Ibid.

31. Ibid.

32. Summary of DK Standing Committee Decisions, April 19–21, 1976, DC-CAM, Document D00695. Many of these purged Eastern Zone cadres would be taken to *Santebal-21*, the centralized torture and execution way station in Phnom Penh, better known by its moniker *Tuol Sleng* or *Santebal-21/S-21*, for interrogation and torture. For the best analysis by far on S-21/Tuol Sleng, see Chandler, *Voices from S-21*, 1999.

33. Luke Hunt, "What Was China's Khmer Rouge Role?" *The Diplomat*, December 17, 2011, available at http://thediplomat.com/2011/12/17/what-was-china's-khmer-rouge-role/, accessed December 19, 2011.

34. Summary of DK Standing Committee Decisions, April 19–21, 1976, DC-CAM, Document D00695.

35. This was especially true after having set precedents of arresting and killing zone leaders, as with Ney Saran (a.k.a. Ya), who led the Northeast Zone until his arrest in 1976. Ya appears to have been arrested and replaced without much difficulty, but that is likely due in part to the fact that he was one of the first to be purged. Colm and Sim, *Khmer Rouge Purges in the Mondul Kiri Highlands*, esp. ch. 6.

36. Ke Pauk, "Ke Pauk's Autobiography from 1949–1985."

37. Becker, *When the War Was Over*, 1986, p. 240.

38. Ke Pauk, "Ke Pauk's Autobiography from 1949–1985."

39. Fabienne Luco, "Between a Tiger and a Crocodile," UNESCO, May 2008, p. 64, available at http://unesdoc.unesco.org/images/0015/001595/159544e.pdf, accessed August 18, 2012.

40. "Transcript of Trial Proceedings Public," Extraordinary Chambers in the Courts of Cambodia, July 20, 2012, Case File 002/19-09-2007-ECCC/TC, pp. 122–123, available at www.eccc.gov.kh/sites/default/files/documents/courtdoc/E1_93.1_TR002_20120720_Final_EN_Pub.pdf, accessed August 18, 2012.

41. Leng Kim (a.k.a. Kung Kim), interviewed in Chiep commune, Toek Phoh district, Kampung [Kampong] Chhnang province, on July 9, 2002, by Ysa Osman, Vanthan Peou Dara, and Phann Sochea. DC-CAM, Document KHI0038/I3939.

42. Ibid.

43. Documents in author's possession.

44. "Request for Opening a New Investigation of So Met and Meas Mut," available at the Investigative Fund website, www.theinvestigativefund.org/files/managed/Cambodia 2nd_Intro_Submission.pdf, accessed July 24, 2012.

45. Ibid.

46. David Shambaugh, *Modernizing China's Military: Progress, Problems, and Prospects* (Berkeley: University of California Press, 2002), pp. 125–126.

47. "Xunlian diji Zhongguo jiefang jun guofang kexue jishu gongye weiyuanhui lishi ceke congshu" [*Training bases of the Chinese People's Liberation Army National Defense Science, Technology and Industry Committee History Information Division Series*], pp. 461–462.

48. Interview with Som Sokhân, Toek Neung village, Chrey Vien commune, Prey Chhor district, Kampong Cham province, August 23, 2003, DC-CAM, Document KCI0441/I03382.

49. Interview 10PP02A, Phnom Penh, March 13, 2010.

50. Interview 12KC01, Kampong Cham, January 4, 2012.

51. Interview 12KC03, Kampong Cham, January 4, 2012.

52. Interview 12KC01, Kampong Cham, January 4, 2012.

53. Interview 12KC02, Kampong Cham, January 4, 2012.

54. Interviews 12KC01, 12KC02, and 12KC03, Kampong Cham, January 4, 2012.

55. Interview 12KC01, Kampong Cham, January 4, 2012.

56. Interview 12KC02, Kampong Cham, January 4, 2012.

57. Interview 10PP02B, Phnom Penh, March 20, 2010.

58. Interview 10PP02A, Phnom Penh, March 13, 2010.

59. Interview 12KC01, Kampong Cham, January 4, 2012.

60. Interviews 12KC01, 12KC02, and 12KC03, Kampong Cham, January 4, 2012.

61. Becker, *When the War Was Over,* pp. 306–308.

62. Ibid., p. 306.

63. Ben Kiernan, "Cambodia: The Eastern Zone Massacres, A Report on Social Conditions and Human Rights Violations in the Eastern Zone of Democratic Kampuchea under the Rule of Pol Pot's (Khmer Rouge) Communist Party of Kampuchea," Columbia University Center for the Study of Human Rights Documentation Series: no. 1, p. 11.

64. Summary of DK Standing Committee Decisions, April 19–21, 1976, DC-CAM, Document D00695.

65. Interview 12KC03, Kampong Cham, January 4, 2012.

66. Interview with An Han, Amleang [Om Leong] commune, Thpong district, Kampong Speu province (undated). Audio transcript available at DC-CAM.

67. Interview with Som Sokhân, Toek Neung village, Chrey Vien commune, Prey Chhor district, Kampong Cham province, August 23, 2003, DC-CAM, Document KCI0441/I03382; interview with Leng Kim (a.k.a. Kung Kim), Chiep commune, Toek Phoh district, Kampung Chhnang province, July 9, 2002, DC-CAM, Document KHI0038/I3939.

CHAPTER 5

1. Diary of Chinese technician, "Meeting of the Chinese Communist Party Committee of the Kampong Som Technical Team," December 1, 1978.

2. Richard Linnett and Roberto Loiederman, *The Eagle Mutiny* (Annapolis, MD: Naval Institute Press, 2001); Ralph Wetterhahn, *The Last Battle: The Mayaguez Incident and the End of the Vietnam War* (New York: Carroll and Graf, 2001).

3. Interview 11BJ01B, Beijing, October 20, 2011.

4. This is in contrast to a number of the DK factories, which retained older, skilled workers from the earlier regime. Interview 12TKM01, Ta Khmau, December 30, 2012.

5. Moeung with Locard, *Prisoner of the Khmer Rouge,* p. 31.

6. Ibid., p. 33.

7. Ibid., pp. 38–39.

8. Ibid., p. 45.

9. Locard, "Khmer Rouge Gulag," p. 6.

10. Interview 11BJ01A, Beijing, October 16, 2011.

11. Ibid.

12. Interview 11LY02, Luoyang, November 15, 2011.

13. See Naughton, "Third Front."

14. Interview 11BJ01B, Beijing, October 20, 2011.

15. Diary of Chinese technician, "Managerial Meeting at Kampong Som," December 12, 1978.

16. Meeting Minutes of DK Military, August 2, 1976, DC-CAM, Document L01373, emphasis mine.

17. Diary of Chinese technician, "Meeting in Kampong Some to Discuss Construction Issues," December 8, 1978.

18. Diary of Chinese technician, "Technical Meeting at Kampong Som Refinery," December 11, 1978.

19. Diary of Chinese technician, "Initial Observations," November 21, 1978.

20. Diary of Chinese technician, "Meeting at Kampong Som Refinery to Discuss Medical Issues," December 9, 1978.

21. Diary of Chinese technician, "Technical Meeting at Kampong Som Refinery," December 11, 1978.

22. Diary of Chinese technician, "Managerial Meeting at Kampong Som," December 12, 1978.

23. Interview 11LY01B, Luoyang, November 15, 2001.

24. Sophearith Chuong, "Excerpts from the Confession of Tuon Sokh Phala," *Searching for Truth* 32 (Phnom Penh: DC-CAM, August 2002): 3.

25. DC-CAM Documents TSL 9957; TSL 10465;, TSL 3024; TSL 5027; TSL 6527; TSL 8218; TSL 9044; TSL 10749; TSL 11441; TSL 11620; TSL 694; and TSL 728.

26. Minutes of Meeting on Public Works, March 10, 1976, DC-CAM, Document D00686.

27. Extraordinary Chambers in the Courts of Cambodia, Closing Order of Case File No. 002/19-09-2007-ECCC-OCIJ, pp. 217, 238.

28. Kiernan, *Pol Pot Regime*, p. 437.

29. Etcheson Report, p. 35.

30. Diary of Chinese technician, "Managerial Meeting at Kampong Som," December 12, 1978.

31. Extraordinary Chambers in the Courts of Cambodia, Closing Order of Case File No. 002/19-09-2007-ECCC-OCIJ, pp. 23–24.

32. Diary of Chinese technician, "Work Meeting to Discuss Problems at Kampong Som," December 13, 1978. In author's possession.

33. Diary of Chinese technician, "Managerial Meeting at Kampong Som," December 12, 1978. These are all based on Chinese approximations of the Khmer names.

34. Ibid.

35. Diary of Chinese technician, "Technical Meeting at Kampong Som Refinery," December 14, 1978.

36. Ibid.

37. For an elite-level perspective of this same period, see Kenneth Lieberthal and Michel Oksenberg, *Policy Making in China: Leaders, Structures, and Processes* (Princeton, NJ: Princeton University Press, 1988), ch. 5.

38. Everything changed when shallow oil deposits were discovered in Daqing in 1958. Oil production was up and running by 1960; by 1972, it was producing 50 million tons of oil.

39. Interview 11LY01A, Luoyang, November 15, 2011.

40. Ibid.

41. Mao Zedong, *tingqu Gu Mu Yu Qiuli huibao jihua gongzuo shi de zhishi* [Instructions given upon hearing Gu Mu and Yu Qiuli report on planning work], Mao Zedong Sixiang Wansui [*Long Live Mao Zedong Thought*], pp. 605–606.

42. Interviews 11LY01A and 11LY02, Luoyang, November 15, 2011.

43. *Zhonghua renmin gongheguo zhongyang zhengfu jigou 1949–1990* [Central party and government organizations of the People's Republic of China, 1949–1990], *jingji kexue chubanshe*, 1993, p. 98; Interview 11LY02, Luoyang, November 15, 2011.

44. *Zhonghua renmin gongheguo zhongyang zhengfu jigou 1949–1990*, p. 104.

45. Ibid., p. 105.

46. Ibid., pp. 44, 116–120.

47. Interviews 11LY01A and 11LY02, Luoyang, November 15, 2011.

48. Ibid.

49. Ibid.

50. Diary of Chinese technician, "Notes on Presentation of Findings to Ambassador Sun Hao," December 22, 1978.

51. As noted, all surnames are pseudonyms.

52. Diary of Chinese technician, "Technical Meeting at Kampong Som Refinery," December 11, 1978.

53. Diary of Chinese technician, "Meeting in Kampong Som to Discuss Construction Issues," December 8, 1978.

54. Ibid.

55. Ibid.

56. Ibid.

57. Diary of Chinese technician, "Meeting in Kampong Som to Discuss Construction Issues," December 9, 1978.

58. Interviews 11LY01B, November 15, 2011; Interview 11LY01C, Luoyang, November 16, 2011.

59. Going against the rules, other foreign Chinese assistance teams in Cambodia began telephoning one another about evacuation plans, with many of them converging on Kampong Som. Interview 11LY01C, Luoyang, November 16, 2011. See also Shui Yun, "An Account of Chinese Diplomats Accompanying the Government of Democratic Kampuchea's Move to the Cardamom Mountains," trans. Paul Marks, *Critical Asian Studies* 34, no. 4 (December 2002).

60. According to one interviewee, Ieng Sary's sale of these items (and pocketing of the money) in the mid-1990s created the final rift between him and the Pol Pot faction of the Khmer Rouge. Interview 13PL04, Pailin, January 5, 2013.

61. Interviews 11LY01B, Luoyang, November 15, 2011; Interview 11LY01C, Luoyang, November 16, 2011.

CHAPTER 6

1. David P. Chandler, Ben Kiernan, and Chanthou Boua, *Pol Pot Plans the Future: Confidential Leadership Documents from Democratic Kampuchea, 1976–1977,* New Haven, CT: Yale Southeast Asia Studies Monograph 33, 1988, p. 47.

2. Kiernan, *Pol Pot Regime,* p. 130. Shipping records at the Cambodian National Archives suggest that this shipment of salt was delivered on May 15, not April 20.

3. *The Complete Register of Imports from China in 1975, Ministry of Commerce,* Cambodian National Archives, File B-1, Number 2, December 30, 1975, p. 6.

4. Interview by John Ciorciari of Loy Unn, Trach village, Kampong Thom province, March 21, 2003. Audio transcript available at DC-CAM.

5. For a comparison of this dynamic in a similar but contemporary Chinese context, see Andrew C. Mertha, *China's Water Warriors: Citizen Action and Policy Change* (Ithaca, NY: Cornell University Press, 2008), pp. 7–8.

6. Interview with Van Rith in Khpop commune, S'ang district, Kandal province, February 20, 2003 by Youk Chhang, DC-CAM, available at http://www.d.dccam.org/Archives/Interviews/Sample_Interviews/Former_Kh_Rouge/Van_Rith.htm, accessed August 10, 2013.

7. Standing Committee of the Communist Party of Kampuchea, March 13, 1976, DC-CAM, Document D00691.

8. Summary of Decision of the Standing Committee of the Communist Party of Kampuchea, April 19–21, 1976, DC-CAM, Document D00695.

9. DK Ministry of Commerce Document No. OI BOTRA/76, Cambodian National Archives, File B-20, June 25, 1976.

10. Minutes of Second Meeting of the DK Council of Ministers, May 31, 1976, DC-CAM, Document D00705.

11. Interview with Van Rith in Khpop commune, S'ang district, Kandal province, February 20, 2003, by Youk Chhang, DC-CAM, available at http://www.d.dccam.org/Archives/Interviews/Sample_Interviews/Former_Kh_Rouge/Van_Rith.htm, accessed August 10, 2013.

12. Ibid.

13. Meeting Minutes of the Standing Committee of the Communist Party of Kampuchea, May 7, 1976, DC-CAM, Document D00697.

14. The address was Ford, Kwan & Company, Chiu Lung Building, 15–23 Chiu Lung Street, 6th Floor, Victoria, Hong Kong.

15. San Sok was eventually recalled to Phnom Penh and executed (he is listed as having resigned from *Ren Fung* on July 5, 1978). He was replaced by the head of the ports committee at Kampong Som, Yim Krinn. Honat is listed as having resigned on November 13, 1978, and killed soon after. The seven thousand shares from San Sok and Honat were transferred to Yim Krinn on November 27, 1978.

16. Interview with Van Rith in Khpop commune, S'ang district, Kandal province, February 20, 2003, by Youk Chhang, DC-CAM, available at www.dccam.org/Archives/Interviews/Sample_Interviews/Former_Kh_Rouge/Van_Rith.htm, accessed May 3, 2011.

17. "Transcript of Trial Proceedings Public," Case File 002/19-09-2007-ECCC/TC, Extraordinary Chambers in the Courts of Cambodia, June 5, 2012, available at www.eccc.gov.kh/sites/default/files/documents/courtdoc/E1_81.1_TR002_20120605_Final_EN_Pub.pdf, accessed April 7, 2013.

18. Interview with Van Rith in Khpop commune, S'ang district, Kandal province, February 20, 2003 by Youk Chhang, DC-CAM, available at www.dccam.org/Archives/Interviews/Sample_Interviews/Former_Kh_Rouge/Van_Rith.htm, accessed May 3, 2011.

19. Martin, "L'Industrie Dans le Kampuchea Démocratique," 106.

20. Meeting Minutes of the Standing Committee of the Communist Party of Kampuchea, August 3, 1976, DC-CAM, Document N0001374. For the spelling of *Yong Kang,* I use the original source Romanization of the time to maintain consistency.

21. Meeting Minutes of the June 26, 1977, Meeting with Communications Delegation from China, Cambodian National Archives 13, box 2.

22. Ibid.

23. Another safety related issue that arose in the meeting was the proper loading procedures and arrangements. The Chinese delegation stressed that the ship must be balanced; for example, it would not sail smoothly if its upper part was too heavy and its lower part was too light. If the goods became endangered, for example by fire, then the ship should take special measures like storing as much water as possible in the lower part of the ship to avoid their being burned. Items that could not be loaded in the lower part of the ship were to be loaded in its upper part; in the event of danger, then those goods could easily be disposed of. The two sides agreed that the ship captain must consider these issues carefully.

24. Cambodian National Archives, File 43, B-06.

25. Report on meeting between Comrade Ieng Sary and Commerce delegates of People's Republic of China (DC-CAM, Document 127) and Report on debate between commerce delegates of Democratic Kampuchea and those of People's Republic of China on December 3rd, 1978 (DC-CAM, Document 132).

26. Democratic Kampuchea Ministry of Commerce, "Using Credit of 140 Million Yuan," October 31, 1977, Cambodian National Archives, File 43, B-06.

27. Cambodian National Archives, File F-74, B-17.

CHAPTER 7

1. Richard Dawkins, *The God Delusion* (New York: Houghton Mifflin, 2006), pp. 204–205.

2. Norbert Klein, "China Provides Additional Aid and Loans of US$1.2 Billion to Develop the Cambodian Economy—Tuesday, 22.12.2009," *Cambodia Mirror,* December 23,

2009, available at http://www.cambodiamirror.org/2009/12/23/china-provides-additional-aid-and-loans-of-us1-2-billion-to-develop-the-cambodian-economy-tuesday-22-12-2009/, accessed August 10, 2013.

3. Mertha, *China's Water Warriors*, ch. 2.

4. Heng Pheakdey, "Cambodia-China Relations: A Positive-Sum Game?" *Journal of Current Southeast Asian Affairs* 2 (2012): 57-85.

5. "Cambodian, Chinese Defense Ministers Ink Military Cooperation Pact," China Defense Blog, May 29, 2012, available at http://china-defense.blogspot.com/2012/05/cambodian-chinese-defense-ministers-ink.html, accessed August 7, 2012.

6. Men Kimseng, "China Offers $20 Million in Military Aid Ahead of Asean Meeting," Voice of America Khmer, May 29, 2012, available at www.voacambodia.com/content/china-offers-20-million-in-military-aid-ahead-of-asean-meeting-155432515/1356122.html, accessed August 7, 2012.

7. Bräutigam, *Dragon's Gift*, p. 11.

8. Daniel C. O'Neill, "Risky Business: The Political Economy of China's Outward Foreign Direct Investment," PhD dissertation, Department of Political Science, Washington University, 2010.

9. Sophal Ear, *Aid Dependence in Cambodia: How Foreign Assistance Undermines Democracy* (New York: Columbia University Press, 2012); Sigfrido Burgos Caceres and Sophal Ear, *The Hungry Dragon: How China's Resource Quest Is Reshaping the World* (London: Routledge, 2013), esp. ch. 5.

10. Graham T. Allison, "Conceptual Models and the Cuban Missile Crisis," *American Political Science Review* 63 (1969): 689–718.

11. Kenneth Lieberthal and Michel Oksenberg, *Bureaucratic Politics and Chinese Energy Development,* Washington, DC: U.S. Department of Commerce, International Trade Administration, U.S. Government Printing Office, 1986; Lieberthal and Oksenberg, *Policy Making in China.*

12. Kjeld Erik Brødsgaard, "'Fragmented Authoritarianism' or 'Integrated Fragmentation?'" and Nis Grünberg, "Revisiting Fragmented Authority in China's Central Energy Administration," papers presented at the panel "China's Fragmented Authoritarianism: An Outdated Notion?" 2013 Annual Conference of the Association for Asian Studies, San Diego, California, March 24, 2013.

13. Grünberg, "Revisiting Fragmented Authority," p. 6.

14. Ibid., p. 5.

15. Ibid., p. 3.

16. Elisabeth Bumiller and Michael Wines, "Test of Stealth Fighter Clouds Gates Visit to China," *New York Times,* January 11, 2011, available at www.nytimes.com/2011/01/12/world/asia/12fighter.html, accessed April 6, 2013.

17. Michael Swaine, "China's Assertive Behavior—Part Three: The Role of the Military in Foreign Policy," Hoover Institution, China Leadership Monitor, no. 36, January 6, 2012, p. 8, available at http://media.hoover.org/sites/default/files/documents/CLM36MS.pdf, accessed June 23, 2013.

18. Michael Swaine, "China's Assertive Behavior—Part Four: The Role of the Military in Foreign Crises," Hoover Institution, China Leadership Monitor, no. 37, April 30, 2012, p. 8, available at http://media.hoover.org/sites/default/files/documents/CLM37MS.pdf, accessed June 23, 2013.

19. Thom Shanker and Mark Mazzetti, "China and U.S. Clash on Naval Fracas," *New York Times,* March 10, 2009, available at www.nytimes.com/2009/03/11/world/asia/11military.html, accessed June 23, 2013.

20. Edward Wong, "Chinese Civilian Boats Roil Disputed Waters," *New York Times,* October 5, 2010, available at www.nytimes.com/2010/10/06/world/asia/06beijing.html,

accessed April 6, 2013; Robert Mackey, "Leaked Video Shows Clash at Sea between Chinese and Japanese Ships," *New York Times,* November 5, 2010, available at http://thelede.blogs.nytimes.com/2010/11/05/leaked-video-shows-clash-at-sea-between-chinese-and-japanese-ships/, accessed April 6, 2013.

21. Swaine, "China's Assertive Behavior—Part Four," p. 7.

22. Mandiant, "Exposing One of China's Cyber Espionage Units," available at http://intelreport.mandiant.com/Mandiant_APT1_Report.pdf, accessed April 7, 2013.

23. Ka Zeng and Andrew Mertha, "Introduction," in *China's Foreign Trade Policy: The New Constituencies,* ed. Ka Zeng (London: Routledge, 2007), pp. 1–19.

24. Andrew Mertha and Ka Zeng, "Political Institutions, Local Resistance, and China's Harmonization with International Law," *China Quarterly* 182 (June 2005): 319–337; Wei Liang, "China's WTO Negotiation Process and its Implications," *Journal of Contemporary China* 11, no. 33 (2002): 683–719.

25. Sebastian Strangio, "Ghosts of the Killing Fields," *South China Morning Post,* June 27, 2011, available at www.sebastianstrangio.com/2011/06/27/ghosts-of-the-killing-fields/, accessed June 23, 2013; Sok Khemara, "In Battambang, Two Tribunal Suspects Remain Elusive," Voice of America Khmer, October 25, 2011, available at www.voacambodia.com/content/in-battambang-two-tribunal-suspects-remain-elusive-132538913/1358353.html, accessed April 7, 2013. Sou Met died on June 14, 2013.

Glossary of Selected Terms

Khmer

Selected Key Individuals

Cheng An	ចេង អន
Chhim Sophon (a.k.a. Touch)	ឈឹម សោភាន់ (ហៅ តូច)
Chhit Choeun (a.k.a. Ta Mok)	ឈិត ជឿន (ហៅ តាម៉ុក)
Hu Nim	ហ៊ូ នីម
Ieng Sary (a.k.a. Van)	អៀង សារី (ហៅ វ៉ាន់)
Ieng Thirith (a.k.a. Phea)	អៀង ធីរិទ្ធ (ហៅ ភា)
Kaing Guek Eev (a.k.a. Duch)	កាំងហ្គេច អ៊ាវ (ហៅ ឌុច)
Ke Pauk	កែ ពក
Khieu Samphan (a.k.a. Haem)	ខៀវ សំផន (ហៅ ហែម)
Koy Thuon (a.k.a. Tuch)	កុយ ធួន (ហៅ ទួច)
Lvei	ល្វៃ
Meas Mut (Khe Mut)	មាស មុត (ខេ មុត)
Mei Prang	ម៉ៃ ប្រាង
Muol Sambath (a.k.a. Nhem Ros)	មួល សម្បត្តិ (ហៅ ញឹម រស់)
Ney Saran (a.k.a. Ya)	ណេ សារ៉ាន់ (ហៅ យ៉ា)
Nuon Chea (b. 劉平坤)	នួន ជា
Nuon Suon	នួន ស្វន
Pang	ប៉ង់
Rochoem Tun (a.k.a. Phi Puon, Chiem)	រ៉ូជឹម ទុន (ហៅ ភី ភួន, ជៀម)
Ros Nhim	រស់ ញឹម

Saloth Sar (a.k.a. Pol Pot)   សាឡុត ស (ហៅ ប៉ុល ពត)

Sao Yann (a.k.a. So Phim/Sao Phim)   សៅ យ៉ាន់ (ហៅ សោ ភីម/សៅ ភីម)

Sar Kimlomouth   ស គឹមលួត

Soeu Vasy (a.k.a. Doeun)   ស្យើ វ៉ាស៊ី (ហៅ ឌឿន)

Sou Met   ស៊ូ ម៉េត

Sok Thuok (a.k.a. Vorn Vet, Von)   (ហៅ វ៉ន វ៉េត, ហៅ វន)

Son Sen (a.k.a. Khieu)   សុន សេន (ហៅ ខ្យេវ)

Tauch Pheaun (a.k.a. Phion)   តូច ភ្លួន (ហៅ ភ្លួន)

Thiounn Prasith   ធួន ប្រសិទ្ធ

Van Rith   វណ្ណ រិទ្ធ

Yun Yat (a.k.a. At)   យ៉ុន យ៉ាត (ហៅ អាត)

Place Names

Akreiy Ksatr   អរិយ៍ក្សត្រ

Anduang Teuk   អណ្ដូងទឹក

Anlong Knagn   អន្លង់ក្បាន

Baray   បារាយ

Baset   បាសែត

Bat Lang   បាត លាង

Boeng Trabek   បឹងត្របែក

Bokor   បូកគោ

Chakrey Ting   ចក្រីទីង

Chamkar Leu   ចំការលើ

Chamkar Mon   ចំការមន

Chamkar Tanget   ចំការតាង៉េត

Cheung Prey   ជើងប្រៃ

Chkae Pruh	ឆ្កែព្រុស
Chraing Chamreh	ច្រាំងចំរេះ
Chroy Changvar	ជ្រោយចង្វារ
Doha Kancho	ដោះកញ្ជរ
Kampong Chhnang	កំពង់ឆ្នាំង
Kampong Siem	កំពង់សៀម
Kampong Som/Sihanoukville	ក្រុងព្រះសីហនុ
Kampong Speu	កំពង់ស្ពឺ
Kampong Svay	កំពង់ស្វាយ
Kang Meas	កងមាស
Kbal Knal	ក្បាលខ្នល់
Kbal Toek	ក្បាលទឹក
Khmeraphoumin	ខេមរៈភូមិន្ទ
Kirirom	គីរីរម្យ
Koh Kong	កោះកុង
Koh Smach	កោះស្មាច់
Kramuon Sar	ក្រមួនសរ
Krang Leav	ក្រាំងលាវ
La Ban Siek	ឡាបានសៀក
Leay Bo	លាយបូ
Mondulkiri	មណ្ឌលគីរី
Om Leong Tbong	អមលាំងត្បូង
Palarng	ប៉ាឡ្បង
Phnom Pitch Nil	ភ្នំពិជនិល
Phnom Touch	ភ្នំតូច
Phnom Traom	ភ្នំគ្រុ

Phsar Touch	ផ្សារតូច
Prek Kdam	ព្រែកក្តាម
Prek Phneou	ព្រែកផ្ញៅ
Prek Prasap	ព្រែកប្រសព្វ
Prey Chhor	ព្រៃឈរ
Prey Kabas	ព្រៃកប្បាស
Prey Nup	ព្រៃនុប
Prey Sar	ព្រៃស
Ratanakiri	រតនគីរី
Samlaut	សំឡូត
Samrong	សំរោង
Santuk	សន្ទុក
Sdok Ach Romeas	ស្តុកអាច់រមាស
Steung Meanchey	ស្ទឹងមានជ័យ
Steung Treng	ស្ទឹងត្រែង
Stung	ស្ទោង
Svay Rieng	ស្វាយរៀង
Ta Khmau	តាខ្មៅ
Tang Kok	តាំងកោក
Thnàl Bèmbèk	ថ្នល់បំបែក
Tmat Porng	ត្មាតពង
Toek Phos	ទឹកផុស
Tram Kak	ត្រាំកក់
Trapaing Krâloeng	ត្រពាំងក្រឡឹង
Trapaing Run	ត្រពាំងរុន
Tuol Kork	ទួលគោក

Tuol Sangke	ទួលសង្កែ	
Uddor Meanchey	ឧត្ដរមានជ័យ	
Veal Renh	វាលរ៉ែញ	
Wat Chom Chao	វត្តចោមចៅ	
Wat Damnak	វត្តដំណាក់	
Wat Koh	វត្តកោះ	
Wat Kok Anhchanh	វត្តគោកអញ្ចាញ	
Wat Sampao Meas	វត្តសំពៅមាស	
Wat Unalom	វត្តឧណ្ណាឡោម	
Yim Krinn	យីម ក្រិន	

Administrative Levels

Angkar	អង្គការ	The Organization
Angkar Loeu	អង្គការលើ	The Center
Phumipheak	ភូមិភាគ	Zone
Phumipheak piseh	ភូមិភាគពិសេស	Zone under Central Administration
Damban	តំបន់	Region
Srok	ស្រុក	District
Khum	ឃុំ	Subdistrict
Sahakar	សហករណ៍	Cooperative
Phum	ភូមិ	Village

Selected Political Terms

Central Committee (Full-Rights) Members	សមាជិកមជ្ឈិមពេញសិទ្ធិ
Central Committee Candidate Members	សមាជិកត្រៀមនៃគណៈកម្មាធិការមជ្ឈិម
Central Committee "Reserve" Members	សមាជិកបំរុង
Central Committee Assistant Members	ជំនួយការគណៈកម្មាធិការ មជ្ឈិម

Anuprâthien	អនុប្រធាន	Vice Chair
Chhlop	ឈ្លប	Militia
Khsae	ខ្សែ	String
Kamaphibal	កម្មាភិបាល	Cadre
Kanak Kamatika	គណៈកម្មាធិការ	Committee
Kanak Montie (Munthi)	គណៈមន្ទីរ	Unit
Kanak Sethekec	គណៈសេដ្ឋកិច្ច	Committee "Steward"
Krasuong	ក្រសួង	Ministry
Khleang Roth	ឃ្លាំងរដ្ឋ	State Warehouse
Prâthien	ប្រធាន	Committee Chair
Sahachip	សហាជីព	Factory Unit
Santebal	សន្តិបាល	Prison/Processing Center
Tung Padevat	ទង់បដិវត្តន៍	*Revolutionary Flag*
Youveak Chon Youveak Neary Padevat	យុវជន យុវនារី បដិវត្តិន៍	*Revolutionary Youth*

Chinese

The Ministry of Foreign Affairs	外事部
The Ministry of Foreign Trade	对外贸易部
The Bureau of Foreign Economic Relations	对外经济联络总局
The Foreign Economic Relations Committee	对外经济联络委员会
The Third Front Construction	三线建设
The *Kelie* Natural Rubber Factory	克列天然橡胶制胶厂
The *Mianmo* Natural Rubber Factory	棉末天然橡胶制胶厂
The *Dabao* Natural Rubber Factory	大保/达包天然橡胶制胶厂
The Ministry of Chemical Industry	化学工业部

The Ministry Communications	交通部
The Ministry of Railways	铁道部
The Ministry of Hydropower and Electricity	水利电力部
The Phnom Penh Number One and Two Electricity Plants	金边火电厂, 金边第二电厂
The Ministry of Petroleum	石油部
Cangzhou Number Thirteen Construction Unit	沧州十三化建
The Lanzhou Petroleum Production Factory	兰州炼油厂
The Luoyang Petroleum Planning Institute	洛阳炼油厂设计院
Direct/centralized control	垂直管理
Personnel and Budgetary Allocations	编制
"Consultation Departments"	参处
Ren Fung (Ying Feng)	英丰

Index

aircraft, 44, 59, 79–83, 86, 93, 117. *See also*
    Krang Leav; RAK air force
Albania, 128
Angkar, 6, 20, 25, 35, 46
    Angkar Loeu, 25 (*see also* Office 870)
    Angkar Padevat, 25
Angkor, 1–2, 8, 30, 99
Anlong Veng, 142
Anti-Rightist Campaign, 58, 113
Arendt, Hanna, 20
artillery, 79–83, 85, 117
ASEAN, 133–134
asymmetry of power, 3–4, 9, 16, 78

Bangladesh, 126
"base" people, 24
Battambang, 8, 30, 38, 42, 49, 52–53, 83–84
bianzhi (budgetary/personnel allocations),
    66–67
broadcasting, 39, 45–47, 79, 92
Brzezinski, Zbigniew, 20

Cangzhou construction unit (Thirteen
    Huajian), 65, 101, 113, 115–116
centralization, 20, 31, 35–36, 39, 44, 55
    Democratic Kampuchea (DK) Military
        (Revolutionary Army of Kampuchea), 87,
        89, 91, 95, 97
    DK Ministry of Commerce, 48
    DK Ministry of Defense, 40–41
    DK Ministry of Foreign Affairs, 38
    DK Ministry of Information and
        Propaganda, 47
    in China, 11, 66
    See also decentralization; *chuizhi guanli*
Cheng An, 28, 47, 49, 54, 127
Chen Yonggui, 7, 17, 19
Chinese ambassador, 1, 3, 67–68, 70–73, 129.
    See also Kang Maozhao; Sun Hao
Chinese Communist Party (CCP) Interna-
    tional Liaison Department, 5, 8, 61
Chinese Embassy, 8, 24, 56, 58–59, 64–68,
    70–73, 104, 109, 114, 117, 118, 129
    Commerce Consultation Department
        (CCD), 65, 67–68

    and DK Ministry of Foreign Affairs, 61
    Economics Consultation Department
        (ECD), 65, 67–73
    Military Consultation Department/Attaché,
        65, 67–68, 90–91
    and Office 870, 61
Chinese leftism, 6–7, 16–19
Chinese Ministries
    Chemical Industry, 63, 65, 113
    Communications, 8, 64–65, 126–127
    Defense, 5, 90
    Foreign Affairs, 14, 66–69, 126
    Foreign Economic Relations, 6, 62–63, 66,
        68, 72, 101, 117, 125
    Foreign Trade, 8, 62, 64, 68, 123, 126, 129
    Hydropower and Electricity, 64–65,
        70–71
    Petroleum, 65–66, 68, 70, 72, 75,
        101–104, 113
    Railways, 8, 64–65
Choeung Ek, 54, 57
Chraing Chamreh, 27
chuizhi guanli, 66
civil aviation, 13, 38
Communist Party of Kampuchea, (CPK)
    Central Committee, 14, 25, 27–28, 32,
        40–41, 48, 54, 108–109, 122
    Central Committee Military Committee, 87
    Standing Committee, 11, 24–29, 32–33,
        35–36, 40–41, 47–48, 55, 61, 79–80, 82,
        85, 95, 108, 123, 125, 128, 139
conditionality, 6, 38, 61–62, 77, 119–120,
    134–135
consultation departments. *See also* Chinese
    Embassy
coordination, 30, 34–39, 48–51, 63, 65–66,
    71, 99, 101–102, 111, 116–117, 120, 123,
    128–130, 138–140
Corfield, Justin, 25, 32
Cultural Revolution, 3, 17, 57, 114
Czechoslovakia, 49

Daqing, 75, 101, 112, 158n38
Dawkins, Richard, 132
Dazhai, 7

CPSIA information can be obtained
at www.ICGtesting.com
Printed in the USA
LVHW091155020119
602461LV00002B/44/P

9 781501 731235